Property Rights, Land Values and
Urban Development

To my daughter, Yuxuan Ouyang
for her smiles and love

Property Rights, Land Values and Urban Development

Betterment and Compensation in China

Li Tian

Tongji University, Shanghai, China

Edward Elgar

Cheltenham, UK • Northampton, MA, USA

Published by
Edward Elgar Publishing Limited
The Lypiatts
15 Lansdown Road
Cheltenham
Glos GL50 2JA
UK

Edward Elgar Publishing, Inc.
William Pratt House
9 Dewey Court
Northampton
Massachusetts 01060
USA

A catalogue record for this book
is available from the British Library

Library of Congress Control Number: 2014947039

This book is available electronically in the ElgarOnline.com Economics Subject Collection, E-ISBN 978 1 78347 640 4

ISBN 978 1 78347 639 8

Typeset by Servis Filmsetting Ltd, Stockport, Cheshire

Contents

Abbreviations

ASP	Average selling price
BMP	Benchmark price
BP	Building permit
EDL	Economic development land
GDP	Gross Domestic Product
GIS	Geographic Information System
GZLRB	Guangzhou Land Resources Bureau
GZUPB	Guangzhou Urban Planning Bureau
IRR	Inner Ring Road
IMGP	Interactive multiple goal programming
LDN	Land Development Notice
LDR	Land development rights
LRB	Land Resources Bureau
LUPP	Land Use Planning Permit
LURs	Land use rights
LVT	Land value tax
ML2	Guangzhou Metro Line 2
MLR	Ministry of Land and Resources
MOHURD	Ministry of Housing and Urban–Rural Development
NICs	Newly industrializing countries
PLL	Projects Location Licence
PRC	People's Republic of China
PRD	Pearl River Delta
RETC	Guangzhou Municipal Real Estate Transaction Center
REB	Real Estate Bureau
SOEs	State-owned enterprises
TOD	Transit-oriented development
TDRs	Transferable development rights
UPB	Urban Planning Bureau
YRD	Yangtze River Delta
ZSAFED	Zoning by special assessment financed eminent domain

Acknowledgements

This book is supported by the National Science Fund of China (Project number: 51222813), and the Publishing Grant of Shanghai Tongji Urban Planning and Design Institute, China. The author wishes to express gratitude to Professor Richard LeGates from San Francisco State University, USA for his generous help in the publication process; Dr Derek Nicholls from the University of Cambridge, UK and Professor Jieming Zhu from the National University of Singapore for their constructive comments; and Mr Zhihao Yao and Mr Pengpeng Lu for their help in data preparation and processing. I also wish to acknowledge the fine editorial work of Elizabeth Clack and her patience and professionalism during the production of this book at Edward Elgar Publishing.

1. Introduction

As the political and economic reforms in China[1] have progressed rapidly, changes in the Chinese economy, society, and urban development have been breathtaking. Among many issues related to the transformation from a planned economy to a market-led economy, the change in the structure of property rights in land is among the most sensitive. Throughout the history of China, major political and economic reforms have been accompanied by the reassignment of property rights in land. It is notable that most land reforms took place almost immediately after the establishment of a new government, and land reform played a key role in political and economic reforms (Li, 1998). This was the case in ancient China, and land tenure changes in contemporary China also occurred when the corrupt Qing Dynasty was overthrown by Sun Yet Sen in 1911, when the People's Republic of China was established in 1949, and when an opening-up reform policy was introduced in 1979. It has long been argued that the failure of the Kuomintang regime was caused by serious income disparity, which was partly caused by land monopoly by a small percentage of the population, and the Communist Party succeeded due to its promise to the underclass and farmers that they could own their own land.

With more attention being paid to the 1980s urban land reform of China, the literature has burgeoned rapidly from different angles. Some papers focus on the significance of establishing a land market (Dowall, 1993; World Bank, 1993), some on the mechanism of land development (Yeh and Wu, 1996; Wu, 1998; Chan, 1999), some on land use and the emergence of a real estate market (Chen, 1993; Walker and Li, 1994; Li, 1998; Zhu, 2002, 2005, 2009), and some on the impact of the land use rights (hereafter LURs) system on city growth (Zhu, 1994; Wu and Yeh, 1999; Ye and Wu, 2014). This literature has focused on the analysis of experiences and problems of the emerging urban land market, but few studies, either overseas or domestic, have focused on the betterment and worsenment generated by government activities under the current institutional framework of the LURs system. This issue, however, reflects the relationship between the state and the individual in the allocation of land interests, and has important implications for the Chinese land market. This is not difficult to understand, for there has been a long tradition in

China that the state has been in the dominant position, and expectations and valuations of the individual have been given much less priority.

A critical factor in understanding urban land markets is the institutional structure of property rights in land, as well as the arrangements of organizations and agents, regulations on the market and the interplay among the actors (Han and Wang, 2003). In explaining betterment and worsenment generated by public actions, property rights can be effective tools. The structure of property rights in land has significant impacts on efficiency and equity. Betterment and worsenment are derived from externalities, and internalizing them can be a critical part of property rights arrangement. Coase (1960) suggests that the parties involved in a dispute arising from the presence of externality could settle their conflict through contracting their property rights, and the 'internalization' of externalities could be greatly affected by transaction costs. Many scholars argue that clearly defined property rights can significantly reduce transaction costs and facilitate economic growth (Demsetz, 1967; Furubotn and Pejovich, 1972; North, 1981; Cheung, 1982; Barzel, 1989; Eggertsson, 1993). On the other hand, the ambiguity in property rights increases uncertainty, encourages corruption, raises costs and reduces the incentive to invest (Putterman, 1996; Zhu, 2004a, 2004b; Desoto, 2003).

In contrast with the radical reform approach of formerly Communist East European countries, China has adopted an incremental economic reform strategy, and change in the area of property rights has been gradual and ambiguous. Cheung (1982: 21) provides interesting explanations for ambiguous property rights in China: one reason is that an idea which is not clearly stated can never be proved clearly wrong; the second reason is that in the absence of clearly drawn boundaries between the nature of one system and another, it is easy to assign all negative characteristics to one and all positive ones to the other. Furthermore, the vagueness of property rights would leave the state free to alter rules at will, spreading benefits or imposing penalties in any way it chose. The ambiguity in property rights in China, therefore, serves as a double-edged sword in economic development. In the short run, the strong state has wielded it to establish a market framework at a very low cost and within a very short time scale; on the other hand, it has incurred uncertainty and impeded long-term economic development because ambiguous property rights are not sufficient to provide order in the absence of formal institutions, and they also make the newly structured property rights being trialled insecure (World Bank, 2002).

With the acceleration of the urban development process, the issues of betterment and worsenment in the land market have become increasingly important in China. Whilst government investment has substantially increased land values in many areas, it is inevitable that government activities may lead to the decrease of land values in other areas because of pollution, noise, and visual disfigurement. How to internalize these externalities is a key constituent part of property rights in land, and the failure to address them can lead to uncertainty and unfairness in the land market. In China, the issues of betterment and worsenment appear to arouse no great concern. For example, no adequate measures have been taken to capture surplus land value or to compensate for the loss of value generated by government investment.

The inability of the government to address betterment and compensation, however, often leads to several problems that are worthy of attention. The first problem is that it worsens an already uneven distribution of income. Among the theoretical and practical studies of betterment and compensation, Henry George ([1879] 1886) is one of the earliest scholars to pay attention to this issue. He attributes the industrial depression to the problem of land monopoly, and argues that the fundamental reason for poverty and inequality was that the benefit of land value increment, which should have accrued to the community, was ultimately monopolized by the possessors of land. Payne (2001) asserts that the concentration of land wealth in the hands of a small percentage of the population is attributed to the government's failure to capture surplus value, whereas the underclass can fall victim to the insufficiency or lack of compensation more easily. The second problem is that the inability to recover surplus land value may weaken the fiscal capability of governments to provide public goods. High urban land cost is often a serious constraint on public goods. If users are not charged for services provided, large benefits may accrue to adjoining landholders, and thus cause the government to lose the opportunity to gain the revenue that should have gone into public coffers. Especially for Chinese cities where the government is faced with limited funding, the failure to capture subsequent land value increments arising from public activities has made the financing of expensive public facilities construction more difficult. The last, but not least, problem is that the inability to recover surplus land value may lead to uncertainty in the land market, therefore impinging on long-term land market development. With the large scale of construction, failure to adequately address windfall gains and hardship, and subsequent uncertainty, have been increasingly distorting the land market price mechanism. Whilst some land developers have enjoyed enormous unearned wealth, other groups have to accept inadequate compensation, or hardship without any compensation payable,[2] even though a loss of value is generated by public works. As a result of uncertainties in the land market, some groups have hesitated to enter the Chinese real estate market, particularly overseas developers. Compared with their counterparts in other fields such as manufacturing and commerce, the participation of overseas developers in the real estate market is much less significant.

Based on the above analysis, how the government can recover surplus land value and mitigate the worsenment generated by its own actions, without seriously affecting private incentives, is very meaningful for urban development in China. In other words, the government has to strike a balance between taking away the gains of development value from benefited owners on the one hand, and keeping the market working on the other hand. The philosophy of Cmnd. 5124 (1972; *Development and Compensation – Putting People First*) is concerned with public and private interests but significantly:

> sees the problem not so much as one of conflict between public and private with its implications of right and wrong but as one of balancing 'a conflict of right with right – the public's undoubted right to have a new road or school or waterworks and the private person's right to enjoy his home and garden undisturbed'. The government believes that all concerned with development must aim to achieve a better balance between provision for the community as a whole and the mitigation of harmful effects on the individual citizen.

1.1   RESEARCH QUESTIONS

Therefore, in order to promote justice, equity, and long-term land market development, it is necessary to draw attention to the issues of betterment and compensation in China. This research is an attempt to examine these issues under the LURs system and focuses on the following three key questions:

1. How and to what extent has the government captured the surplus value and compensated the hardship generated by public activities under the LURs system?
2. What are the impacts on land markets of the current measures for addressing the betterment and compensation issues?
3. What are the obstacles to implementing effective schemes of land value capture and compensation?

1.2   TERMINOLOGY

1.2.1   'Betterment', 'Worsenment' and 'Compensation'

Palgrave's *Dictionary of Political Economy* defines 'betterment' as follows:

> persons benefited by public expenditure should contribute to such expenditure to the extent of the increased value of their property, not only if the

improvement effected by the public authority was carried out for the purpose of conferring a benefit on such property, but also if the resulting benefit was purely accidental, the expenditure having been undertaken for a totally different purpose.

This definition is limited since it only considers particular improvements carried out at public expense, but betterment may also occur without any public expenditure at all: for example, the change of planning parameters. The 1942 Uthwatt Report (p. 104) thus defines the term 'betterment' as 'any increase in land value (including the buildings thereon) arising from central or local government action, whether positive, e.g., by the execution of public works or improvements, or negative, e.g., by the imposition of restrictions on other land'. According to Hagman (1978), betterment is any increase in the value of land arising from central or local government action, excluding increases due to general inflation, the efforts and expenditure of the owner.

In this book, the term 'betterment' does not include the land value increment arising from general community influences such as population growth, general inflation or land user's investment in land, for it is generally difficult to prove the extent to which any increase in value can properly be attributed to any of these factors. Therefore betterment is defined as the land value increase generated by government activities such as infrastructure investment and change of planning parameters. Likewise, the term 'worsenment' means any decrease in the value of real estate generated by government actions other than one caused by land users or general deflation. In some countries, say the USA, 'betterment' and 'worsenment' are also called 'windfall' and 'wipeout' respectively.

'Compensation' in this book not only means compensation for worsenment, but also includes compensation for land acquisition. In China, there is no compensation for the decrease of land value caused by government activities. Therefore, the term 'compensation' in this volume focuses on the discussion of compensation standards and compulsory purchase in land acquisition.

1.2.2 'Land Market' and 'Real Estate Market'

Owing to the institutional difference between China and the Western world, the terms 'land market' and 'real estate market' have different meanings under the LURs system. In the Western world where freehold is the dominant land tenure, there are no distinct differences between real estate markets and land markets. According to *Black's Law Dictionary*, real estate includes the land and anything fixed, immovable, or permanently attached to it such as buildings, walls, fixtures, improvements, roads, trees, shrubs, fences, roads, sewers, structures, and utility systems. However, for technical purposes, some scholars prefer to distinguish real estate, referring to the land and fixtures themselves, from real property, referring to ownership rights over real estate. Seabrooke and How (2004) differentiate the concepts of 'land' and 'real estate' in the way that real estate is not defined simply by the physical characteristics of the land or the buildings on it, but by the enforceable rights that allow the use of land and buildings thereon to be exercised, protected, and transferred. Basically, the real estate market includes markets for various property types, such as an office market, housing markets, and the commercial market.

Under the LURs system, the land ownership and the LURs are separated, that is, the state owns the land, but not structures on the land. Therefore, 'land market' and 'real estate market' are slightly different concepts under the LURs system. Usually the transfer of land property rights is divided into three levels in urban land markets (Figure 1.1). The first level is named the primary market, which means both the conversion of collective land into state land and the transfer of LURs between the state and individuals or corporations; in theory, the primary market should be monopolized by the state. The secondary market refers to the outright transfer of LURs as a bundle of rights between individuals or corporations with the permission of the government. If the government needs land for the construction of public facilities, it can acquire collective land in the primary market or purchase LURs from other land users in the secondary market. The tertiary market means the partial transfer of LURs between individuals or corporations, for instance the rental or mortgage of LURs.

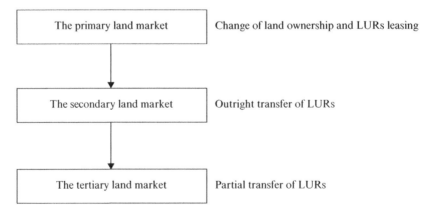

The primary land market	Change of land ownership and LURs leasing
The secondary land market	Outright transfer of LURs
The tertiary land market	Partial transfer of LURs

Figure 1.1   Stratification of land markets under the LURs system

Generally speaking, land leasing means the transfer of LURs between the government and individuals or corporations in the primary market.

1.3   THE STRUCTURE OF THE BOOK

Chapter 1   Introduction

This chapter outlines the background, the scope, and the objectives of this research. It also identifies research questions and indicates the structure of this book. Several terms are also defined in this chapter.

Chapter 2   The nature of land rent and land value capture

This chapter examines the classic theories of land rent and land value, and focuses on the fundamental questions: What is the nature of land value and real property? Who are entitled to capture the land value increments?

Chapter 3   Studying betterment and compensation from the perspective of property rights

This chapter adopts an analytical framework derived from the New Institutional Economics to examine the following betterment and compensation issues:

1.   Externalities, transaction costs, betterment and worsenment.
2.   Property rights as a tool of economic development and public policy.
3.   The theory of the state.

These theories are employed to develop an analytical framework for how the land market is affected by property rights arrangements, and what role the government has been playing in land markets.

Chapter 4   Assessing and addressing betterment and compensation: international experiences

This chapter firstly presents the methods that are frequently applied to assess the land value change generated by certain events. Then it describes various international practical approaches to addressing betterment and compensation, and analyses their strength and weakness. The complexity and costliness of these approaches are analyzed to explain why it is difficult to enforce betterment and compensation policies in practice.

Chapter 5 Urban land reform and the evolution of the land market in China

This chapter provides an introduction to the institutional context and process of urban land reform in 1988. Firstly, the historical evolution of Chinese land tenure, particularly the land tenure of contemporary China – the Republic of China after 1911 – is reviewed. Then the traditional land use system from 1949 to 1987 is explained and its consequences are analysed. The chapter then introduces the legal and administrative frameworks of the LURs system. Finally, the urban land market since the 1988 land reform is described to illustrate its problems and prospects.

Chapter 6 Betterment and compensation schemes under the LURs system

Under the LURs system, current mechanisms for dealing with betterment and compensation, such as LURs fees, land taxation, land requisition approaches, and compensation standards, are described in this chapter, and their deficiency and influences on land markets are analysed. Then the role of the state in addressing betterment and compensation is examined. The chapter concludes with an analysis of the obstacles to addressing betterment and compensation.

Chapter 7 Assessing and addressing betterment and compensation in Guangzhou: empirical evidence

This chapter adopts a case study approach at two levels. At the municipal level, Guangzhou is selected as a case. In evaluating its betterment approach, the main attributes, including land revenue and real estate taxes, the proportion of land revenue in local revenue, and infrastructure investment are used as evaluation indicators. It is very difficult to evaluate compensation quantitatively at the municipal level. Therefore the evaluation is mainly a descriptive analysis.

At the project level, the Inner Ring Road and the Metro Line 2 are selected as case studies. A repeat-sales model and hedonic regression model are applied to evaluate to what extent the government action has affected the land and property value.

Chapter 8 Institutional evolution in the land market of Guangzhou

This chapter provides a wider institutional context in which to understand the current schemes of betterment and compensation. It examines the evolutionary path of the institutional arrangements and property rights in the land market of Guangzhou, such as changes in the land administrative framework, and the coexistence of formal and informal property rights. The chapter ends with reflections on institutional arrangements in the transitional land market.

Chapter 9 Conclusion

This chapter summarizes the analyses and findings above, and explores policy implications germane to betterment and compensation in China, including the role of the state, the establishment of information structures, and further reform of property rights in land. It concludes with a recommendation for further research.

NOTES

1. In this research China refers to Mainland of China, excluding Hong Kong, Macao, and Taiwan. Hong Kong and Macao were returned to China in 1997 and 1999, respectively, and they are highly autonomous economically as well as politically. Taiwan is still independent of the control of Beijing. All of these areas are implementing different policies and management frameworks from Mainland China.
2. Under the situation where their occupied land is compulsorily acquired, they can be paid compensation based on the existing market value of their property at the time of land acquisition.

2. The nature of land rent and land value capture

Land rent is the price paid by individuals to landowners for the use of a parcel of property. The nature of land ownership varies from society to society, reflecting the particular social relations between people in that society. Rent directly reflects the social relations of the agent of land with the users of the land. According to Jaèger (2003), land rent theory does not have a coherent and widely accepted theoretical corpus, but consists of varied concepts, even of its central categories. This chapter describes the rent theories in classical, neoclassical and modern Western economics, including the nature, the law, and the forms of land rent. Additionally, this chapter explores the nature of land value capture in relation to social structure.

2.1 EVOLUTION OF LAND RENT THEORY

2.1.1 Emergence of Concept of Land Rent

The classical economy regards rent as a regular payment for the use of land, as well as a specific historical social institution (the latter was particularly emphasized by Marx), which regulates the relationship between landowner and capitalist or producer (Jaèger, 2003). British classical political economist William Petty made a pioneering contribution to the theory of rent and developed a theory of value. Petty argued that all things ought to be valued by two natural denominations: land and labour. The natural rent of a land is the excess of what a labourer produces on it in a year over what he eats himself and trades for necessities (Petty, 1662).

A representative of the French physiocratic school, Turgot, published his best-known work, *Reflections on the Formation and Distribution of Wealth* (Turgot, [1766] 2012). It argues that the surplus of agriculture products is generated from the special kind of natural productivity that is the natural gift of 'pure products'. The 'pure products' are the wealth of agricultural workers obtained by their labour, and this can be labelled as rent. The owner of the land can reap these 'pure products' (rent) without sowing, because they have the legal protection of land ownership. Turgot reveals the preliminary relationship between land rent and land ownership.

Adam Smith (1723–1790) was the first economist to study rent systematically. He maintained that rent emerged after the appearance of private ownership. Smith considered rent as the price paid for the use of land, and rent is naturally the highest which the tenant can afford to pay. The rent of the land, therefore, is naturally a monopoly price. It is not proportioned according to what the landlord may have laid out upon the improvement of the land, or to what he can afford to take, but to what the farmer can afford to give. Rent is therefore different from wages and profit. High or low wages and profit trigger high or low prices, but rent is the effect of price. Smith ([1776] 1976) concludes that improvements in labor production increase with the real wealth of the society and the quantity of useful labour employed within it, and this tends indirectly to raise the real rent of land.

Notwithstanding Adam Smith's important contribution on the theory of rent, there exists some confusion and inconsistency in his views. On the one hand, Smith acknowledges that rent is the product of labour. On the other hand, however, he considers that rent and profit are not dependent on workers' labour, but are independently generated by the land and capital. Thus, Marx (in Marx and Engels, 1961) points out that in Smith the most profound insights and the most ridiculous notion are strangely intertwined.

Ricardo ([1817] 1871) argues that land rent is determined by the excess of its production over that which the same application can secure from the least productive land in use. He defines rent as 'the difference between the produce obtained by the employment of two equal quantities of capital and labour', and 'that portion of the produce of the earth, which is paid to the landlord for the use of the original and indestructible powers of the soil'. He clearly holds that land rent was a transfer payment from one class (the capitalists) to another (the landowners), and this division of surplus was much less 'natural' for him than it had appeared to Adam Smith half a century earlier (Deák, 1985).

Thomas Malthus (1776–1834) proposed that rent is the total price of the remaining portion, the remaining part of the total price of the product after deduction of labour wages and profits (Malthus, 1798). He argues that rent is natural, the gifts of God are granted to mankind, and it has nothing to do with other monopolies. He further states that with the development of society, rents inevitably increase. Rent growth is inevitable as the bourgeois economists believe it is consistent with the development of social trends and conforms to the interests of all consumers. Malthus attributes the rent to natural causes and a natural principle, similar to the law of gravity, and portrays landowners as significant contributors to social development; therefore they are supposed to own land rent.

Opposite to the viewpoints of Malthus, Marx (1894) believes there are three classes in the capitalist relationship in the production of agriculture: wage-labourers, capitalists and landowners. He notes that farmers pay the landowner a sum of money at definite periods fixed by contract; for instance, annually for the right to invest capital in a specific sphere of production. This sum of money is called ground-rent, no matter whether it is paid for agricultural land, building plots, mines, fishing grounds or forests, and so on. Ground-rent, therefore, is here that form in which property in land is realized economically; that is, produces value. Essentially, rent is the economic realization of land property, and individuals have an exclusive right to certain parts of our planet. Virtually all ground-rent is surplus value, and the product of surplus labour, which is generated by monopoly of land possession and management, and its excess profits. Land rent is established as a result of the struggle between tenant and landlord.

2.1.2   Types of Land Rent

The writings of the economic classics on rent (Marx, 1894; Ricardo, [1817] 1821) concentrate mainly on the issue of agricultural rent (with a few exceptions, such as Engels, [1884] 2010; Marx, [1863] 1988: 782) and have already determined the principal types of rent, such as intensive and extensive differential rent, monopoly rent and absolute rent (Jaèger, 2003).

Absolute rent
Absolute rent is a concept put forward by Marx and refers originally to a land tribute which was paid by agriculture due to a lower organic composition of capital (Jaèger, 2003). It involves the integration of two of Marx's major discoveries – the deviation of prices from values and the historical specificity of the capitalist mode of production – as observed in the distribution of surplus value to land-based products (Emsley, 1998).

Adam Smith ([1776] 1976) identifies the existence of absolute rent, however he never explicitly puts forward the concept of absolute rent. Ricardo ([1817] 1921) completely denies the existence of absolute rent, mainly because he confuses the concepts of price and value. Thünen (1826) denies the existence of absolute rent in theory. But he recognizes the existence of it in another way. He states that when the price of agricultural products equals the sum of production and transportation costs, rent is zero. In the second volume of *The Isolated State*, he realizes the fact that landowners get access to the land rent by the right of private ownership of land monopoly.

According to Marx (1844), absolute ground rent is explained as the rent which landowners can extract because they monopolise the access to or supply of land. Absolute rent cannot exist when the organic composition of capital (the ratio C/V, a ratio of constant capital to variable capital) in agriculture becomes higher than the social average and the value of output produced is persistently higher than the production price of that output. Physically, the manifestation of absolute rent has been excess profits from agriculture. 'At any rate this absolute rent arising out of the excess of value over the price of production is but a portion of the agricultural surplus-value, a conversion of this surplus-value into rent, its being filched by the landlord' (Marx, 1894).

Economakis (2003) states that Marx studies the issue of surplus value in the sphere of agricultural production, however, he does not take into account the possibility that a rise in labour productivity may accompany the rise in the organic composition of capital (*ceteris paribus*). Therefore, he does not examine the possible consequence of this increased productivity: the increase in the rate of surplus value. Thus, substantiation of absolute rent on the basis of differences in the composition of capital demands a specific combination of outcomes, for instance, those that give rise to an overabundance of surplus value in the sphere of agricultural production.

Differential rent
William Petty (1662) initially lays the foundation for differential rent, and he states that the differences of soil fertility levels and farming techniques, as well as the different distances from origin to market, bring about the difference of land rents and price. British economist James Anderson (1800–1864) first studied the basic features of the theory of differential rent, and Marx regarded him as 'the founder of the modern theory of land rent'. He stresses that it is not land rent which determines prices of products, but the price of the product which determines the land rent. Among the theories of land rent, Ricardian and Marxian differential rent theories are the most influential among the classical economists.

Ricardo ([1817] 1821: 59) clarifies differential rent on the basis of labour theory: 'Rent is always the difference between the produce obtained by the employment of two equal quantities of capital and labour'. His differential rent theory starts out from two basic assumptions regarding agricultural production: (1) the undisputable assumption of diminishing returns related to the concrete conditions of production on land; (2) the controversial assumption of marginal return equalizing investment related to decisions of the capitalist farmer prior to the existence of rent (Deák, 1985). Ricardo mainly observes and studies differential rent under different degrees of fertile land, due to the comparison between inferior and superior to the middle cultivated ground. Since land is neither unlimited in quantity nor uniform in quality, Ricardo regards the range of cultivated land from superior to inferior as the precondition for the generation of differential land rent.

Ricardo assumes the best-quality farm land would be the first to be cultivated, and that goods are sold in a competitive, single-price market. While only one grade of land is used for cultivation, rent will not exist; but when multiple grades of land are utilized, rent will be charged on the higher grades and will increase as the grade increases:

> With every step in the progress of population, which shall oblige a country to have recourse to land of a worse quality, to enable it to raise its supply of food, rent, on all the more fertile land, will rise. The amount of that rent depends on the difference in the quality of these two portions of land. (Ricardo, [1817] 1821)

The Ricardian theory of rent was challenged by Richard Jones (1790–1855), who considers Ricardian differential rent theory as an unrealistic logical inference drawn from historical and geographical information. Jones finds that the rent institutions of ancient and foreign countries were not similar with that of the United Kingdom, while for cultivators and landlords, the distribution of gains are not necessarily in accordance with Ricardo's law.

Van Thünen (1826) describes his theory of land rent, which is similar to the Ricardian land rent theory without reading Ricardo's principles, in the first volume of his book, *The Isolated State*. Based on large amounts of empirical and experimental data, Thünen improves the differential rent theory. The superiority of the location of individual estates and the superiority of soil fertility are the two elements that Thünen states bring about land rent; and thus land rent as Thünen discusses explicitly is the first form of differential rent. Nevertheless, he does not take the differences of soil fertility of the whole territory into consideration, but focuses on the location of land. In this sense, his research on differential rent is unilateral.

Marx's theory of rent has been far more developed in both depth and detail than Ricardo's. The main difference between the two is that for Marx, rent is a historical form rather than a natural form (Deák, 1985). Marx notes that differential rent invariably arises from the difference between the individual production price of a particular capital over the monopolized natural force and general production price of the total capital invested in the sphere of production concerned. Thus, the excess profits are ultimately reaped by landowners.

There are three reasons which account for differences in land rent: the fertility of the land, the location of the land, and labour productivity resulting from continuous investment in the same piece of land. These differences result in varied land productivity when each type of land has the same amount of labour input, forming the material conditions and base for differential rent. Marx attributes differential rent to the difference of fertility and location of the land, and the difference in labour productivity resulting from the successive investment of capital in the same land can be termed as 'differential rent II'. Differential rent exists not only in agriculture but also in the mining and construction industries. Differential rent is formed as a result of differences in the productivity of labour produced by inequality of natural conditions for the exploitation and use of minerals, forest lands, and so on (Prokhorov, 1969).

'Differential rent I' shows how extra profit is transformed into rent by equal quantities of capital being invested on different lands of unequal productivity. 'Differential rent I' is directly related to differences in the fertility and location of plots of land. The individual production price of a unit of agricultural produce which comes from a better portion of land actually turns out to have a lower cost. This occurs because with all other conditions being equal, the labour applied to more fertile soil is more productive and expenditures for the delivery of agricultural goods to market are less for lands situated relatively closer to the market.

Agricultural goods are sold on the basis of the social price of production, which in agriculture expresses the social value of these goods determined by the conditions of production on the poorer plots of land (Prokhorov, 1969). 'Differential rent I' arises because land is limited, and the agricultural produce created only on the comparatively superior lands is insufficient to meet the social demands for this produce. The market also demands the produce created on the average and poorer lands. Farmers operating on the better and average lands sell their produce at market prices and receive additional profits in the form of differential rents. Historically, this form of differential rent arose earlier than 'differential rent II', and it increases with the development of agriculture, industry and the system of communications.

'Differential rent II' is the additional profit that arises as a result of successive capital investments on specific parcels of land. The increased quantity and rate of this form of differential rent reflects the growth in productivity of additional capital investments, a growth which becomes basic and decisive in times of scientific and technical progress despite the so-called law of declining fertility of the soil. Until a tenant lease terminates, the super-profits obtained as a result of additional capital investments go to the tenant farmer. But when a new lease is signed, the landowner, by virtue of the supremacy of the monopoly of private property in land, appropriates this additional profit by increasing the rental fee. As a result, the landowner obtains a portion of this form of differential rent. This is the basis of the struggle between tenant capitalists and land-owners over the rental period (Prokhorov, 1969).

Monopoly rent

The normal forms rent takes are 'absolute' and 'differential'. Apart from these two forms, rent can be based only upon an actual monopoly price, which is determined neither by price of production nor by value of commodities, but by the buyers' needs and ability to pay – a special form of land rent in a capitalist economy; it occurs in connection with the sale of goods at monopoly prices in excess of their value.

Certain land that has special natural features often produces scarce or luxurious products. In agriculture, monopoly rent is derived from lands on which uncommon crops, for example wine with a special flavor, may be produced by particular raw materials (including water) on certain land plots. In the mining industry, such rents are related to the mining of rare metals. Because of the limited amount of land especially suitable for the production of rare commodities, and because of the high demand for the products, it becomes possible not only that these kinds of products are sold for much higher than the price of production, but also that their price exceeds their value. The monopoly price is then determined by the purchasing desire and ability to buy (the market), regardless of the production price and the value of the product. In all such cases, the capitalists renting such land must make very high payments to the landowners; the basis of the payments emerges as monopoly rent. These rental payments take the form of additional income for the landowner. Thus monopoly rent represents that portion of the surplus value produced by wage labour that is appropriated by the landowner through the redistribution of such surplus value (Prokhorov, 1969). The excess profits generated by the monopoly price fall into the hands of the landowner which are then transformed into monopoly rents.

2.1.3   Development of Land Rent Theory

With the advent of the industrial revolution in the mid-nineteenth century, the world economy achieved unprecedented growth. Meanwhile, social inequalities enlarged significantly, compared with times when societies were largely agrarian. Compared with before the mid-nineteenth century, the role of land rent in society has also drawn more attention from economists and philosophers alike, bringing with it a variety of theories.

One of most influential economists on land rent, Henry George ([1879] 1886), argues that rent is the price of monopoly. It arises from individual ownership of natural elements which human exertion can neither produce nor increase. George regards the law of rent as the relation under the circumstances of free competition among all parties. George argues that the law of rent is a consequence of the law of competition. The ownership of land grants the owner the power to appropriate the wealth produced by labour and capital, and the surplus profit is then reaped by landowners (George, [1879] 1886).

George is also best known for his argument that the economic rent of land should be shared equally by the people of a society rather than being owned privately, the idea of a single land value tax (LVT), by standard economic theory. Nobel laureate Milton Friedman described Henry George's tax on unimproved value of land as the 'least bad tax', since unlike other taxes it would not impose an excess burden on economic activity, leading to 'deadweight loss' (Foldvary, 2005).

Alfred Marshall ([1890] 1997) believes that rent generally consists of several parts, including original value, private value, and public value. The private value of land refers to the income of investment and labour input by the landowners for the purpose of improvement of land and buildings. The public value refers to the betterment of land due to the improvement of land use efficiency generated by the investment of public infrastructure. The original value of the land is the revenue granted from nature, and the outcome of interactions between supply and demand of the land. Therefore, land rent can be regarded as the equilibrium price of supply and demand.

In the political-economic theoretical tradition, land rent theory has been considered essential in explaining socio-economic phenomena. Since the end of the 1980s only a few theoretical contributions to land rent theory in a political-economic tradition have been made (Haila, 1988; KraÈtke, 1992; Emsley, 1998; Evans, 1999) and rarely has empirical analysis been applied to it. Contrary to this development (or rather, lack of development) of the past decade, there was a lively theoretical debate from the 1970s to the mid-1980s (Jaèger, 2003). Haila (1988) notes that a consensus – that urban land rent was a social relation – was reached in the 1970s and 1980s. For instance, Stiglitz (1977) argues that increase in land rents results from public improvement in infrastructure and facilities along with progressive urbanization which attracts migrants demanding land and space. The close linkage with the theoretical work of the classics (centred on the question of agricultural rent) and the orthodox interpretation of the writings, particularly in France, as well as the predominant use of the concept of absolute rent at the beginning of the debate, contributed to a very particular way of answering contemporary urban questions (Jaèger, 2003). Since the beginning of the 1990s, the theoretical development of rent theory has virtually stagnated.

2.2   NATURE OF LAND VALUE CAPTURE

Who has created land value and how to capture land value have remained two hotly debated issues for the last several centuries. Should governments reap the land value increment attributed to regulations or public works? Or should governments be obliged to compensate the worsenment due to regulations or public works? These issues carry fundamental social, economic, and justice implications. Before discussing these issues and relevant tools of value capture, I first address a philosophical debate: is real property the epitome of private rights, or a social good? (Alterman, 2011b).

2.2.1   Hobbesian Solution or Lockean Position

When discussing who should capture the land value increment, we should not ignore two famous and influential thinkers, Thomas Hobbes and John Locke, who hold opposite views on property rights. Hobbes, the defender of absolute sovereign power, emphasizes the selfish behaviour of selfish individuals in a world without any external authority to restrain their appetites and passions. He puts forward the critical question: how can one escape the omnipresent peril of a state of nature and exchange it for personal security and social order? His solution is simple: the surrender of liberty and property in exchange for security (Hobbes, [1651] 2012). Hobbes's position has encountered many critiques. Undoubtedly the sovereign is the biggest winner in his solution, and the legal monopolist will act like any other unconstrained monopolist. His laws and rules will expropriate most of the benefits by allowing each individual only the minimum inducement to remain quiescent (Epstein, 1985). In contrast, Locke seeks to create a sovereign that could maintain good order without extracting monopoly rents from the exclusive legitimate use of force. He argues that private real property preceded the civil state and deserves its protection in law, and land ownership is closely linked to human autonomy. The work invested by individuals in obtaining and cultivating land is the basis for private property rights (Locke, 1690). The organization of the state does not require the surrender of all natural rights to the sovereign, and the sovereign has no absolute power to generate profits. The state gets what it needs to rule: its costs, and nothing more. Meanwhile, the bulwark of the individual is no longer the absolute protection of their property. If any portion of their property has been taken from them, they must receive from the state some equivalent of greater benefit as part of the same transaction (Epstein, 1985).

The continuing relevance of these classical philosophers' positions is evident in current debates about property rights. Scholars and political leaders who sanction unbridled private ownership have their roots in Locke's thinking (Alterman, 2011b). They argue that unfettered or only mildly regulated land ownership will utilize land more efficiently by means of market forces, compared with government regulations (Fischel, 1995; Yandle, 1995). Morevoer, excessive land use and environmental regulations and financial obligations are partly to blame for the high cost of housing and other built-up products (Glaeser, 2007; Quigley, 2007).

2.2.2 The Nature of Real Property: Private Goods or Social Goods?

According to classical liberalism, property is an individual right that is limited only by the rights of others and the public interest. Therefore, the holder of this right can use, reap the benefits of, and dispose of their assets in an appropriate manner, on the condition that the law is followed and the common good is not violated (Lomasky, 1990). The assumption is that people are essentially autonomous and rational beings, and they have the ability to articulate, transform, and try to realize life plans by making use of reason (Foster, 2011). Meanwhile, opponents of classical liberal property argue that private property has caused social inequity, and they propose the abolition of private ownership and strong government intervention in the rights to property in order to achieve redistributive aims, for example, egalitarian liberalism, socialism, and communism (Marx, 1844).

Between classical liberalism and socialism, the most influential concept in the twentieth century is the social function of property put forward by French jurist León Duguit, one of the most revolutionary legal thinkers of his generation. Duguit argues that property is not a right but rather a social function, and the owner has obligations to make it productive. The wealth controlled by owners should be put at the service of the community by means of economic transactions. As a consequence, the state should protect property only when it fulfills its social function.

Influenced by the social function theory, some legal scholars (Alexander, 2006; Foster, 2011) recognize the existence of social obligations in US law. Foster (2011) regards that the social obligation norm is a concept with much plasticity, and property owners owe affirmative obligations to the welfare of others, and to societal welfare more generally, which can fit into different ideological orientations, including classical liberalism. According to Alexander (2006), the individual is not an isolated, self-sufficient being, but a social animal. Therefore, dependency and interdependency are constitutive parts of the human condition, and society ought to promote through entitling each person to use material resources to develop their capabilities essential to human flourishing. Social obligation values have been reflected in eminent domain cases and cases adjudicating remedies for nuisance, both of which involve state-sanctioned forced sales of private property for the common good or community best interest.

To summarize, the nature of real property reflects the plurality of values, that property should serve the goals of both individual development and social obligation, and it is up to the legal system to negotiate them in defining the contours of private property rights. However, what form this negotiation assumes varies significantly depending upon the legal, political, and social culture of a particular society (Foster, 2011). How to balance private rights and social obligation has been a hotly debated topic, and international experiences in attempting to achieve balance will be discussed in Chapter 4.

2.2.3 Direct Value Capture and Indirect Value Capture

In today's world, many countries have adopted the social obligations view of property. Almost all countries have land use regulations and real property, without following a purist Locke position. The mainstream debates about property rights today no longer revolve around the big ideological issues about whether private property should exist. Instead, the debates focus on specific issues such as the appropriate degrees of land use and environmental regulation, the extent of government powers to take land for public needs, and the level of compensation for injurious regulation (Alterman, 2011b).

Alterman (2011a, 2011b) conducted a comparative study of land-use regulations and compensation rights across the world, but she did not include China. Based on the international experiences, she categorizes value capture tools as direct instruments and indirect instruments, and identifies direct value capture as instruments that 'seek to capture all or some of the value rise in real property under the explicit rationale that it is a legal or moral obligation for landowners to contribute a share of their community-derived wealth to the public pocket' (Altherman, 2011: 765). A direct value capture tool is often regarded as a tax similar to capital gains tax, or annual property tax. Different from direct value capture, indirect instruments do not seek to capture the added value for its own sake, but in order to generate revenues (or in-kind substitutes) for specific public services, for instance exactions in the USA, and planning gains and obligations in the UK, which will be discussed in detail in Chapter 4.

According to Alterman (2011b), direct capture instruments are usually enacted or adopted from the top down, and are applied within an entire jurisdiction. This is mostly because in well-governed countries, authority for direct value capture entails enabling legislation, and sometimes even constitutional amendments. By contrast, indirect instruments often emerge 'from the bottom' by dispersed locally grown policies. If the instruments are viewed as successful and survive legal challenges, they are likely to be extended to other localities. Recently, indirect value capture tools have proliferated widely across the world. Compared with direct value capture tools, indirect value capture tools have more realistic potential for funding public services. Meanwhile, Alterman (2011b: 778–779) addresses the preconditions of applying indirect value capture tools:

> Governments should have well-trained professionals (planners or real estate experts) to negotiate with the developers or to develop preset formulas of impact assessment . . .

Local government should conduct monitoring of fluctuations in land prices in order to be able to challenge developers' arguments that the exactions in fact raise the cost of housing or other products. This type of argument may generate public opposition even though it is not necessarily true in all market situations.

- There should be enough transparency in negotiated exactions to help withstand legal challenges (yet full disclosure is often not possible in order to protect the legitimate economic interests of the developers).
- Countries or local authorities known for high levels of corruption should refrain from adopting indirect value capture instruments with discretionary elements. A reasonable good level of trust in government is a precondition for their successful operation.

SUMMARY

The evolution of land rent theory underlines the importance of the institutional context for an understanding of rent (Jaèger, 2003). This chapter has examined theories of land rent from classical liberalism to socialism since the seventeenth century. Although nowadays nearly all societies have reached a consensus that property rights have both social and individual functions, and land rent should be captured by both the individual and the public, it is hard to decide how the appropriate proportion should be distributed between them, which depends highly on local politics, culture, and economic systems. The following chapter will examine the allocation of land value increment and compensation from a property rights perspective.

3. Studying betterment and compensation from the perspective of property rights

China's 1988 land use rights (LURs) system marketized property rights in land, which used to be administratively allocated. As a result, a land market was established and triggered more economic growth in China. The current LURs management framework, however, has not been sophisticated enough to internalize externalities of betterment and worsenment. This chapter examines the issues of betterment and compensation at a theoretical level, using the analytic framework of property rights and the theory of the state initiated by New Institutional Economics.

3.1 BETTERMENT AND WORSENMENT, EXTERNALITY AND THE COASE THEOREM

3.1.1 Betterment, Worsenment and Externality

Land value largely depends on location advantages and decisions concerning the use of neighbouring sites. This interdependent quality of urban land is referred to by economists in terms of externalities: those impacts (positive or negative) that are not reflected in the pricing system of land (Loughlin, 1988). Betterment and worsenment are typically derived from externalities: betterment is a positive externality generated neither by the capital investment nor by the decisions of land users themselves; worsenment is a negative externality in the same way. In dealing with the externality issue, the Pigovian argument and the Coase theorem are most influential.

The Pigovian approach to internalizing an externality is through taxation and regulation (Pigou, [1920] 1929). For instance, a factory emits smoke that pollutes the environment, thereby incurring damage to the community. The costs of polluting, however, are not incorporated into the production costs of the factory. Thus a divergence between 'marginal social net product and marginal private net product' emerges. To attain efficiency, the factory owner's behaviour must be altered by government actions such as taxation and regulation of the amount of pollution.

The Pigovian formula, however, makes two implicit assumptions: (1) the cost of administering government intervention is zero; and (2) an unrealistic one, is that political executives act solely to maximize social efficiency without regard to their own utility (Burton, 1978; Cheung, 1978). In real life, however, government behaviour cannot be explained solely by social benefits. Niskanen (1973) argues that power, prestige and income tend to be related to the size of the agency, and bureaucrats have an incentive to expand the size of their budget allocation or agency. This will lead to 'overcorrection' of externalities and an inefficient allocation of resources. The Pigovian formula is thus oversimplistic as a rule for government externalities policy (Burton, 1978).

In Coase's view ([1960] 1973), the problem of externalities is a reciprocal one. He argues that Pigou's approach can incur more harm on one party than is gained by the other party, and thus entail loss. On efficiency grounds the solution is not simply to restrain the damaging party, but to allow the involved parties to establish a mutually agreed-upon scheme to share the responsibility of 'internalizing' the negative externality, Therefore contracts play a key role in internalizing externalities. Cheung (1970) attributes the mushrooming of alleged 'externalities' to the following factors: (1) the absence of the right to contract; (2) the presence of a contract but with incomplete stipulations; and (3) the presence of stipulations that are somehow inconsistent with some marginal equalities.

3.1.2 Transaction Costs and Externality

The theory of transaction costs originated by Ronald H. Coase can be an effective tool in analysing the externality issue. Coase ([1960] 1973) defines transaction costs as the costs of information and bargaining, and of policing and enforcing property rights and contracts. In his seminal article 'The nature of the firm', Coase ([1937] 1973) argues that the existence of a firm is due to the reduction of marketing costs and organizing costs. Then, Coase developed the idea of 'transaction costs' in another renowned article, 'The problem of social cost' ([1960] 1973), and discusses how transaction costs may affect the 'internalization' of externalities. In a world of zero transaction costs, the parties involved in a dispute arising from the presence of an externality could settle their conflict through contracting their property rights.

The Coase theorem is based on the following assumptions: (1) there are fully developed rights and zero transaction costs; and (2) the identity of owners has no resource allocation consequences. Therefore, Coase's analysis concludes that social cost and private cost will be brought into equality through market negotiations, regardless of which party is assigned the responsibility for bearing the cost. As a result, income effects are ignored (Cheung, 1978; Demsetz, 1990).

In reality, transaction costs are never zero. Many scholars, such as Demsetz (1967), Cheung (1978), Barzel ([1989] 1997) and North (1990a), have followed Coase's idea of transaction costs, but have treated transaction costs as being significant rather than negligible. Coase ([1960] 1973) himself realizes that only in the absence of transaction costs does the neoclassical paradigm yield the implied allocative results; with positive transaction costs, resource allocations are altered by property rights structures. Transaction costs can block mutually beneficial exchange and cooperation because discovering an agreed solution might require extensive negotiation, whilst enforcing it might require monitoring and policing. Cheung (1982) broadly identifies transaction costs as the primary constraint in determining institutional arrangements. When transaction costs arise, institutions emerge to reduce them and shape the resultant market structure.

North (1990a) notes that transaction costs arise because information is costly and asymmetrically held by the parties to an exchange, and the way that the actors develop institutions leads to market imperfections. The costliness of information and enforcement, plus measurement costs, together determine the costs of transacting. Eggertsson (1990) further demonstrates that when transaction costs are introduced, the role of the state can have a crucial effect on resource allocation. Transaction costs may block the reassignment of rights, and the initial partitioning of property rights may have important consequences for the general economy.

3.1.3 Transaction Costs of Addressing Betterment and Compensation

By extending Coase's idea, the costs of managing betterment and compensation can be identified as follows: (1) delineation of parties' rights in land; (2) negotiation between the state and the affected individuals; (3) maintenance of the economic and legal basis for property rights in land, for example the cost of establishing and maintaining a computerized system and land valuation; and (4) enforcement and administrative costs.

While addressing betterment and worsenment, there is always uncertainty and debate over who has the right to recover the surplus land value, what portion of the increased value can go to the government, and what portion of the loss of value can be compensated by the government. Empirical evidence from many countries has revealed that the tax or compensation rate is controversial. For instance, if the property tax rate is set high, it may incur broad resistance, but if the tax rate is too low, it cannot even cover the cost of evaluation and collection. Moreover, the assessment of betterment and worsenment involves a large amount of expertise and fees, which developing countries are short of. In an emerging land market such as China where the government has insufficient experience and expertise, high transaction costs can be a major barrier to implementing and maintaining betterment and compensation schemes. How institutions can be arranged to minimize prohibitive cost is therefore the key to addressing betterment and compensation.

3.2 PROPERTY RIGHTS AS A TOOL OF ECONOMIC DEVELOPMENT AND PUBLIC POLICY

Before the early 1960s, classical and neoclassical economists focused on studies of market institutions, and issues of property rights were paid little attention (Hong, 1995). Not until the late 1960s was the role of property rights in reducing transaction costs and facilitating economic growth emphasized by many scholars (Demsetz, 1967; Furubotn and Pejovich, 1972; Alchian, 1977; North, 1981, 1990b; Cheung, 1978, 1982; Barzel, [1989] 1997; Eggertsson, 1993), and a vast amount of research and literature has accumulated.

Property rights have been likened to a bundle of sticks, where each stick represents a right or stream of benefits, such as the right to sell, lease, mortgage, donate, subdivide, grant easements, and so on. The community also has a bundle of rights, such as to tax, take for public use, regulate use, and so on (Barber, 2005). Nonetheless, 'no definition of ownership is wholly satisfactory for all purposes' (Ryan, 1987: 1029). Property rights consisting of a bundle of rights vary in their components and elements, their combinations and restrictions under different contexts (Omura, 2004).

3.2.1 Property Rights as Economic, Social and Political Relations

Demsetz (1967) points out that the primary function of property rights is to guide incentives to achieve a greater internalization of externalities. Property rights develop to internalize externalities when the gains of internalization become larger than the costs of internalization. Through the analysis of the land ownership paradigm among Indian hunters in the eastern part of Canada, Demsetz emphasizes that the externality of private property rights presents a lesser degree. More important, the negotiating cost over the externality that accompanies private owner-ship can be reduced greatly. Following the same rationale, Furubotn and Pejovich (1974) state that the property rights system is the sum of economic and social relations with respect to scarce resources in which individual members stand to each other, and a more complete and definite specification of individual property rights diminishes uncertainty and tends to promote efficient allocation and use of resources. Bromley (1991) further indicates that property is not an empirical possession but rather is a social relation that defines the property holder with respect to something of value against all others. Therefore, property rights are also a factor of production. Property rights can be altered among individuals and groups to accomplish certain desired ends.

Cheung (1982) elaborates that the key factor in defining any economic system is the structure of property rights, comprising all the limitations, constraints or rules subject to which people in society compete and inter-act. Barzel ([1989] 1997) advances transaction costs and property rights as an analytical tool of the multiplicity of economic structures. He argues that rights to assets will not be perfectly delineated when transaction costs are positive. Since property rights have never been perfectly delineated, some valued assets will be left in the public domain, subject to open access. Capture of values in the public domain is nevertheless not costless, and the resources spent by competing parties are sometimes dissipated since these assets are not secured.

In view of such an important role of property rights in economic growth, Eggertsson (1990) concludes that subtle changes in the content of property rights can change the macro-performance of an economic system and lead to economic growth or stagnation. Besides, the assignment of dif-ferent property rights has important implications for resource allocation. McKean (1972) indicates that alternative property right assignments may have different impacts on equity, production processes and costs, alloca-tion of resources among uses, and the options open to consumers given the existence of transaction costs. Very often transaction costs vary markedly with different assignments of property rights. Therefore it is important to know more about the variation of transaction costs under alternative insti-tutions, and about the implications for wealth distribution and resource allocation under different contexts.

Property rights involve not only economic and social relations, but also political performance. Riker and Sened (1996) criticize Demsetz's expla-nation of 'the emergence of property rights' as suffering from the typical defect of neoclassical political economy of specifying the conditions for, and properties of, equilibrium. Whilst Demsetz deliberately excludes pol-itics in order to understand the economic features of perfect competition,

North (1981, 1993a, 1993b) introduces politics into the analysis of property rights, and argues that polities significantly shape economic performance because they define and enforce economic rules. Property rights are the relative power of individuals to control valuable resources. Therefore, an essential part of development policy is the creation of polities that will create and enforce efficient property rights. North (1990a, 1990b) further indicates the deficiencies of neoclassical economists through challenging their behavioural assumption, instrumental rationality,[1] which may be more applicable in economic markets than in political markets. Political markets are inherently highly imperfect due to the high cost of information and the low pay-off to the individual constituent of acquiring information, and they are far more prone to inefficiency. In communist and Third World countries, the imperfections of such markets are the root cause of their poor economic performance since it is polities which devise and enforce property rights that diminish the incentive of economies.

3.2.2   Laws, Transaction Costs and Property Rights

The importance of legal institutions for economic growth has long been paid much attention. According to Coase ([1937] 1973), when transaction costs are positive in contracting, the parties may rely on laws to settle disputes arising from economic exchanges. Many scholars have conducted research in the field of law and economics, and it has long been argued that when negotiation costs among parties are high, the law will become important in reducing these costs.

Barzel ([1989] 1997) defines property rights in two ways: economic rights and legal rights. Economic rights are the rights of an individual over assets through exercising their ability to consume or exchange the services of the asset; legal rights are defined as what the government delineates and enforces as a person's property. Whilst economic rights are the end, legal rights are the means to achieve the end. Bromley (1991) emphasizes that the courts play two important roles in the delineation of rights. The first is indirect: when the parties choose to settle their disputes without resorting to the courts, their actions are influenced by their perceptions of how the courts would have acted in their disputes. The second is direct: the disputes are actually settled by the courts. McKean (1972) stresses the importance of legal enforcement. He claims that the rarely enforced law only incurs modest cost to people violating it. High enforcement costs, or lax enforcement, may erode the ability of anyone to appropriate rewards from deals that might be mutually advantageous.

Furubotn and Pejovich (1972), however, challenge the function of law in economic growth. They note that some externalities are generated by legal constraints on the use and exchange of resources, rather than high transaction costs. In other words, under some situations, the disparity between social and private benefits and costs should be ascribed not to transaction costs but to the fact that transaction costs are made prohibitively high by law. Realizing this problem, North (1981, 1990b) initiated research on informal institutions and economic performance. He defines institutions as formal and informal rules that constrain individual behaviour and shape human interaction. Formal rules include political and judicial rules, economic rules and contracts. Informal constraints are embodied in customs, traditions and codes of conduct. A major role of informal constraints is to modify, supplement or extend formal rules. Formal and informal rules together define the incentive structure of societies and, specifically, economics. Although formal rules may change overnight as the result of political or judicial decisions, informal constraints are much more impervious to deliberate policies. However, formal rules can complement and increase the effectiveness of informal constraints. North (1993a) and Eggertsson (1993) argue that limited understanding of the relation between formal and informal institutions often leads to the failure of aid programmes from industrial countries for developing countries. Why the introduction of particular formal rules is sometimes futile can be explained by their mismatch with informal rules. Conversely, a better understanding of the role of informal institutions can be of help in designing formal rules that take advantage of existing informal rules to rely extensively on self-enforcement.

3.2.3 Diversity of Property Rights Regimes

The usual distinction made about property rights is between private and state ownership. The justification for state ownership is based on equality for every citizen. Nevertheless, for everyone to be equal would mean that individual risk preferences and incentives would have to be ignored, which usually results in a free-rider problem (Bertaud and Renaud, 1997). The collapse of state ownership in the former Soviet Union and East European countries has proved that the goal of absolute equity is hard to achieve.

The fear of the monopoly power of the state has led to many advocates of private ownership in the Western world. Scully's (1988) investigation into the compound growth rates per capita output for 115 market economies over the period of 1960–1980 shows that the institutional framework has significant and large effects on the efficiency and growth rate of economies. Politically open societies with strong individual freedom grew economically at three times the rate, and were two-and-a-half times as efficient, as societies that limited those freedoms in favor of the state. Jaffe and Louziotis (1996) hold that strong property rights reduce the risk associated with receiving future returns that property can potentially generate.

Nevertheless, private property rights do not necessarily mean security of property rights. Bromley (1991) criticizes the position which holds any property regime other than private property is inefficient as being prone to overuse and abuse. He argues that the spread of private property rights has undermined traditional collective management regimes, and is concerned with the economic feasibility of investing scarce development resources and time in natural resources; and he asserts that how they are managed, rather than who owns them, is the key to efficiency.

In terms of property rights in land, one has to be more cautious in concluding that private property rights are more secure. For instance, a short lease that is by custom always renewed may provide greater security of tenure than a longer lease or freehold ownership that may be subject to arbitrary public acquisition (Dunkerley, 1983: 12). The issue of equity in a strong private property rights scheme is another focus worthy of attention. As Payne (1997: 3) states: 'Notwithstanding the obvious advantage of freehold – a powerful incentive to stimulating investment in land and house improvements – a significant and permanent under-class may be created and distortions in the land and housing markets may be generated by the monopoly'. Many analysts argue that a public land leasehold system can allow the government to capture surplus land value and balance public and private interests more easily and efficiently than a land freehold system (Archer, 1974; Payne, 1997). The significance of a public land leasehold system also includes mitigating uncertainty in decision-making and curbing excessive land speculation, overcoming barriers in the organization of space and allocation of land (Montgomery, 1987), and financing urban development. If the administration is efficient and incorruptible, and a sophisticated legal system can be established, the equity in the land market can be advanced and the monopoly can be reduced; hence, the balance between efficiency and equity can be achieved. It is clear that no single land tenure system can be applied to all countries. As Feder and Feeny (1991) have shown, changes in population density, technology and political power generate changes in the assignment of property rights and in the institutional arrangements associated with these rights. Land tenure choice must be based on the historical context, cultural diversity and institutional arrangements.

Reviewing evidence from some cities such as Hong Kong, Singapore, Amsterdam, Stockholm, London and Honolulu, one can argue that the leasehold method is not an obstacle to market-led reform (World Bank,

1993). Government ownership of land may create positive impacts while the land can be leased to individuals, especially for countries with a high population density and limited land, where land use needs to be recycled at intervals to meet community needs. Archer (1972) recommends the use of a public leasehold land system to finance urban development in Canberra and argues that it can provide efficient urban development with a maximum private enterprise role. The justification for leasehold tenure in Canberra is that speculation in undeveloped land can be avoided, and future increases in the value of land will remain in the public purse. Montgomery (1987), in his analysis of the significance of public owner-ship of land in Oxford and Sheffield in the UK, argues that public land ownership can overcome barriers in the organization of space and alloca-tion of land. Castells et al. (1990) suggest that there may be an indirect relationship between Hong Kong's miraculous economic growth and its land policy.

Nevertheless, the theoretical advantages of public ownership must be traded off against bureaucratic disadvantages. Public ownership is unlikely to achieve improved equitable access unless there is both political commitment and administrative capability (Doebele, 1982). The inexperi-ence of the policy-makers in developing countries, however, often makes success of a public leasehold system uncertain.

3.2.4 Property Rights and Chinese Economic Reform

Compared with the radical departures from the past, change in the area of property rights has been ambiguous in China. The role that property rights have played in China's reforming economy is debatable. Two oppo-site views coexist (Putterman, 1996): China offers evidence of the viability of a market socialist option, but the transformation of property rights remains a major hurdle on the road to an economy that can support sus-tained growth. On the one hand, institutional changes have been regarded as paving the way for China's successful economic reform, and they have removed constraints on local government autonomy and injected strong economic incentives for local government to be entrepreneurial. Qian (1999) argues that the unconventional economic reform of China can be more productive than 'best practice institutions' for a certain period of time because of the second-best principle. On the other hand, Chinese reform has often been criticized for its unsystematic approach and opaque rules, leading to increased uncertainty, corruption, and the reduction of incentives to invest (Putterman, 1996).

In contrast to the 'big bang' approach adopted by former East European socialist countries that transitioned abruptly to a market economy, China's economic reform has been described as partial. Market elements have been introduced on a gradual and incremental basis (Li, 2000). The Chinese economic reform approach of trial and error, gradualism, and permitting new and old systems to coexist, has been reflected in major economic and institutional changes. In his article 'Will China go "capitalist"', Cheung (1982) provides insightful thinking on the vague nature of the Chinese Constitution. He states that the survival of the communist system in China has been abetted by ambiguities within the Marx–Lenin–Mao doctrines, which offer opportunities for exploitation. Thus, 'the Chinese Constitution, rather than establishing a structure of rights for social and economic interaction, merely serves to confuse' (p. 26).

While neoclassical economists claim that formal, full private rights have been advanced in conventional economic theories, there is a prevalence of informal de facto property rights in developing countries where the formalization of these rights lags behind, due to the limited capacity of state administrations (Omura, 2004). Contrary to conventional theories, ambiguous property rights have been regarded as a second-best institution which facilitates economic growth in China during the transitional period, in the absence of clear-cut property rights (Li, 1996; Qian, 1999). Li (1996) argues that the arrangement of ambiguous property rights is a response to the market imperfection in China during the transitional economy. Oi (1996) asserts that entrepreneurial local governments have made significant contribution to the economic growth of China, and the complete clarification of property rights is not the only way to stimulate economic growth.

Ambiguous property rights, however, are deemed to be tentative during the transitional period (Zhu, 2005). The evolutionary trajectory of property rights in China has shown that their marketability and strength have been increasing and they are moving towards more formal titles. China's institutions have been changed to carry out the tasks of reform and modernization. Property rights which lag behind changes in the environment can act as brakes on economic development and growth (Eggertsson, 1990). Zhu (2002, 2005) notes that ambiguous delineation of property rights over urban land drove oversupply of property in China in the 1990s and caused massive rent dissipation. As a consequence, costs incurred by ambiguous property rights are gradually overtaking the benefits. After the market structure has been established, more clarification of property rights is needed to facilitate long-term economic growth.

3.3 THE STATE, THE INDIVIDUAL AND PROPERTY RIGHTS

In the realm of land policy-making, the relationship between the state and the private property owner has always been an important and sensitive issue, politically and economically. According to Payne (1997: 3), 'the key factor in any system of land tenure and property rights is the relationship of an individual to the group, and of different groups to each other and the state, and their collective impact on land'. In most cases, the security level of a land tenure system is defined by the state through a series of tools such as land laws, land use regulations and land taxation, and is vulnerable to changes of political regime and economic system. The state, however, is not free of restraints in defining property rights in land. On the one hand, the state has its own national planning aims and preferences in different development periods. Property rights over land as basic instruments of overall development policy perform both an indirect, facilitating role and a direct and active one, and therefore exert a great impact on urban development in terms of both efficiency and equity (Doebele, 1987; Payne, 1997); on the other hand, the state cannot go too far for its own interests or impede the security of tenure, for the security is essential to stimulate the individual initiative necessary for economic development. The state therefore has to strike a balance between efficiency and equity.

3.3.1 The Rationale of State Intervention in Land Markets

The laws of supply and demand cannot operate satisfactorily in land markets, because the supply side has a built-in element of monopoly – built in by nature (Bryant, 1972); in other words, land is distinguished from other commodities in that its supply is more or less fixed. Due to the heterogeneity of land plots in terms of location and quality, the urban land market is inherently imperfect (Zhu, 2002). Alterman (2011b) addresses other well-known special attributes of land: it provides the essential context for social and political life, it often embeds symbolic or religious values, and it is largely irreplaceable.

Market mechanisms, even with zoning controls, cannot produce a perfect allocation of land use. The existence of significant externalities in the functioning of urban land markets is generally regarded as a major reason for state intervention. Moreover, land use control is too important to be left to private greed (Bromley, 1991). For these reasons state intervention has become inevitable in urban land markets, although in varying degrees. State regulation of land development thus aims to minimize the disruptive effect of externalities on the efficient functioning of market processes (Loughlin, 1988).

3.3.2   Debates over the State

It has long been established that property rights are mainly delineated by the state. As Furubotn and Pejovich (1974) claim, a theory of property rights cannot be truly complete without a theory of the state. Most restrictions established by the state can attenuate property rights by limiting the owner's right to use or transfer rights in their asset. Therefore, changes in the content of property rights depend on the relationship between an *ex ante* estimate of benefits to the ruling class and the *ex ante* or even *ex post* estimates of the costs to be incurred in policing and enforcing the changed structure of rights. North (1981) argues that the state has a central role in determining the structure of property rights, and he advances the theory of the state to analyse economic growth. Property rights are specified and enforced by polities; therefore, without an in-depth understanding of the way polities evolve, it is impossible to understand the way in which property rights evolve. Eggertsson (1990, 1996) maintains that historically the state has lowered transaction costs of the contracting of individual actors by providing clear and stable property rights and a consistent system of enforcement, and by introducing and maintaining a stable economy.

The role of the state in economic growth, however, has been frequently challenged in the Western world where the individualistic tradition of property rights has had the tendency to protect private property against the state (Donahue, 1980). Basically, there are two fundamental issues of questioning the state. The first one is the predatory state approach, which views the state as a 'predator' which tries to maximize its own profits even at the cost of the society (Vandergeest, 1997). Public-choice scholars reject the assumption of a benevolent government. Government is treated as a self-interested strategic player that attempts to maximize its own utility in the form of maximized revenue or political support (Buchanan, 1975; Sened, 1997). Booth (1996) argues that the search for material interests turns the controlling authority from impartial adjudicator into an equal partner with the developer. Therefore, the idea of government as an impartial adjudicator acting in the public interest is an inherently false model. The second challenges the implicit assumption of the sufficient capability of the state to achieve its own objectives. Coase ([1960] 1973) states that government actions that are not subject to the rule of markets may lead to misallocation of resources. North (1981) asserts that there is overwhelming historical evidence that the state typically does not supply structures of property rights that are appropriate for economic growth. On the one hand, the state acts as a wealth maximizer of the ruler or ruling class, and trades a group of services for revenue; on the other hand, the state is constrained by the opportunity cost of its constituents since there are always potential rivals to provide the same set of services. Therefore, the state has to face two constraints: a competitive constraint and a transaction cost constraint. Both typically produce inefficient property rights. In effect, the property rights structure that will maximize rents to the ruler (or ruling class) is in conflict with that that would produce economic growth.

Realizing the shortcoming of the state, Cheung (1978) and Burton (1978)[2] advocate that governments should play a minimal role in the economy, except to protect private property rights, but their judgement is not compelling because they do not evaluate clearly the 'costs' and 'benefits' of government intervention. Cheung (1978: 50) himself realizes that, 'Whatever government is, its economic role in society must remain unclear until we can pinpoint the activities where governmental intervention incurs lower costs than private contracting.'

Despite the critical views about the state, the necessity of the state is generally accepted. The argument mainly focuses on to what extent the state should be involved in economic activities. Oi (1996) divides the role of the state into three levels: the first is the laissez-faire minimalist state whose role is limited to ensuring a stable and secure environment so that contracts, property rights and other institutions of the market can be honoured; the second is the centrally planned Leninist states that directly replace the market with bureaucratic allocation and planning, such as the former Soviet Union and China under the command economy. Between these two extremes are the capitalist developmental states of Japan and the East Asian newly industrializing countries (NICs) that are neither communist nor laissez-faire, but exhibit characteristics of both.

While the minimal role of the state has been vigorously advocated in some Western countries such as the USA, evidence from some other countries and cities supports the idea that government intervention may play a positive role in economic growth. Stiglitz (1994) attributes the Asia miracle – rapid growth of Japan, Korea, Singapore and Taiwan – to the crucial role of government in 'governing the market', and argues that transforming to a market economy does not entail a withering away of the state but a redefinition of its role. Duncan (1988) concludes that Swedish state intervention into the supply of development land has increased social welfare and economic efficiency because speculation in land is severely constrained, and most development land is acquired by state authorities in publicly owned land banks for release to developers. Swedish state intervention in land markets has created a socially just and economically effective society. Castells et al. (1990: 2) point out that: 'It is generally accepted today in specialized literature that the state has been the engine of the process of hypergrowth in the leading Asian economies, first in Japan, and then in South Korea, Taiwan, and Singapore'. Zhu (1997) argues that government intervention within the framework of a free market economy can contribute considerably to an efficient property market through his research on property markets in Singapore in the 1980s. Based on research on East European reform, Koslowski (1992) favours the role of the state in economic reform, and stresses the importance of the state in the establishment of market institutions and the institutionalization of property rights. Liew's (1995) research about Chinese gradualist reform leads to a conclusion that a strong central state is more fundamental in Chinese economic reform, as only a strong central state can provide conditions that will enable the creation and enlargement of a constituent of government and party officials in favour of reform. A strong state itself, however, does not guarantee a successful development process; the role of the state must be integrated in a broader framework of interactions in the international economy (Castells et al., 1990).

Therefore, it is impossible to simply conclude what role the state should play in economic growth. This role varies according to different contexts. North's elaboration (1981, 1990b) about the state is very comprehensive. He argues that the state has been playing a paradoxical role in economic growth: on the one hand, it is critical for economic development; on the other hand, it is the source of man-made economic decline. The influence of the state on the economy is mainly reflected in its role of specifying and enforcing property rights, which is responsible for growth, stagnation or economic decline. In his book, *Institutions, Institutional Change and Economic Performance*, North (1990b: 128) emphasizes the role of the state in economic evolution: 'there was continuous interplay between the fiscal needs of the state and its credibility in its relationships with merchants and the citizenry in general'. However, as a main form of third-party enforcement in impersonal exchange, the state has never been ideal or perfect in enforcement, due to the arbitrary behaviour of rulers. Therefore, it is critical to consider how the state can be organized so as to provide the necessary political foundations for market capitalism without posing potential dangers to the continued functioning of efficient production and exchange.

3.3.3   The Individual and Property Rights

Although the state has a comparative advantage over individuals in the use of violence to protect property rights and reduce uncertainty, political actors are constrained by their physical and social environment and do not have unlimited capacity to structure property rights (North, 1981; Riker and Sened, 1996). Furthermore, the power exercised by the state sometimes leads to a situation where a strong government is capable of both protection of private property rights and confiscation of the wealth of its citizens. North (1990b) and Weignast (1993) argue that unrestrained, undisciplined state power creates a strong disincentive for decentralized investors, and maintain that the evolution of modern industrial economies in North-Western Europe is closely related to success in introducing the rule of law and constraining the state from randomly overriding individual property rights.

Notwithstanding the dominant role of the state in property rights formation, Barzel ([1989] 1997) demonstrates that the delineation of property rights is also subject to individuals' optimization. Individuals have a comparative advantage over the government in various delineation activities, and actually undertake many of them. When the value of rights in the public domain increases, people will tend to spend more resources to capture them and turn them into private property. Such transfer from the public domain to private ownership sometimes enables much clearer delineation of property rights. Therefore, individuals' behaviour must be considered in the study of rights formation. Eggertsson (1990, 1996) indicates that the enforcement of exclusive rights is usually undertaken by both individual owners and the state. He supports the view that rational individuals will compete not only to maximize their utility within a given set of rules, but also to seek to change the rules and achieve more favourable outcomes than was possible under the old regime. Individuals can better their position not only by investing in economic activity within a given framework of institutions, but also, in the long run, by investing in strengthening their property rights through altering the institutional framework. Barzel ([1989] 1997: 152) emphasizes the role of the individual in the formation of rights: 'Whereas individuals are always ready to expend resources to increase their share of the pie, they will also seek out methods and organizations by which to better delineate rights to it, thereby dividing the pie without shrinking it too much'.

Kiser and Ostrom (1982: 184) advance a three-level micro-institutional approach starting from the individual as a basic unit of analysis to explain and predict individual behaviour, and resulting aggregated outcomes. One is the operational level, which explains the world of action. The second is the collective level, which explains the world of authoritative decision-making. The third is the constitutional level, which explains the design of collective-choice mechanisms. Constitutional decisions establish institutional arrangements and their enforcement for collective choice. Collective decisions, in turn, establish institutional arrangements and their enforcement for individual action. The enforcement is crucial for individuals to follow rules. Nevertheless, the enforcement alone is not enough to assume that rules are followed: people have to share a belief that the rules are fair, otherwise enforcement will be too expensive to maintain regularity and predictability in ongoing human relationships.

3.3.4   The State of China in Economic Reform

According to Oi (1996) and Zhu (1999a), China has adopted a distinctive form of state-led growth. The core of the growth is that local governments have played a unique role in economic growth, and they act as both regulators and advocates of local enterprise growth. The decentralization in the early 1990s has made local governments fully fledged economic actors, not just administrative service providers as they are in other countries. Each local government is keen to generate 'extra-budgetary' revenues for its own purposes in 'entrepreneurial' ways. Local officials are highly motivated to maximize local revenues due to their own interests; in other words, the local revenue has become an essential criterion of evaluating the performance of top officials, and opening up opportunities for local officials to enlarge their own income. A coalition between local government and local industries is thus formed (Zhu, 1999a).

China's reforms typically involve what might be termed 'enabling measures' rather than compulsory changes. It is the government that initiates partial reform measures (Putterman, 1996). The success of Chinese economic reform has been greatly attributed to the role of the state in economic development. Cheung (1982: 38–43) puts it: 'Subject to existing constraints, society will always choose that institution which imposes the lowest transaction costs... Major obstacles to institutional change are observed in the cost of obtaining correct information about other institutional arrangements and the cost of persuading or forcing the privileged group to acquiesce'. However, he observes that the costs of institutional change have been declining in China, and rules conflicting with the current structure of property rights have been gradually altered. Unlike the former Soviet Union, which undertook political reform before beginning the task of economic restructuring, and unlike the weak authoritarian states of Africa and Latin America, China maintained its ability to rein in economic activity after reforms began. Liew (1995) argues that the presence of a strong central government that could enforce the delivery of plans has contributed to the success of the gradual strategy. Oi (1996) further asserts that not only is the political strength of a regime on the eve of reform crucial to determining its capacity to structure economic change, but a regime must also ensure that it retains sufficient capacity to control the course of reform.

Generally speaking, the Chinese government has been successful in its economic reform, although its political system is not founded on democracy, which Western scholars regard as critical for restriction on the power of the state (Tiebout, 1956; Weingast, 1993). Nevertheless, even under a democratic political system there are always problems associated with the polity, such as 'political free ridership' (North, 1981: 31), 'transaction cost log-rolling' or 'vote trading', and the inflexibility of the Congressional committee system to meet changing public preferences (Shepsle, 1992). So far there has been very little progress in creating a polity of checks and balance to maximize the social well-being, as North (1994: 366) claims: 'Polities significantly shape economic performance because they define and enforce the economic rules. Therefore, an essential part of development policy is the creation of polities that will create and enforce efficient property rights. However, we know very little about how to create such polities'.

SUMMARY

The concept of property rights is fundamental to economic activities, for they are regarded as providing incentives to management and allocation of resources. This chapter has explored issues germane to betterment and worsenment as externalities. Special attention was given to the role of property rights in promoting economic growth and reducing transaction costs. Emphasis was also given to property rights as economic, social and political relations. Next, the argument of the state as an institution was discussed, given its paradoxical role in economic development. Government intervention has been regarded as indispensable in the land market, but its influences vary from country to country. Furthermore, it is noteworthy that the perspective of the individual has an important impact on the formation of property rights. Although it is hard to build consensus on the distribution of property rights, and the resultant effect on the relative power between the state and the individual, it is universally accepted that every society must establish its own equilibrium between private rights and social responsibilities. A system of checks and balances is needed for long-term economic growth.

This chapter has applied the framework of property rights to analyse Chinese economic reform and the role of the Chinese government in the transitional economy. Whilst an approach of property rights has been intensively and extensively applied in the Western world, it will inevitably introduce some biases into the developing world. Specifically the concept of property rights is regarded as being affected by the historical experiences characterized by Western culture. A property rights framework has been found to be workable but has never perfectly explained the Chinese economic reform. The biggest challenge of the application of a Western property rights framework in China is whether it can satisfactorily maintain that a strong state and the ambiguity of property rights have helped to reduce transaction costs and establish a market framework within a short time period, which is a fascinating and challenging task facing economists, but that is beyond the scope of this book. In the following chapters, property rights in land will be examined in detail to analyse their influences on Chinese land markets and urban development.

NOTES

1. Instrumental rationality means that the actors either have correct models by which to interpret the world around them or receive information feedback that will lead them to revise and correct their initially incorrect theories. North (1990a) asserts that there are no institutions in neoclassical economic theory because the instrumental rationality postulate renders them superfluous. Once one introduces institutions into the model, a necessary corollary is recognition that instrumental rationality is not the correct behavioural assumption.
2. See Cheung (1978: 64): 'any government action can be speciously justified on efficiency grounds by the simple expedient of assuming that transaction costs in the market are high and that costs of governmental control are low'. And Burton (1978: 90): 'Government intervention is best kept as a "solution of the last resort": to be used only when and where high and irreducible transaction costs prevent the internalisation of externalities by private action.'

4. Assessing and addressing betterment and compensation: international experiences

Given the lack of experience of China in addressing betterment and compensation, it is highly desirable to gain an understanding of international experiences. The purposes of this chapter are to highlight some techniques adopted in other countries and to explore their potential applicability in China. In reading about national experiences from different countries, the author has been struck by the differences in national responses and the diversity of approaches. Britain has played the leading role in land value capture across the world, and it is well known for its volatile policies and various attempts to deal with compensation and betterment. While the whole emphasis of the Labour government was on preventing landowners benefiting from the 'unearned increment' in land by means of national taxes, the Conservative Party went to the other extreme and simply abolished them during the 1960s and 1970s (Hallett, 1985). In the USA, by the end of the 1960s, 'unearned increment' seemed to arouse no concern at all, and correspondingly, no compensation was payable to owners whose property lost value as the result of a planning decision (Delafons, 1969). Over the last two decades, and even before this, constrained by the cut of federal and state intergovernmental revenues, local governments throughout the US have been looking for additional sources of revenue, and municipalities have been allowed to impose impact fees to generate revenue for funding or recouping the cost of new capital improvements or facility expansions necessitated by new development (Adams et al., 1999). Korea, Japan and Taiwan apply the tool of land readjustment to recoup the cost of urban investment and finance urban construction. The public land leasehold system, which has been adopted in China, Canberra, Singapore, Amsterdam, Stockholm, the inner city of London and Honolulu, is often regarded as an effective tool to recover betterment and compensate worsenment. Approaches vary from country to country and city to city, and any approach has its own merits and drawbacks.

4.1   ASSESSMENT OF BETTERMENT AND WORSENMENT

The extent to which land value has been changed by public actions has been debated heatedly for over a century. Empirical evidence has shown different impacts of various public actions on land value change, and demonstrates that the context is important and should be seen as an input to any analysis. For instance, a survey of 150 references on the topic of land value and public transport conducted by the Royal Institution of Chartered Surveyors (RICS, 2002) reveals that similar transport investments have a different impact in locations depending on whether local economic situations are vibrant or stagnant, and according to different population densities. While Wegener's (1995) collection of evidence from North American cities shows that locations close to rail stations in general have not attracted more development and not generated higher land values than more remote locations, Banister and Berechman (2000) conclude that in Japan, where population densities are quite high, rail transport dictates development patterns in Tokyo and the other major Japanese cities as employment is highly centralized with limited parking, making land values a function of travel time to Tokyo and other cities. They realize that transit may have clearer impact on the economy in developing countries where the transport network is sparse and of a lower quality than in developed countries where the transport network has been more developed. Thus it is not possible to generalize with regard to the strength of impact of public actions across the world. While assessing property price change, two basic models, hedonic and repeat sales, have been suggested for building price indexes.

4.1.1   Hedonic Pricing Model

The hedonic pricing method is based on the assumption that people value the characteristics of a good, or the services it provides, rather than the good itself. Thus, prices reflect the value of a set of characteristics, such as plot size, living area, the layout of houses, proximity to public transport facilities, and surrounding environment and facilities, all of which people consider important when purchasing the good (RICS, 2002). Hedonic valuation models have often been used to account for the prices of heterogeneous goods, for example, real estate rents and capitalized values for land and buildings. In this context, heterogeneity means that the properties of one good can differ markedly from the properties of another. It is therefore impossible to make a direct comparison of the market prices of such goods. On the basis of recent prices that have been paid for property, a proven statistical method (multiple linear regression) can be used to calculate the proportion of the total value accounted for by each of a property's individual features (Llewelyn et al., 2004).

A simplified equation of hedonic pricing[1] can be expressed as follows:

$$P_i = \beta_0 + \beta_1(X_1) + \beta_2(X_2) + \ldots + \beta_N(X_N) \qquad (4.1)$$

where P_i denotes the most recent selling price of the ith observation, β is the regression coefficient, and X means different explanatory variables such as plot size, living area, building age, distance from transport facilities, and surrounding public facilities. Depending on different contexts, equation (4.1) can be revised.

Hedonic regression, however, is very demanding on both assumptions and data. If there are unobservable characteristics that are correlated with those included, hedonic regression estimates may be severely biased. One of the hedonic model's key assumptions is identical preference among households, but preferences are not identical even among households with similar socio-economic and demographic characteristics (Giuliano, 1995). Furthermore, the adoption of hedonic methods requires a considerable data collection effort, as not only product prices but also their related characteristics are needed (Bover and Velilla, 2002). Since the hedonic method was first applied in the USA in the 1950s, it has also been officially used in the Netherlands, Norway, Sweden and the UK.

4.1.2 Repeat-Sales Model

The idea of the repeated sales regression is to use observations on houses that have been sold more than once to estimate a quality corrected index. It assumes that the characteristics of the same property, such as living area, surrounding public facilities and open space, do not change as time goes by. Therefore, a housing price index of properties whose value is affected by transport services can be constructed to compare with the overall housing price index to see how much the difference is.

The housing price index of affected property can be expressed as:

$$P_i = P_1 (1 + r_1)^{D1}(1 + r_2)^{D2} \ldots (1 + r_n)^{Dn} \qquad (4.2)$$

where P_1 is the initial transaction price; P_i is the ith transaction price; $1 + r_n$ is the cumulative index of appreciation at period of t; D_t is an exponent equal to -1 if period t is second most recent sale, $+1$ if it is the most recent sale, and 0 for all other t.[2] To normalize the index, D_1 is set equal to 0. Taking the natural log of (4.2) yields:

$$LN(P_i/P_1) = D_1 LN (1 + r_1) + \ldots + D_n LN (1 + r_n) \qquad (4.3)$$

Then the r_n can be compared with the housing price index of the entire city to conclude the impact of transport services (Gatzlaff and Smith, 1993). This technique, however, has been criticized because of the small sample size involved after discarding all the information on houses sold only once, which may result in large sampling errors (Bover and Velilla, 2002). Also, changes in asset composition and characteristics quality between sales, such as the change of house structure and neighbour-hood characteristics, are difficult to measure and may go unobserved (Hill et al., 1997).

Therefore, in terms of methodological issues, the hedonic and repeat sales methods are both inherently imperfect. Furthermore, both of these techniques require a sophisticated housing registration system, which records transactional data and relevant characteristics of houses. Banister and Lichfield (1995) argue that there is no single methodology available to test the relationship between transit and economic development, as the counterfactual situation is difficult to determine and the question of causality is not addressed. Even where clear methodological approaches have been tried, problems arise concerning available data and the inherent complexity of the relationships. The links between land use, transport and development are much more profound than just an examination of physical, social and economic relationships might produce. Institutional, organizational and financial concerns are equally important. Therefore, no model can be generally applied across geographic areas because of its sensitivity to small changes in model parameters and assumptions.

There have been numerous empirical studies, designed to present some quantitative and qualitative evidence on the evaluation of public facilities on economic growth at the macro level as well as land value changes at the micro level (Gatzlaff and Smith, 1993; Banister and Lichfield, 1995; Banister and Berechman, 2000; Bover and Velilla, 2002; Startup and Rossiter, 2003), but these have to be used with care, as they are often based on particular locations, and for more rigorous analysis they need to be combined with context (Llewelyn et al., 2004).

4.2 APPROACHES TO ADDRESSING BETTERMENT AND COMPENSATION

4.2.1 Betterment Capture Approaches

Land taxation

Land taxation has been the most important and popular tool for governments to capture betterment. Under some situations where land prices rise as a direct result of public activities, it seems perfectly reasonable for the concerned authority to recoup the surplus land value through taxing a proportion of development value. According to Dunkerley (1983), land taxes can be categorized into two main types. One is taxes applied to the value of land or property in general; the other is betterment levies or special assessments that are based on increases in land or property values within the zone of influence of individual projects. Hallett (1985) divides land taxes into:

- property taxes;
- betterment levies;
- infrastructure charges;
- taxes on development value.[3]

Land taxation has proved an effective way to recoup surplus land value and finance public infrastructure construction. Failure to implement land taxes and charges would result in windfall gains, and cause the surplus value to accrue to present holders. Nevertheless, although land taxation is often advocated for its theoretical advantages, in reality there are many practical difficulties. The imposition of land taxes is vulnerable to strong opposition, particularly in the case of the introduction of taxes or charges based on flows of surplus value that are already occurring or anticipated (Dunkerley, 1983). Local property tax, one of most widely adopted land taxation methods, can highlight these difficulties. In most communities, property tax is based on periodic assessments of the capital value of houses and other properties, with the tax rate being determined by the local community. It is not easily evaded, and provides an independent source of revenue to local communities, but many analysts, including economists from the World Bank (1993: 89), consider the property tax to be an unsatisfactory instrument for the following reasons:

- Property taxes can be extremely politically unpopular as they often represent one of the few instances where a large percentage of households confront a tax bill.

● Assessments of property tax are complex, and they require an expertise that might not be available in many developing countries. The cost of collecting property tax is not negligible, and it requires not only the completion of a plot-by-plot cadastre but also a computerised system to update the cadastre.

Even in developed countries, theoretically favourable land taxes can generate undesirable consequences. In Britain, development tax has proved to be politically a hot potato. The development charge of 100 per cent introduced in 1947 was regarded as throttling the land market and adversely affecting the economy, and it was finally abolished by the Conservative administration in 1953. In 1967, the Labour administration introduced a 40 per cent tax on betterment, but this was again repealed by the incoming Conservative administration in 1971. In 1976, the Labour administration introduced betterment taxation at rates varying from 66.6 per cent to 80 per cent on betterment in excess of £10000. In 1980, the Conservative administration raised this threshold to £50000 and introduced a single top rate of 60 per cent. In 1985, it abolished the tax together, and this has remained unchanged (Corkindale, 2004). Similarly, development impact fees in the USA have sparked much debate since they increase housing costs, reduce housing affordability and disproportionately affect the poor (Boutin, 1999).

Realizing that taxes on the entire value of improved real estate tend to prevent improvement, rehabilitation or even change in the character of improved land uses, some scholars advocate land value (site value) as an alternative to total property value for the real estate tax base (Bryant, 1972; Harvey and Clark, 1972; Shoup, 1983). Site value taxation means the imposition of a tax on the land value only and not on the collective value of land and improvements. Advocates of site value taxation claim that its advantages include: (1) curbing land speculation; (2) stimulation of the redevelopment of slum areas, by making continued ownership of slum properties uneconomic; and (3) shifting the burden of municipal taxation from home owners to the owners of other types of property in an urban community (Plunkett, 1972). In particular, Georgists applaud using raw land as a base, because that land is relatively fixed in supply, and is a constant rather than created by the expenditure of labour and capital. A technical reason for favouring site value taxation is that betterment capture and worsenment mitigation would cause fewer economic distortions (Hagman and Misczynski, 1978).

Theoretical arguments strongly favour taxation of site value, and site value taxes are regarded as effective tools to capture betterment, but evidence only weakly confirms the predicted benefits of exempting improvement value from the tax base. Even in Georgist countries such as Australia and New Zealand where the use of site value taxation has been determined by local option, it is apparently the lure of reduced taxation that enables residential property owners to sanction its introduction. The main difficulty lies in assessment problems. A major argument against site valuation is that it is very difficult to separate the land value and the value of improvements (Hagman and Misczynski, 1978). Startup and Rossiter (2003) assert that although the argument is in favour of taxing property values, it does not lie in an untenable distinction between 'land' and 'property'. Besides, advocates of site value taxation often tend to overlook the important issue of the 'ability to pay' principle while they emphasize that site value taxation can stimulate the redevelopment of slum areas (Plunkett, 1972).

Land banking

Land banking usually refers either to advance acquisition of sites for government use or to larger-scale public ownership of undeveloped land planned for future urban use (Shoup, 1983). Flechner (1974) groups land banking into two broad categories: the former is called project or special land banking, and the latter is called general land banking.

Public acquisition arises when an authority purchases more land than is necessary for the construction of an improvement and subsequently sells or leases the surplus at a higher figure reflecting the enhancement in value due to the improvement. The early acquisition in the open market of land for a project has many advantages. Land banking can be used to influence the direction of urban development through the development of urban infrastructure, which will inevitably affect the direction of urban growth in the future (Farvacque and McAuslan, 1992). Besides, land banking can act as a buffer against price inflation in the open land market, and help to iron out fluctuations in land prices (Tse, 1998). Prices are lower because the new use has not yet increased the value, and there is a wider choice of sites (Dunkerley, 1983). Land banking is also an effective tool in capturing increases in land value created by governmental investment and lowering the cost of public improvements and services. Land banking is therefore regarded as powerful in controlling the land market and regulating land use planning.

Land banking is widely adopted in some Western European countries where crowded conditions, a relative land shortage and war damage generate acceptance of public intervention in land ownership. In Britain and the Scandinavian countries, there is a political theory that all land belongs to the Crown (Flechner, 1974). The City of Stockholm provides a successful example of land banking. The publicly owned land in Stockholm

County constitutes the largest land bank of any metropolitan area in Western Europe. At the beginning of the twentieth century, the city began to buy up land through a grant from the Crown and loans. By the end of the 1980s, the city owned 74 per cent of all land there. Over 80 per cent of new housing was built on land released from local authority (commune) land banks. Atmer (1987) indicates that land acquisition long in advance of development enabled Stockholm to control the timing and location of development and to subsidize housing. Duncan (1988) summarizes the three major results of large-scale use of land banking. Firstly, the costs of purchasing raw land, as a proportion of the production costs for new dwelling, average less than 5 per cent. As a corollary, the substantial part of land development gains are socialized and/or passed on to housing consumers in the form of cheaper housing, better-quality housing, better-planned environments, more accessible housing and capital gains to owner-occupiers. Secondly, a major source of unearned income for private landowners and/or builders is substantially reduced. Finally, for urban planners it is more possible to plan rationally: sufficient land will be available in advance. The municipal government of Amsterdam provides another successful example of land banking. For decades most Dutch municipalities have bought land a few years in advance of development, prepared it for development, and then sold or leased the actual development sites, retaining a substantial portion of the land for roads, parks and community facilities. Land banking has been the first step towards plan implementation, making it possible to provide housing sites in an attractive setting at moderate cost and to develop land in an efficient and orderly manner (Strong, 1979).

The public acquisition of large tracts, the installation of services, and their resale, have theoretical advantages in terms of efficiency, but in practice have proved to be problematic, particularly in many developing countries. According to Flechner (1974) and Shoup (1983), potential problems can be:

● Political problems, including fear of corruption in the land-purchase programme and fear of widespread use of condemnation of private property.
● Economic costs, including acquisition cost, land holding or interest cost, management and improvement cost, acquisition and disposition transaction costs. These costs may be substantial. Considerable opportunity cost may also be incurred in pre-empting public funds that could have been used for other purposes. Furthermore, the government may confront the risk of land price decreasing below acquisition cost.

• Operational issues, including government having a hard time evict-
ing interim users when the time comes to build. One obvious temp-
tation is to use banked land for public use when another location
would actually be better, and this has allegedly been a problem with
some site-and-service projects. Besides, the danger of acquiring
unneeded properties exists.

Even in Sweden and the Netherlands where land banking has been
regarded as fairly successful, the failure to adjust the base rate at frequent
intervals to reflect changes in site value has been criticized. Cities have
given many lessees a windfall and simultaneously denied themselves a fair
return on their investment, and this has prevented their land banks from
becoming self-supporting (Strong, 1979).

Until now land banking has been applied successfully in a few developed countries such as Sweden and the Netherlands where it has been
established since the early 1900s. In the 1960s Singapore and Hong Kong
achieved rapid urban redevelopment through applying the land banking
tool. However, Atmer (1987) is cautious about the transferability of
Stockholm's experience: Stockholm's growth pressures are insignificant
when compared to those of the developing world; the Swedish traditionally have accepted a large degree of public control of land use. Moreover,
Stockholm has maintained excellent records, enabling it to manage the
land acquisition and leasehold system efficiently.

Exactions and planning gains

Exactions are a type of windfall recapture device. City expansion requires
the installation of public facilities. Traditionally these services have been
provided by the community. In the early 1960s, local governments of
the USA, seeking ways to reduce financial burdens caused by development, began to require developers to reserve land for parks, school
sites and recreation areas, as a condition for obtaining development
permission. Thus local governments could avoid the expense of acquiring land for these facilities by purchase or condemnation (Jacobsen and
McHenry, 1978).

The land dedication requirement is the first device used by local governments to shift improvement costs to developers and new residents. From
the land dedication requirements, municipalities progressed to require the
construction and dedication of on-site improvements (Adams et al., 1999).
In the late 1970s, as a result of the criticism of urban sprawl and high
property taxes, impact fees were introduced to require that each development pay its proportionate share of the cost of providing the off-site
public facilities required by new development (Gomez-Ibanez, 1996). The

demand that growth should pay its own way attracted public support. As a result, municipalities have shifted their emphasis from general taxation toward user fees. Impact fees have become increasingly popular. Other exaction types include linkage and conditional zoning. Under the linkage programme, developers of high-value commercial schemes in downtown locations are required to contribute to specified uses such as an affordable housing scheme in the suburbs, on the premise that further commercial property development in the city will raise housing prices and drive out poorer would-be homeowners. Under the conditional zoning programme, a developer may choose either to develop at the density permitted by zoning ordinances, or increase the density provided that they pay a linkage fee, or set aside some land for public purposes (Callies and Grant, 1995). Since the late 1980s, required exactions and dedications of land within the proposed land development have been replaced by impact fees, because many local governments found it easier to require a fee rather than requiring land dedication as a condition of a permit.

Impact fees as a type of exaction are paid in the form of predetermined set amounts. According to Adams et al. (1999) and Wakeford (1990), their advantages include heightened user equity, more political support, reduced borrowing by local government, and promotion of local land use, economic and community planning. Disadvantages accompanying impact fees, however, cannot be ignored, such as the negative effect of increased new house prices on affordable housing, the opposition of developers attributed to increasingly burdensome exaction, and the equity argument that existing residents never have to pay impact fees so new residents and businesses should not be obligated to do so. More importantly, negoti- ated exactions are regarded as softening the hard edge of certainty inher- ent in traditional subdivision and zoning ordinances. Furthermore, in a period of recession, impact fees stifle real estate development and thus will usually stunt economic growth.

Somewhat similar to exactions of the USA, Britain has introduced plan- ning gains to recoup betterment during the last three decades in order to help finance the provision of infrastructure and other public facilities, and mitigate development impacts. In the past, planning gain has been defined as:

> a term which has come to be applied whenever, in connection with a grant of planning permission, a local planning authority seeks to impose on a developer an obligation to carry out works not included in the development for which per- mission has been sought, or to make some payment or confer some extraneous right or benefit in return for permitting development to take place. Planning gain is perhaps seen as the community's share of the profits to be made from a development. (Morgan and Nott, 1995: 310)

According to the government's Property Advisory Group report in July 1981, planning gains are 'the arrangements whereby local authorities, in granting planning permission, achieve planning and other community gains at the expense of developers' (RTPI, 2000).

In Britain, there is no formal test of a proportional relationship between the need generated by the development and the sum contributed, and deals are negotiated individually. Moreover, there is no general requirement that the contribution be earmarked for a specified purpose (Callies and Grant, 1995). The planning gains policy, therefore, has incurred some criticisms. The Royal Town Planning Institute (RTPI, 2000) summarizes these problems as follows:

- The negotiation of planning gains itself takes time and is a potent source of delay.
- Its incidence is unfair and capricious.
- The details of negotiations between local authorities and developers is so covered by a cloak of commercial confidentiality that it warps confidence in the planning system.

The success of the planning gains approach largely depends on two factors: (1) a fair and transparent means of assessment; and (2) a generally acceptable means of apportionment. For reasons of equity, it is essential that there should be a demonstrable and rational nexus between the infrastructure requirement and the development being charged for it; in other words, consideration should always be given as to whether it is desirable, or equitable, for the whole cost of infrastructure provision to fall upon developers. In many situations, the benefits of an infrastructure project may be shared between the development and the existing community or other users of the project, therefore it may be too onerous for the developers to bear all costs.

Public land leasehold system

Archer (1974) notes that there are many problems of land freehold in urban fringe areas, namely: significant external costs and benefits in decision-making; divergent and conflicting landowner goals; public works finance shortages; and excessive land speculation, which is generated by the small size of urban land parcels in many separate ownerships. Therefore, he advocates a land leasehold system on the grounds that it can meet the cost of land development and redevelopment works, and can recover the urban land values it generates as land rents and lease premiums. Furthermore, it has the advantage of solving the problem of windfall gains and hardship, while being a less extreme measure than compulsory purchase and land nationalization.

Montgomery (1987), in his analysis of the significance of public owner-ship of land in Oxford and Sheffield in the UK, argues that the institu-tional structure of private land ownership is a barrier to land uses, and public land ownership can overcome barriers in the organization of space and allocation of land. Land can be taken into public ownership in order to facilitate the development of a major infrastructure project. Taking the example of the city of Stockholm, Atmer (1987) argues that the advan-tages of a leasehold system include the following: (1) the increase in land value goes to the municipality; (2) it gives the city continuous control of the built-up areas and of construction, and makes it easier to arrange common facilities; (3) the possibility to reclaim land and use it for other purposes is a great advantage; and (4) the city has influence on the land value and can counteract unreasonable rises. Castells et al. (1990) attribute the success of the Hong Kong new towns and public housing scheme to its public land leasehold system. They claim that this system has provided key financial resources to the government; furthermore, it has been used to finance the necessary infrastructure for growth without having to resort to heavy direct taxation that would have undermined the business climate.

Compared with the land freehold system, the leasehold system has more tools to capture the land value increment. For example, the government can recoup the betterment through land leasing, land taxation, and re-grant of land leases under the leasehold system. Under the freehold system such as that of the US, however, choices of land value capture instruments could be limited to land taxation and exactions (Hong, 1998).

The major limitations of public land ownership stem from the capability and integrity of administrative systems and their ability to respond effi-ciently to changes in demand (Payne, 1997). In practice, the effectiveness of public land ownership or control depends largely upon the capacity, competence and integrity of the administrative system, and political commitment (Doebele, 1982). Where the administration framework is weak – for example, the government is corrupt or does not have enough information to decide correctly on the allocation of land resources – the evidence suggests that in the long term, public land ownership is not able to guarantee either efficiency or equity.

Land readjustment
Land readjustment is a technique for carrying out the unified servicing and subdivision of separate land holdings for planned urban development (Farvacque and McAuslan, 1992). By taking a relatively small proportion of the land benefited into the government's own hands, land readjust-ment can make the provision of public services virtually costless (Doebele, 1982). This would suggest that land readjustment could be applied to

informal settlements and inner city high-density low-income settlements (Farvacque and McAuslan, 1992). It is designed as a vehicle to be applicable in countries with rapid growth, rapid increasing land value and insufficient funds to provide urban services. It has been widely applied in some cities in Australia, Taiwan, Korea, Japan and Germany. Unlike outright purchase, land readjustment returns to each owner a substantial portion of the land originally owned in a location as close as possible to the original site. Therefore it is more politically acceptable than outright purchase or expropriation, which requires reducing all land values to specific cash sums. It also has advantages over various systems of land taxation in that it permits a relatively quick recovery of public capital investment.

In spite of many advantages, land readjustment is not universally applicable. Land readjustment has a number of important prerequisites for success, such as clear cadastre and title registration, an adequate corps of well-trained and objective real property appraisers, dedicated and energetic municipal staff, and support from the national, provincial and municipal governments. Since land readjustment reduces the area of every owner's property, it will be attractive only where infrastructure is difficult to obtain by other means, and where the demand for serviced land is strong enough to compensate the owner for the loss of area by making the remaining property more valuable, even though it is smaller (Farvacque and McAuslan, 1992). More importantly, the scale of the project must be large enough and the increased land value must be sufficient to both cover the project cost and return to the landowners a significant increase in land values.

Overall, land readjustment is an attractive tool for financing urbanization, but its application may be limited due to the technical complexities, land users' attitudes and equity issues during the readjustment.

Land nationalization
The term 'land nationalization' does not necessarily mean the confiscation of land, and it also may mean the nationalization of land development rights. The idea of land nationalization can be traced back more than 100 years. In 1870, Sir John Stuart Mill advocated a resumption of accruing land value increment in the future, realizing the essential injustice of private property in land. Mill's plan was that a fair and even liberal estimate should be made of the market value of all the land in the kingdom, and that future additions to that value less the improvements made by the proprietor should be taken by the state.

Alfred Russel Wallace develops Mill's idea. His two most important writings on land are *Land Nationalization*, published in 1883, and *The 'Why' and the 'How' of Land Nationalization*, also published in 1883.

Wallace argues that the state should, over the long term, buy out large land holdings and then institute an elaborate rent system based on a combination of location-specific considerations and considerations of value added by the renter. In *Land Nationalization* (1883) he lays out his programme. The state is to assume title to all land after compensating present landowners. Compensation is to be an annuity limited to the duration of lives in being. Individual lessees are to have secure tenure, and tenant rights to improvements. These rents will be based on the assessed 'inherent value' of land, depending only on natural and social conditions. Present holders will lose the right to sell, to bequeath and to let land. They can only hold what they have occupied and used themselves (Gaffney, 1987).

Henry ([1879] 1886: 283–284) argues that Mill's plan for nationalizing the future 'unearned increase in the value of land', by fixing the present market value of all lands and appropriating to the state the future increase in value, would not remedy the injustice of the present distribution of wealth. This plan will leave, for all the future, one class in possession of enormous advantage. He comes to the conclusion that the solution of modern social problems lies in the nationalization of land, through the medium of the single tax. George's view is that land rent is the only source of poverty and industrial depression.

The 1942 Uthwatt Report in the UK, 'Final Report of Expert Committee on Compensation and Betterment' (Uthwatt et al., 1942), remains the most complete and authoritative document available on compensation and betterment. It makes a proposal for a 'once and for all' solution: a large degree of public ownership of land, considering the problems of shifting value, floating value,[4] high value of properties in central areas, and the multiplicity of ownerships in central areas which lead to costly delays in acquiring property (Parker, 1965). The details of the solution as proposed by Uthwatt are that the state should immediately acquire development rights in all land outside built-up areas on payment of compensation. This compensation is to be assessed for the whole country as a single sum. The Uthwatt Report has been praised due to its advantages in forestalling speculation, removing the conflict between the state and public, and ensuring harmonious and coordinated development (Bryant, 1972).

This report, however, has incurred much criticism. Farrier and McAuslan (1975) criticize the Uthwatt Report on the ground that it is based on the fundamental premise of the necessity and efficacy of national planning and fails to take people's lives and the environment into account. The overriding need for beneficial effects of comprehensive land planning and subordination of private to public good is regarded as naïve by neoliberals. This report was rejected on the ground that it was politically unacceptable because it was regarded as being of little help in securing good development.

4.2.2 Compensation Approaches

While most countries provide compensation for compulsory acquisition of land,[5] no compensation is payable for the lost value arising from a planning decision or public works in many countries. Delafons (1969) criticizes the lack of resources to pay compensation for the loss of development value in the US, which he claims has made it impossible to secure some of the most important objectives of land use planning. While the American system can be quite effective in resolving conflicts of private interest and in enforcing good standards of private development, its scope for resolving conflicts of public and private interests in land use is far more limited: it cannot reserve land needed for public use or protect high agricultural or amenity value from development.

Special assessment
Special assessment has been popular in the United States since the early 1900s. It particularly focuses on circumstances in which the need for a capital improvement is clearly attributable to a particular development project or to development in a defined geographic area. Some property owners in that area clearly benefit from these projects, whereas other property owners may be adversely affected (Leitner, 1995).

Another situation of special assessment is generated by 'downzoning'. When a significant amount of some property is downzoned, landowners not downzoned may receive a windfall from the shifting of value. However, the landowners who benefit from the shifting value may be specially assessed to finance the payment of compensation. Harsh zoning therefore could be made 'zoning by special assessment financed eminent domain' (ZSAFED). ZSAFED makes payments from one set of property owners to another set. Under the early ZSAFED, each restricted residential district was assumed to be a separate externality-internalizing instrument. Historically, ZSAFED was initiated by a landowner. It is not necessary to consider the compensatory payment to be a purchase of an interest by government. It can be considered as the payment of damages, particularly if windfall recapture is provided (Hagman and Misczynski, 1978). Special assessment is not simply a compensation tool, but a comprehensive windfall recapture and wipeout mitigation system.

Special assessments are attractive partly because they are not perceived as taxes, but more like a fee for a government service. They do not engender general public objection because they affect only a limited area. Usually a special assessment district is created to levy the special assessment. A common problem is how to determine the boundaries of the district. Particularly where there are both special and general benefits at issue, the determination is more difficult, since it is very difficult to separate value increments attributable to the improvement from other contextual changes that might affect value (Melnick, 1995).

Transferable Development Rights (TDRs)
A conceptual key to TDRs is the notion that the development potential of a parcel may be severed from the physical location of that parcel. The rights may be sold, or the owner of the restricted parcel may use them on land that he owns in the transfer area. These development rights in effect compensate the owner of restricted land for the wipeout caused by the restrictions there.

TDRs have emerged as a land management device, based on the underlying principle that the development potential of privately held land is in part a community asset that government may allocate to enhance the general welfare. In concept, TDR serves the development potential from the land and treats it as a separately marketable item. It is viewed as a means of providing an equitable return on land invest-ment to property owners whose returns otherwise would be lessened by regulatory activity.

TDRs are useful in three main contexts: with historical building preser-vation, with open space preservation and with traditional zoning. A plan-ning authority uses TDRs to establish conservation zones and transfer zones. This transfer allows the marketplace to compensate the owner of land where development is restricted by allowing them to sell that density to transfer zone landowners. Strong (1987) considers the ambitious pro-gramme in the New Jersey Pinelands to use TDRs as achieving public land use goals by stimulating private market action. Because the environmental protection plan severely limits the development potential of much private land, TDRs were chosen to offer some compensation for the denial of development opportunity.

Several issues must be addressed in devising a TDR programme. They include establishing the boundaries of the conservation and developable areas, defining the nature of development rights and selecting the number and type to be issued, deciding how to allocate the rights among landown-ers, dealing with taxation of development rights, assuring their market-ability, as well as policies for retiring excess development rights and for issuing additional rights.

Blight notice

Britain provides compensation to an owner from whom no land has been acquired in certain circumstances. For example, injury to interests caused by the execution of works and the depreciation in land value caused by the use of public works, such as the construction of a new or widened road and the declaration of a clearance area under the Housing Acts, can be compensated. Under the circumstances where the affected homeowner is unable to develop their land or to sell it, they can claim a 'blight notice' which requires the authority to buy the land in advance. A blight notice, if accepted, effectively becomes a compulsory purchase. That 'full' compensation package varies depending on the affected landowner's status, but by and large it would include the market value of the property, together with a 10 per cent (minimum £1500, maximum £15000) uplift called a Home Loss Payment to represent the trauma of being removed. These arrangements, however, only apply in tightly defined circumstances, for instance where the owner-occupier of premises has tried to sell their property in the open market but cannot find a buyer except at a reduced price because of the authority's proposal.

4.3   THE COMPLEXITY AND COSTLINESS OF BETTERMENT AND COMPENSATION POLICIES

Scholars and analysts in both developed and developing countries have debated betterment and compensation approaches for many years, and have struggled with the implementation of various policies. However, it is difficult to build a consensus as to which policies have been successful. As Hallett (1985: 206) points out, 'the issues involved here are of great complexity, and no perfect solution is to be expected'. Alterman (2011b: 755) concludes that 'This topic has trailed planning policy for a long time, yet is no closer today to being resolved in a politically or legally sustainable manner.'

4.3.1   Difficulty in Separating Land Value Increments Caused by Different Factors

The fundamental reason why the distribution of land value changes is so problematic is the multiple determinants of land value. The change of land value can be categorized into at least five elements:

- change of locational advantages as towns and cities expand;
- the general growth of urban population;

- changes in permitted use as land use is rezoned;
- public investment in highways, bridges and other infrastructure; and
- private investment in land.

In theory, land users should be entitled to the portion of increased land value due to their investments in land and willingness to bear the risk involved, and be compensated for the lost value of their land arising from public works. The government and the community should obtain the portion of land value increment created by the improvements of public expenditure and city growth, and compensate for the adversely affected land users owing to public activities (Hong, 1995). In reality, however, it is very difficult to draw a line between the land value changes incurred by different activities and to decide how much should accrue to land users, government and communities, respectively. As Strong (1979) indicates, there is no clear methodology for separating out value attributable to public actions from other causes for increasing land value. Both land users and government can claim that they own the land benefit, and usually it is complicated and time-consuming to build a consensus on how to divide the land value increment between them.

4.3.2   Debates over Compensation

'Taking' or 'regulating'?
The difficulty in the area of compensation for worsenment is where to draw the line between compensatable damage and non-compensatable damage (Garner, 1975), namely, 'taking' or 'regulating'. For the questions under which situations and how much compensation should be paid, there are many different answers.

Firstly, the question whether compensation should be paid for the refusal of planning permission remains controversial. The UK and the USA treat development rights differently: in the UK development rights have rested with the state since the 1947 Town and Country Planning Act nationalized development rights, except in certain narrowly defined cases. The 1947 Act dealt with the compensation and betterment problem on a 'once and for all' basis. All development values were acquired by the state, and payments were made for their liquidation value from a £300 million fund. The £300 million fund was not a 'compensation' fund; instead, it was a fund from which *ex gratia* payments were to be made on account of 'hardship' (Cullingworth and Nadin 2006). No development was to take place without the permission of local authorities. If a development application was refused, no compensation would be paid. Therefore, the cost to the developer of a refused planning permission is not a planning issue

(Morgan and Nott, 1995). Americans, however, value private property rights very highly as an important freedom, and there is great resistance to any government action that appears to result in a reduction of land value. The refusal of planning permission often leads to litigation. Many American local governments have been confronting difficulties in deciding how far they can go without becoming liable to pay compensation (Wakeford, 1990).

Secondly, whether a landowner whose interests are indirectly affected by the activities of public authorities should be compensated, and how to compensate them, are reasonably well settled. The English law compensates not only the landowner for compulsory purchase but also the injurious impact on land where no actual land or interest in land has been acquired from an owner. For instance, the injury to interests caused by the execution of works and the depreciation of an interest in land caused by the use of public works are both compensated, but the principle is that the damage must be material, not trifling. English law has never protected a right to a view and no compensation is payable for injury caused merely by the visible presence of the public works (Garner, 1975). In some other countries such as China, only landowners whose land is requisitioned can receive compensation, and no compensation is available for the land that is adversely affected by public activities.

Compensation standard
The measurement of compensation is also debatable. The common controversy is about whether the existing market value or the expected value should be adopted as the compensation standard. Evans (1983) claims that land (and real property) is often valued by their owners at above market price, reflecting consumer surplus. Thus, a farmer who owns his land would not be induced to sell by an offer equal to the land value in agricultural use. He would require, in addition, a sum to compensate him for the other benefits that he enjoys from his land. The 1942 Uthwatt Report, however, argues that the greatest obstacle to effective planning has been the fear of planning authorities of incurring indefinite liabilities in the matter of compensation should the extreme step of forbidding development be taken. Therefore the report strongly proposes that compensation should be based on the existing market value. Bryant (1972) follows the idea of the 1942 Uthwatt Report and argues that compensation should be based on the existing use value in order to guarantee the benefits and needs of the government. Farrier and McAuslen (1975) criticizes the fact that the 1942 Uthwatt Report overemphasizes national interests and ignores the needs of individuals. He lays much emphasis on the expectation and valuation of homeowners, in other words, the floating value of the land.

In practice, many countries with successful land management experiences adopt the current market value as their compensation standard, although they may apply different valuation methods. Doebele (1987) emphasizes that, given the highly speculative nature of land markets in most cities and the ease with which existing large landowners can ascertain government intentions in advance, compensation based on the full market value is increasingly prohibitive. For example, in the US, governments often have to resort to other means in addition to direct cash compensation. TDRs are an interesting experiment concerned with ways of achieving public land policy goals without buying land in fee simple. In Sweden, according to the new 1972 expropriation law, the price paid in expropriation is the market value of the land ten years prior to expropriation,[6] determined by looking at comparable sales. The compensation standard of the Netherlands is also based on current use rather than potential future use. French law states that in land banking programmes the compensation for land requisition is to be its existing use value one year prior to the initiation of specified condemnation or pre-emption, and it is to exclude expectations of increases due to public investments or to the probable relaxation of land use controls (Strong, 1979). The 1962 Land Administration Act of Puerto Rico stipulates that just compensation is the market value exclusive of any increase in value occasioned by expectations that the land or nearby land would be publicly acquired by the Land Administration or the Commonwealth, and exclusive of any increase in value attributable to public involvements. In Singapore, the 1973 Land Acquisition Act states that compensation for acquired land shall be based on the market value of the land in November 1973, or the date of public notification, whichever is lower. Market value is determined on the basis of existing land use or zoning, whichever is lower; the potential value is not counted. Besides, it asserts that when the value of land has been increased by reason of development in the neighbourhood by the provision of roads, drains, electricity, water, gas or sewerage, or social or educational facilities by any public or statutory authority at its expense within seven years from the date of declaration of acquisition, the amount of such increase shall not be taken into account in assessing the compensation award when the land is subsequently acquired. In general, prices paid by the Housing Development Board for acquired lands are much lower than market prices (Castells et al., 1990). According to a random analysis of appeals reported in the press, awards made for private land compulsorily acquired in 1979 and 1980 by the government were less than 20 per cent of the values claimed by the owners and assessed by chartered land appraisers (Motha, 1981).

Compensation, however, should be measured not only in purely financial terms, but also in terms of general social benefits in some special instances. For example, the British Parliament may well intend that in some cases compensation should be less than financial equivalence or perhaps be in some other form of satisfaction besides money. The Leasehold Reform Act 1967 authorizes the power of compulsory purchase for private individuals to remove certain social injustices. Under this legislation a freeholder was not properly compensated, because it is said that the objective of this Act would not be achieved if an enfranchising tenant was obliged to pay the full market value of the freehold interest (Green, 1986). Besides, in a case where a hardship may be generated by compensating at the current market use value, a higher compensation standard should be considered. In Amsterdam, compensation includes payment not only for land and structures, but also for consequential losses, such as moving expenses, losses realized on the sale of stock or equipment, and any decrease in value of the remaining property. Actually this value is often much higher than the agrarian value, so that the owner of land purchased compulsorily can receive more yields than he used to earn from his farm (Strong, 1979).

Finally, very often the government and landowners do not have the same bargaining strength, even in some developed countries. Green (1986) examines land compensation claims in England from 1979 to 1983, and finds that in nearly half of the cases determined by the Land Tribunals, on average the claimants receive awards about two and a half times that of the compensating authority's offer. Compensation is supposed to even out the inequalities between the expropriatee and the rest of society, but in some cases the inequity is exacerbated. In many developing countries, many expropriatees with low income have discovered that compensation based on the market value is not enough for them to relocate in another area. The inequity caused by compensation often leaves society vulnerable to political unrest.

SUMMARY

Starting from an introduction of assessment methods of land value changes engendered by public activities, this chapter has examined various betterment and compensation approaches adopted in Europe, the US and some Asian countries. The frequently used betterment capture tools include land taxation, land banking, exactions or planning gains, public land leasehold systems, land readjustment, and land nationalization. The compensation schemes include special assessment, TDRs and blight notice. Their strength and shortcomings were analysed in order to provide some quick references and a background for the discussion of betterment and compensation schemes under the LURs system in the following chapters.

The diversity and complexity of betterment and compensation schemes demonstrate that there is no universally accepted method that can be adopted on a worldwide basis. The selection and adoption of these schemes depend greatly on local context, including social, economic and political environments. After analysing international experiences, betterment and compensation schemes under the land use rights (LURs) system will be examined and their merits and problems will be assessed.

NOTES

1. Please refer to Gatzlaff and Smith (1993: 54–69) for more details.
2. This model was first introduced by Bailey et al. (1963).
3. Hallett (1985) makes a distinction between the 'betterment tax' and 'tax on development value'. He points out that the term of 'betterment levy' used by the Labour government in Britain is misleading because this tax was not levied on owners who had benefited from specific public investment, but levied only when there was development, or a transfer of property.
4. The 1942 Uthwatt Report defines the 'floating value' as potential development value, and identifies it as naturally speculative.
5. This is called 'compulsory purchase' in Britain, 'expropriation' in other European countries, and 'eminent domain' in the United States.
6. In Sweden there is little variation in the value of land a decade or more away from development, other than variation due to the natural characteristics of the land.

5. Urban land reform and the evolution of the land market in China

This chapter aims to illustrate the context for betterment and compensation under the Chinese land use rights (LURs) system. It begins with a brief overview of ancient and contemporary Chinese land tenure, indicating the complicated political and economic implications of land tenure reform. Next it examines the administrative land allocation system in the pre-reform era to analyse the institutional context of land reform in 1988. Then it describes the legal and administrative frameworks of the LURs system, reviews the urban land market since the 1988 urban land reform and identifies the problems and prospects of the land market.

5.1 EVOLUTION OF CHINESE LAND TENURE

In ancient China, where an agriculture-based economy was dominant, land management was always a political rather than an economic issue, and most land was controlled by a powerful landed class. One of the interesting phenomena that can be observed from the evolution of land management is that when new dynasties came to power, there was an attempt to reintroduce a public land ownership system, but once a dynasty had become established, state-allocated land tended to return to private hands by one means or another (Li, 1998). Throughout history, however, land belonged to the emperor and was allocated to members of the royal family and ministers who showed loyalty to the emperor or contributed to the empire under the feudal society. 'Over the nation, there are only Crown lands; over the land, there are only subjects of the King' was the famous cry of the ruling class.

The 1911 revolution changed China from a monarchy to a republic, but land concentration remained almost unchanged. President Sun Yet Sen proposed the idea of 'equalization of land rights' in order to promote equity in the land market. Instead of abolishing private land ownership, in 1924 President Sun introduced a land-value-based tax and a capital gains tax to suppress land price and forestall land speculation. The land value tax was based on land value calculated by the owners or by government valuers, and the capital gains tax was based on profits or unearned income when land was transferred. After the death of Sun, in 1930 the Kuomintang government enacted the first land law to manage land use, land surveys, land taxes, land rights and so on. The law clearly stated that all land was state land and belonged to the state on behalf of the people, except for the land that had been transferred or conveyed legally, so that private ownership could be preserved. Therefore, the framework of public land ownership was not really established since private land ownership was maintained, and the introduction of state ownership did not change the dominant private ownership. Land was mainly owned by a small percentage of the upper class and land monopoly was prevalent. Meanwhile, rural land reform was very difficult to implement due to opposition from the monopoly of landlords and gentry who regarded the land law as a threat to their interests (Li, 1998). The income disparity generated by the land monopoly led to a large class of proletariat without land. Therefore, the idea to 'confiscate all private land and reallocate the land on the base of household size' put forward by the Communist Party since the late 1920s soon gained the support of the urban low-income class and landless farmers – the majority of the national population. In this regard, the victory of the Communist Party in China's civil war was no exception to the subversion of old dynasties in Chinese history: that is, the revolution of land tenure paved the way for the establishment of a new regime. It also suggests that the failure of land reform indirectly led to the collapse of the Kuomintang regime in China.

5.2   INSTITUTIONAL CONTEXTS OF THE 1988 URBAN LAND REFORM

5.2.1   The Traditional System and Its Consequences

Urban land in China has been nationalized since the Chinese Communist Party took power in 1949, based on the ideology and political promise that all land was common property. During the pre-reform era (from 1949 to 1978), land was publicly owned, and nominally worthless, although the nationalization of urban land was not officially finalized until the promulgation of the Constitution of 1982 which stated: 'No organization or individual may seize, buy, sell land or make any other unlawful transfer of land'. The acquisition of land was nothing more than a bureaucratic arrangement. Land use could be classified as political rather than economic (Walker and Li, 1994).

The traditional system has led to a number of problems in China. Firstly, because land was not considered a commodity, with the assignment of land free of charge reflecting neither economic nor social opportunity costs, users have no incentive to economize on their land use (Dowall, 1993). Bertaud and Renaud (1992) show that in most planned economies, land use patterns are not determined by economic efficiency, but are subject to social and political pressures. Residential land is usually squeezed out in favour of industrial land in urban core areas, since housing has been classified as 'non-productive' and deemed a much lower priority than manufacturing industry (Chen, 1998). Industrial land accounted for 20.5 per cent of the total city centre area in Shanghai and 34.15 per cent in Guangzhou before the urban land reform. The absence of land markets impaired the ability to allocate and recycle urban land (Bertaud and Renaud, 1997).

The second consequence is the serious free-rider problem. Administrative land allocation free of charge caused government agencies and state-owned enterprises to claim more land than they needed, thus land was wasted and misused. Tang (1989) defines the wastage in the utilization of land resources as 'public squatting'; the logic of public squatting is that a publicly owned firm is automatically entitled to a piece of land for its production. Examples of deliberate waste and low efficiency of land use are common; for instance, a research institute in Dalian city requested a 50000 m^2 building site when it only needed 600 m^2 (Tang, 1989).

The final, but not the least important, problem is the huge loss of state revenue due to the free land allocation. This can be highlighted through a comparison with Hong Kong. According to Hong Kong government statistics, the proportion of government revenue from property and the construction industry on average amounted to 33.5 per cent of total revenue between 1983 and 1993 (Li, 1998). The Chinese government, however, gained nothing from land. Furthermore, it was heavily burdened with the cost of housing that was provided as a benefit for government employees at a very low nominal rent.

5.2.2 The Rationale of Establishing Land Markets

Since the launch of economic reform in 1978, market elements have been gradually introduced into agriculture, manufacturing, labour, housing and other industries. Urban land reform, however, did not start with the overall economic reforms, because land is 'more politically sensitive than other commodities in Chinese societies' (Li, 1998: 18). Urban land reform, however, is no exception to the Chinese gradualist reform framework.

Although the official urban land reform began in 1988, the change of attitude towards land use had already happened in 1979 when the People's Republic of China (PRC) law on co-operative ventures allowed indigenous enterprises to use their land as capital to cooperate with foreign investors. Between 1982 and 1987, pilot schemes in various cities were set up to collect land use fees (Ling and Isaac, 1994). Meanwhile, pushed by overseas investors who have been accustomed to well-defined property rights, governments at central and local levels realized that land leasing could open up resources for revenue. The experiences of the public land leasehold systems of Hong Kong and Singapore proved instructive. Therefore, the government adopted a pragmatic attitude and decided to introduce a new land allocation system (World Bank, 1993).

The initial rationale for urban land reform, however, remains controversial. The World Bank (1993) argues that it was either to increase administrative controls over land or to generate some revenue from its use, not to establish a market allocation scheme. Ding (2003) states that the LURs system was developed to accommodate the needs of foreign direct investment. Whatever the rationale is, the adoption of the LURs system has been regarded as helping to establish land markets and improve land use efficiency, enabling municipal governments to launch large-scale infrastructure projects and enhance land management.

5.3   THE FRAMEWORK OF THE LURs SYSTEM

In November 1987, the State Council decided to conduct a pilot reform in land use in Shenzhen, Shanghai, Tianjin, GuangZhou, Xiamen and Fuzhou. The first land leasing in the Shenzhen Special Economic Zone initiated the urban land reform of China. On 1 December 1987, Shenzhen sold the first LURs of 8588 m^2 for 50 years by auction. Forty-four enterprises with corporate qualifications in Shenzhen competed vigorously for the land, one of which won the competition by paying 5250000 yuan. Following this, land leasing was gradually implemented throughout the rest of China. In 1988 the government adopted a LURs system that was established on a leasehold basis and allowed the lessees to buy, transfer and mortgage LURs within a certain period of time.[1]

The LURs system, literally the 'paid transfer of land use rights' (*tudi youchang zhuanran*), was made official by an amendment to the Constitution of the People's Republic of China in 1988. 'The right of land use can be transferred in accordance with the relevant legislation' was added into the Constitution. Land still belongs to the state, making LURs acceptable on the basis of the socialist doctrine. Therefore, the urban land privatization programme in China is basically a programme to release the leasehold value of land, not the real freehold ownership (Li, 1998).

5.3.1 The Legal Framework

At the national level, the rudimentary legal framework under the LURs system is provided by:

1. The 1988 PRC Land Management Law as amended by the People's Congress in 1998.
2. The 1990 Provisional Regulations on the Conveyance, Granting and Transferring of the State LURs in Cities and Towns (hereafter the 1990 Provision), adopted by the State Council, 1990.
3. The Urban Real Estate Administration Law of the PRC (effective 1 January 1995), adopted by the People's Congress in 1994 and amended in 2007.

The Land Management Law mainly deals with the general policy of LURs reform. It reaffirms the ownership structure of property rights in land: state ownership in urban land and collective ownership in rural land. Meanwhile, it emphasizes the principle of separation of land ownership and land use rights. Furthermore, it imposes a limitation on the area of cultivated land being requisitioned by the government or developer. Finally, it defines the compensation criteria that apply to farmers whose land is being converted into urban land and urban land users whose land is compulsorily purchased for public benefits.

The 1990 Provision illustrates the granting, transfer, leasing, mortgaging and termination of LURs. It stipulates that the longest leasehold term is 70 years for residential use, 50 years for industrial use, 50 years for educational and cultural use, and 40 years for commercial and office use. LURs can be granted through auction, tender or negotiation. Within the lease period, they can be transferred and traded with the permission of the government. In practice, almost all LURs are sold for the maximum period, and purchasers pay a lump sum premium, instead of annual rents (Cao, 2003).

The Urban Real Estate Administration Law of the PRC was enacted to enhance the management of urban real estate property. It lays downs conditions and procedures for the allocation of LURs for real estate development, the procedures for real estate transactions, and the management of registration of property rights. At the provincial and municipal level, the general policies and guidelines of the national legislation are often amended according to the special needs of localities. The city government mainly implements the policy and law. In general, the lower the level of government, the more detailed the provisions for implementation (Li, 1998).

5.3.2 The Administrative Framework

At the national level, the Ministry of Land and Resources (hereafter MLR) and the Ministry of Housing and Urban–Rural Development (hereafter MOHURD) are in charge of land and real estate issues. The National Development and Reform Commission has much less involvement in actual land administration, but it is responsible for providing macro-level policy guidance on land resources development and utilization, determining the location of large-scale industry, and analysing its effect on land resources. Therefore, the Commission has an important influence on land administration.

The main functions of the MLR are:

● To formulate land policy principles and regulations and to organize, supervise and inspect their implementation.
● To carry out cadastral surveys, land registration, land appraisal, and settle land ownership disputes.
● To be responsible for land requisition, allocation and granting, and to convert rural land into state land.
● To undertake the administrative management of land markets. To inspect and supervise the transfer, leasing and mortgaging of LURs, and to assist the financial and tax departments to collect land use fees and taxes.

The responsibilities of the MOHURD relative to land include:

● To direct national urban planning, and examine and approve city master plans designated by the State Council. To participate in national and regional land planning.
● To provide guidance on the transfer of LURs, the development and operation of real estate and commercialization of housing.

Correspondingly, at the provincial and autonomous regional level (Figure 5.1), land management is the task of the Land Resources Department and HURD Department. Their functions correspond to those of the MLR and MOHURD. The Provincial Development and Reform Commission is responsible for the land use strategy of the whole province. At the city level, the Construction Commission, the

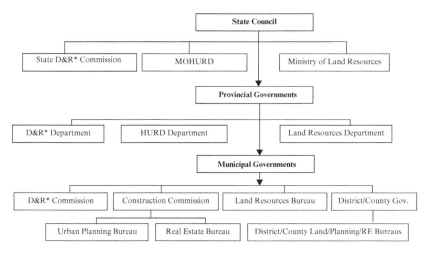

Note: * D&R – development and reform.

Figure 5.1 Organization and authorities related to land management in China

Land Resources Bureau (LRB), the Real Estate Bureau (REB)[2] and the Urban Planning Bureau (UPB) are responsible for land and real estate management. The Construction Commission is the main institution in charge of urban construction, under the leadership of a deputy mayor. The LRB acts as the executive arm of the MLR, and is responsible for land title registration, land requisition approval, and LURs transfer administration, the collection of land use taxes and fees, and the management of public housing. The LRB also administers the urban demolition and relocation process. The responsibilities of the REB include: controlling public housing stock; collecting rent and maintaining public properties; selling public housing to individuals; as well as administering the urban demolition and relocation process. The UPB is responsible for drafting and executing the city master plan and site development plan, approving land use proposals for state construction, project designs, and the issuance of construction permission. In some cities, the UPB and REB are under the leadership of the Construction Commission, but in others, they are independent agencies and report directly to the deputy mayor.

In practice, government departments at the national and provincial levels are more involved in policy formulation and supervision. The municipal governments have most power in controlling land and real estate affairs, and institutional arrangements are complex. Different departments claim that they have power over land and real estate management, resulting in the overlap of their functions. In view of such a complex administrative structure, it is understandable that acquiring LURs involves an extensive administrative approval process.

The way of acquiring LURs is institutionalized through the 2008 City Planning Act, and it varies according to different applicants. For government agencies, the army and state-owned enterprises, it is mainly administrative allocation free of charge. Private developers and quasi-state-owned development companies can achieve LURs through private treaty, auction or tender.

The procedure of acquiring LURs (see Figure 5.2) can be summarized as follows:

1. The applicant submits a project proposal to the Development and Reform Commission.

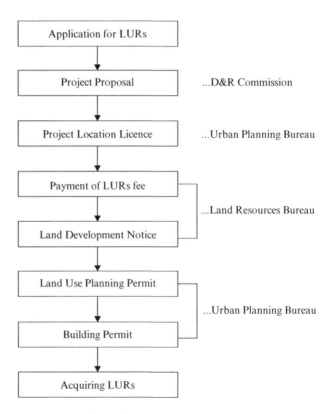

Figure 5.2   The procedure of acquiring LURs

2. After the proposal is approved, the applicant prepares a project feasibility report, and submits it to the Development and Reform Commission.
3. The applicant applies to the UPB for authorized Projects Location Licence (PLL). The PLL is attached with land use planning parameters such as permitted land use type, land size, plot ratio, plot coverage ratio,[3] building height, car parking minimum standard and population density. Then the applicant pays the LURs assignment fee and signs a land contract with the LRB to obtain a Land Development Notice (LDN).
4. When all formalities for a land transaction are complete, the applicant applies for a Land Use Planning Permit (LUPP). PLLs and LUPPs are issued by the UPB to ensure that site selection and land use are consistent with the city master plan and site development plan.
5. When the LUPP is approved, the developer can proceed to employ architects to design the buildings, and building design must comply with planning parameters attached in the PLL and building codes. Next the developer submits an application to the UPB to obtain a Building Permit (BP). Only then can LURs be acquired.

Among all certificates, PLLs, LUPPs and BPs are most crucial to obtain LURs. According to the 1990 City Planning Act, this procedure of development control is the so-called 'one licence, two permits' system (Zhu, 2002). The above procedure is for land users who achieve LURs through negotiable leases. The land users who acquire LURs through auction or tender automatically receive all documents after paying the LURs fee.

5.4   AN OVERVIEW OF THE URBAN LAND MARKET SINCE THE 1988 LAND REFORM

5.4.1   Three Phases of the Urban Land Market: Policy Changes and their Impacts

The Chinese urban land market has experienced several highs and lows since the urban land reform. It can be divided into three phases since 1988 (Tian and Ma, 2009).

The establishment of LURs (1988 to 1995)
With the establishment of the LURs, China's real estate market started to emerge and the land market gradually came into being. As the political situation and economic growth stabilized and foreign investment

increased, the real estate market flourished. In the early 1990s, China's real estate market reached its peak in terms of growth speed. The profit from real estate development was surprisingly high. Local government agencies, banks, enterprises and individuals all plunged into the real estate market and the nation was gripped by 'real estate fever' (Chen, 1998). Housing prices increased rapidly and the provision of luxury housing was substantial. In Shenzhen, for example, the average house price increased from 3000 yuan/m^2 at the beginning of 1991 to 4000 yuan/m^2 by the end of the year (Zhu, 1997). In July 1993, the government announced measures to strengthen control over the country's overheated real estate market along with efforts to tighten monetary policy and speed up banking system reform (Chen, 1998).

The establishment of land market mechanism and land banking system (1996 to mid-2003)
With the establishment of the LURs, land leasing revenue has become a major resource of local revenue. Realizing the substantial increase of land value, various de facto land holders, such as state-owned enterprises (SOEs), *danwei*,[4] collectives and army organizations, all plunged into land leasing, either through forming a development partnership with the private sector, or through transferring their free allocated land to developers illegally, which has incurred chaotic land supply and weakened the ability of municipalities to control land markets and city development.

Realizing the importance of land banking for enhancing government intervention, circumscribing land speculation and increasing local revenue, Shanghai established the first land banking agency of China in 1996. Hangzhou city set up its land banking centre in 1997, which has been regarded as the most successful among Chinese cities in terms of raising public funds. In 2001, the State Council issued a notice which encouraged local governments to learn from the experiences of the Hangzhou land banking centre and establish land banks. To date, more than 3000 cities and counties have set up their own land banking organizations. As a consequence of setting up land banks, the role of the government in urban land markets has been substantially enhanced. Theoretically, the government has become the single supplier of land in the primary market, and *danwei* and SOEs no longer enjoy the privilege of allocated land free of charge.

Usually the land in the bank will be sold through auction or tender several years or just after the municipalities acquire the land, depending on the market demand. Since August 1997 when the Land Banking Center was established, Hangzhou has acquired land of more than 667 ha, leased 260 ha, and received revenue of more than 5 billion yuan by the end of

2003, of which only 45 per cent was for land costs such as compensation, land servicing and land administration, showing the huge benefit of land banking (http://www.lifeweek.com.cn/2004-10-19/000539901.shtml, accessed 27/11/2006).

Initially, land banking was proposed for stabilizing housing prices and enhancing the ability of government to control land supply. Ironically, it has been criticized for resulting in the rise of average housing price within the last several years (Liu, 2003). The national average land price increased by 10 per cent within the first half of 2002 when the nationwide land banking system was introduced. The average house price of Hangzhou was around 2700 yuan/m^2 of building area in 1997, but it jumped to 5565 yuan/m^2 in 2004 (http://house.focus.cn, accessed 17/11/2006). It has been argued that the increasing monopolization by the government and complete implementation of auction or tender in profitable land supply have resulted in the rise in land prices, leading to considerable increase in house prices, thus making houses unaffordable for many households.

Meanwhile, the method of acquiring land has changed greatly. LURs used to be acquired through negotiation, tender and auction. In the late 1980s and 1990s, negotiation was the main way to acquire LURs, which provides local governments with large discretion in setting land prices, and allows space for rent-seeking. In order to avoid problems generated by under-the-table negotiations and to create a fair and transparent land transaction system, in the late 1990s tender and auction were gradually introduced into land supply in some coastal cities such as Shanghai, Guangzhou and Shenzhen. In March 2002, the MLR issued the No. 11 circular, which requires negotiation to be abolished in the supply of all for-profit developable land. The land for commerce, tourism, recreation, finance, services and commodity housing must be supplied through auction or tender after July 2002.

While control of the land supply had been more stringent at the local level, the central government also enhanced its governance over the land market. In May 1997 it announced a one-year moratorium on arable land conversion to non-agricultural use, and in April 2004 it again froze on agricultural land conversion for six months. In 1998, the central government substantially revised the Land Administration Law to address the importance of agricultural land preservation and restrict the autonomy of local government in land conversion.

Land policy as a part of national macro-control system (late 2003 to present)

Since the early 2000s, the Chinese economy has entered a new period of development. A prominent feature of this round of economic development is that heavy industry contributes a great deal to the manufacturing sector, and the strong demand for energy, electricity, raw materials and other products has fuelled a large amount of investment. The government had to take a series of measures to deal with the overheated economy, including raising interest rates and reserve requirements of banks in order to cool down the economy (Xinhua, 2005).

Meanwhile, the government believes that illegal land supply is a leading cause of runaway investment[5] (Xinhua, 2006). In September 2003, the central government announced that land policy would be applied as a major part of national macro control measures, together with fiscal policy and monetary policy. Considering the importance of regime stability and farmland preservation, the central government established a land quota system, and has attempted to control the total amount of construction land at the subnational level by setting mandatory land quotas. These quotas are distributed in a top-down way: firstly the central government sets national quotas and disaggregates them to provinces; each province then disaggregates its quotas to its municipalities, and each municipality to its counties (Cai, 2011). Under the land quota system, the land conversion autonomy of local government has been seriously restricted.

Meanwhile, in order to contain speculative demand and continuously increasing house prices, in 2004 the State Council issued 'Eight Measures' and 'Fifteen Measures' requiring an increased supply of small flats, raising the proportion of downpayments and requiring a sales tax if a house is resold within five years. Since 2006, the land supply policy has been transformed from quantity control to structure control. In May, the State Council put forward 'Six Measures' to address six issues: the structure of housing supply, taxation, mortgaging of real estate, land supply, low-rent housing and affordable housing. These policies, however, exerted limited influence on rocketing housing prices. The year 2010 is regarded as a turning point, when the Second Home Purchase Restriction was officially released. On 30 April 2010, Beijing ordered restrictions on purchase of second homes. Each household is only allowed to buy one new apartment unit, and those who own more than one house are not allowed to purchase any more. Additionally, downpayments and mortgage rates have been increased for second homes. Then, municipalities directly under the central government, provincial capital cities, and some other cities issued restrictions on second-home purchases. After a period of overheating in 2009 and the implementation of tightening policies in 2010, prices cooled to some extent (http://thediplomat.com/china-power/real-estate-restrictions-tighten-in-china/, accessed 7/3/2013).

According to research by the China Land and Mine Resources Law Center (2007), changes in land policy since 2003 have had significant impacts on city development and housing affordability, although their consequences have been debatable. In general, the positive consequences include the following. Firstly, land policy has been playing an active role in the improvement of industry structure through forbidding land leasing to projects which are not consistent with national industrial policy, and development planning and entry standards. Secondly, the area of land supply has greatly decreased due to stringent controls. In 2004, the total LURs sales area was 219 670 ha, decreased by 23.3 per cent compared with 2003. In 2005, the land supply area was reduced to 180 326 ha. Meanwhile, gross domestic product (GDP) generated per hectare of developable land has increased substantially. In 2004, GDP per hectare of land was 73 million yuan, and this figure climbed to 101 million yuan in 2005. Thirdly, brownfield land has replaced greenfield land to become the major source of land supply. Since 2004 brownfield land development overtook greenfield development for the first time, and accounted for more than 55 per cent in 2005. As a result, the loss of arable land has been alleviated. In 2005, the farmland that is converted into development land was reduced 37 per cent compared with 2004 (Tian and Ma, 2009).

Overall, it is noteworthy that every high and low has been driven not only by market forces, but also by political force, involving many non-economic factors, as well as the fact that the development of the urban land market has been fairly stagnant. For example, the property boom in the early 1990s was facilitated and reinforced by market inefficiency and pitfalls in the system. Extensive and intensive state intervention in the urban land market exacerbated instability in the real estate market. An obvious feature of the Chinese land market is the variability of policies over short time frames. It is not difficult to understand the frequency of policy adjustments, as decision-makers are not experienced enough to deal with the infant real estate market. Several dramatic policy changes since the 1990s, including the Land Management Law amendment, land supply policy and the Second Home Purchase Restriction order, have exerted significant influence on land markets.

5.4.2 Land Financing Regime: A Double-Edged Sword

With the development of a real estate market, LURs fees have become an increasingly important source of government revenue, which has been widely identified as 'land financing' in China. Land financing, however, has been proved to be a double-edged sword. On the one hand, under the land financing regime, expensive infrastructure construction has been largely financed by land lease revenue, and city growth has been facilitated in China. On the other hand, driven by the incentive to maximize benefits of land leasing and the pressure from developers to acquire land, local governments have been trapped by an oversupply of land, leading to urban sprawl and housing affordability problems.

Rationale of land financing
Land-centred development is often regarded as the most significant feature of China's urbanization (Heikkila, 2007; Lin, 2007). This is mainly attributed to the economic and fiscal system of China. Land-centred urban politics has been regarded as one of the most important driving forces behind the spectacular expansion of Chinese cites and urbanization of China since the mid-1990s (Deng et al., 2010; Ye and Wu, 2014). During the period of 1978–1993, the fiscal contracting system granted local governments residual rights over local revenue (Oi, 1992, 1996). In 1994, however, the central government set up its own tax collection bureaus at the local level and launched the tax-sharing system. According to Ye and Wu (2014), from 1980 to 2010 the central government collected over 51 per cent of the national fiscal revenue, but only covered 20 per cent of the expenditures. In contrast, local governments were responsible for over 80 per cent of the social expenditures, but only received less than 50 per cent of the revenue. As a consequence, local governments have to look for extra-budgetary revenue out of the control of the central government, and land financing has been found to be a powerful tool to achieve this. Based on Ye and Wu's (2014) panel data of all 286 prefecture-level cities during the period of 1999–2009, a 1 per cent increase in LURs fees as a share of local budgetary revenue is positively associated with a 0.0157–0.0179 per cent increase in expansion of land.

Land market and general economy
The 1988 land reform is a critical turning point in the Chinese urban development process. The LURs system was established which allows municipalities to lease state-owned land to developers. The leasing of urban land opened up sources of local revenue and to a great extent and financed the construction of public facilities. The provision of cheap land has also become a way to attract foreign investors (Zhu, 1994). The LURs system has triggered more rapid economic growth in China since 1988. A comparison reveals that real estate investment in 2010 grew by 444 times compared with that in 1988, whereas GDP in 2010 was only 26 times that in 1988. Thus the urban land reform and establishment of a real estate market have brought more revenue to the government and enhanced overall economic growth.

   Figure 5.3 compares the changes in the growth rates of GDP and real estate investment from 1988 to 2010. While GDP has been increasing

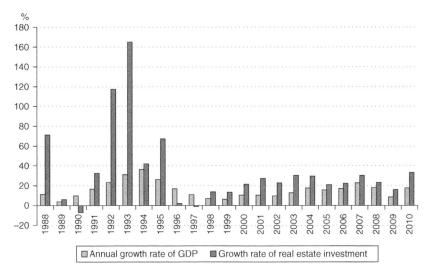

Source: China Statistics Yearbook (1989–2012).

Figure 5.3   Comparison between the growth of GDP and real estate investment

steadily, the real estate investment has shown a fluctuating tendency. In 1992 and 1993, GDP growth rate was 14.2 per cent and 13.5 per cent, respectively; meanwhile real estate investment increased by 117.6 per cent and 165 per cent, respectively (China Statistics Yearbook, 1994). The sudden drop in 1990 was the result of political unrest: the Tiananmen Square event in 1989. During the early 1990s, the investment in real estate rose remarkably and peaked in 1993, as a consequence of the famous southern tour of China's pioneer of economic reform, Deng Xiaoping, from 18 to 21 January 1992.[6] After 1993, growth slowed down due to macroeconomic policy adjustments. In 1997, the real estate investment dropped for the first time since 1990. This, however, was not because of the market change, but due to an ordinance issued by the State Council which required a suspension of land supply for profitable use in the whole year. After this, real estate investment began to increase in a relatively stable fashion. The sudden drop of GDP and real estate investment in 2009 was the result of the 2008 global financial crisis, but they went up immediately in 2010 due to the stimulation of 'Four Trillion Plan' issued by the State Council of China as an attempt to minimize the impact of the global financial crisis on China through public investment in November 2008.

The real estate industry has achieved breathtaking progress since the 1988 urban land reform. In 1978, the added value of the real estate industry was only 2.2 per cent of GDP. This figure rose to 4 per cent in 1998, and reached 5.46 per cent in 2010 (Liu, 2010), not considering the multiplier effect of the real estate industry for other industries such as steel, finance and property decoration. The real estate industry has therefore been regarded as one of China's most profitable industries (http://www.ttpaihang.com/news/daynews/2010/10032650436.htm, accessed 6/12/2014).

Urban sprawl and loss of cultivated land
Zhang (2000) defines the rapid city growth in the early 1990s as the Chinese version of urban sprawl. According to Table 5.1, the average annual growth rate of built-up city areas was 6.3 per cent from 1981 to 2010, much higher than that of urban population growth at 4.21 per cent, and urbanization at 3.11 per cent. The much more rapid growth rate of the urbanized area was driven not only by the demand of the increasing urban population but also by the ambition of local governments to raise local revenues and attract investment through land leasing. The huge amount of vacant land can partly explain why the urbanized area is growing much faster than the urban population. From 1989 to 1997, the land area of 15000 km^2 was leased for economic development zones, but the actual built-up area was less than 1852 km^2.

With rapid city growth, per capita cultivated land has decreased by

Table 5.1   Changes of urbanization, population and built-up city areas in China since the 1980s

Year	Urbanization (%)	Urban population (million)	City built-up area (km^2)
1981	20.12	199.70	7438
1985	23.71	250.94	9386
1990	26.41	301.91	12856
1995	29.04	351.74	19264
2000	36.22	459.06	22439
2005	42.99	562.12	32521
2006	43.90	582.88	33660
2007	44.94	606.33	35470
2008	45.68	624.03	36295
2009	46.6	645.12	38107
2010	49.7	669.78	40058

Sources: China Statistics Yearbook (1990–2012), China City Construction Statistics Yearbook (1995–2012).

Table 5.2   Changes of cultivated land area and per capita cultivated land area in China

Year	Cultivated land area (km²)	Population (1000)	Per capita cultivated land area (m²)
1900	565 200	366 810	1540
1949	978 700	541 670	1807
1957	1 118 000	646 530	1729
1980	993 400	987 050	1006
1990	956 700	1 143 330	836
1993	954 200	1 185 170	805
1995	949 700	1 211 210	784
2000	1 282 331	1 265 830	966
2003	1 233 922	1 292 270	955
2005	1 220 827	1 307 560	933
2010	1 217 200	1 340 910	907

Sources: China Statistics Yearbook and MLR.

more than 40 per cent within one century (see Table 5.2). The loss of cultivated land has jeopardized the objective of food self-sufficiency set by the state, and caught the attention of the central government. Therefore, at the end of 1996, the State Council issued an administrative order that no more cultivated land was allowed to change to other uses for the whole year of 1997. The 1998 Land Management Law introduced two key articles to prevent the loss of farmland. One mandates no net loss of basic farmland, and the other is that developers have to either exploit or reclaim an amount of farmland equivalent to the amount lost due to development in order to guarantee no loss of cultivated land as a result of urban development (Ding, 2003). Owing to these stringent controls, the area of cultivated land increased during the period from 1995 to 2000; it slowed after 2000. However there is evidence that the increment of farmland is mainly from the reclamation of wasteland, and that the high-quality farmland is still disappearing rapidly at the periphery of the cities (Bao and Hu, 2003).

Housing affordability
Although the central government has issued many policies to increase housing affordability, these policies have been criticized for being unable to achieve the stated objectives. In 2010 the fixed asset investment reached 27 814 billion yuan, an increase of 23.8 per cent compared with 2009, and enthusiasm for investment was not contained. In many cities, house prices did not drop as expected even after the issuance of the Second

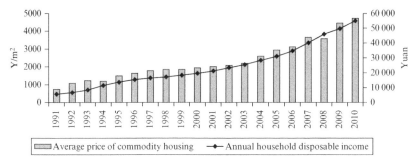

Source: China Statistics Yearbook (1992–2005).

Figure 5.4   Changes of house price and household income from 1991 to 2010

Home Purchase Restriction policy. Since there is a time lag between policy changes and their actual consequence, one cannot hastily conclude that these policies have failed. Nevertheless, the excessive dependence on administrative control instead of market measures has been extensively criticized due to policy-makers' lack of experience (Lin, 2006).

According to the China Statistics Yearbook, the growth rate of household income has been greater than that of residential housing prices in the whole country (Figure 5.4). Nevertheless, in the first-tier cities, house prices have been growing much faster than family income. For instance, in Beijing, the average price of commodity houses[7] was 4456 yuan/m^2 in 2003, and it rose to 21929 yuan/m^2 in 2011, 4.92 times of that in 2003 (Zhang Xiaosong, *New Jing Newspaper*, 11/11/2011). During the same period, disposable household income only increased by 1.37 times (Beijing Statistics Yearbook, 2012). It takes 20 years for a household to purchase an apartment of 90 m^2. In Shanghai, a house price index released by Fudan University has revealed that the average price of commodity houses increased by 2.53 times from 2004 to 2011, 1.9 times higher than the growth speed of disposable income (http://www.sina.com.cn, accessed 8/11/2011). Housing is becoming more and more unaffordable in these cities.

SUMMARY

The Chinese economic reform is gradual, incremental and experimental in nature. Public ownership and the role of the state in production are rigorously maintained. Urban land reform in China has been under way for more than two decades, and it has followed a top-down approach. It was prompted by the need for economic efficiency and was not a by-product of China's political reforms. The urban land reform is proceeding within the framework of a socialist economy (Li, 1998). Following the revival of land and property as economic assets in the early 1980s, China's urban land market started in the late 1980s and has experienced peaks and troughs.

Starting with a background to China's urban land reform, this chapter has illustrated the problems such as low land use efficiency and the loss of state revenue under the traditional land administrative allocation system, which arises due to the lack of a market mechanism. The legal framework of the LURs system is mainly reflected in the 1998 Land Management Law, the 1990 Provisional Regulations on the Conveyance, Granting and Transferring of the State LURs in Cities and Towns, and the Urban Real Estate Administration Law of the PRC. The administrative framework of the LURs system is based on a hierarchical structure: state–province–municipality–district/county. The land management mechanism, however, is not a simple top-down scheme, and local governments, particularly municipal governments, have significant influence on land management under the development-oriented approach.

Based on an analysis of the three-stage land market since the late 1980s, this chapter has examined the merits and problems of urban land markets. On the one hand, the growth of a real estate market has driven the national economy growth significantly during the previous two decades. On the other hand, urban sprawl, consequent loss of cultivated land, and housing affordability problems are consequences of the unsophisticated land law and management. The ups and downs in land markets can be attributed to the major policy and macroeconomic situation changes. Nevertheless, in spite of the informality and a lack of clear definitions of property rights, the potential value of land and buildings has been widely acknowledged and is anticipated to appreciate in time, in the context of long-pent-up demand for premises and a relative scarcity of urban land stock due to the looming magnitude of rural to urban migration (Zhu, 2002).

From 1981 to 2011, the urbanization rate of China increased from 20.12 per cent to 51.27 per cent, at a rate of more than 1 per cent per year, and nearly 500 million people flooded into cities and towns from rural areas. According to a projection by McKinsey & Company, the urban population of China will reach 925 million by 2025 (http://finance.eastmoney.com/news/1352,20120910250079055.html, accessed 1/2/2013), and more than 200 million rural people will move to cities and towns in the following decade. According to research by the Tsinghua University Institute of Real Estate Studies, annual housing demand will be around 540 million m² of floor space every year from 2004 until 2020. Likewise, the demand for retail and office space engendered by the swarming of new households into cities is likely to be huge.

Overall, despite the problems, prospects of urban real estate market development are encouraging. The positive outlook arises from elements that favour vigorous development. Fundamental factors such as growth of the urban population and of jobs, increases in income, greater population mobility and a generally favourable development environment, will all contribute to higher demand for housing. On the supply side, both the market and government policies are working in directing more resources toward basic residential housing construction to meet the increased demand.

NOTES

1. Readers interested in the evolution of the LURs system may refer to Walker and Li (1994) and Chan (1999).
2. In many cities, such as Beijing, Shanghai and Guangzhou, the LRB and REB are merged into one department.
3. Plot coverage ratio is the footprint area of the building divided by the plot size.
4. Literally, *danwei* is a work unit. According to Lv and Perry (1997), *danwei* refers to a variety of state-owned enterprises, non-profit institutes and governmental bureaus where most urban residents were employed during China's centralized system. A *danwei* is a work unit that has such attributes as personnel administration, communal facilities, urban or non-agricultural purview and being in the public sector.
5. A survey of 16 cities by the Ministry of Land and Resources in 2005 showed that nearly 50 per cent of the new land under development was acquired illegally. The figure was as high as 90 per cent in some cities.
6. After the 1989 Tiananmen Square event, many Chinese were confused about the economic reform of China. In his southern tour to Shenzhen and Zhuhai, Deng Xiaoping asked local officials to accelerate the economic reform process, and he emphasized that the market economy was not a hallmark of a capitalist society. His speech was regarded as a turning point in the economic reform process of China.
7. In China, 'commodity houses' are commercially provided houses, and 'commodity property' is commercially provided property. They are named 'commodity' to differentiate them from buildings built by the government agencies or state-owned enterprises.

6. Betterment and compensation schemes under the LURs system

The major policy objectives of the Chinese government in establishing the land use rights (LURs) system can be summarized as to: (1) raise public funds to promote the construction of infrastructure and public facilities; (2) establish a land market to accommodate the economic reform; and (3) manage urban development. In this chapter, different schemes that are employed by the Chinese government to raise public funds, recover betterment and compensate the requisitioned land user are presented, their strength and weakness are analysed, and their impacts on the urban land market are illustrated. After this exposition, the chapter discusses the role of government in the land market, and the obstacles to addressing betterment and compensation, in order to respond to research questions put forward in Chapter 1.

6.1 LAND VALUE CAPTURE SCHEMES

As mentioned in Chapter 4, under either the land freehold or land leasehold system, various approaches are applied to recoup the government investment in public facilities. Compared with the land freehold system, the LURs system has more tools to capture the surplus value. Among the countries that have adopted land leasing to manage part of their public land, China is unique in terms of extending the land leasehold system countrywide. Under the LURs system, there are four main mechanisms to capture the surplus land value.

6.1.1 LURs Assignment Fee

Under the LURs system, the government assigns LURs to land users based on contractual arrangements. Besides specifying planning parameters, lease duration and the type of property rights in land, the land-use contract indicates the amount of the LURs assignment fee. Only after paying the LURs assignment fee and satisfying other requirements of the land use contract can the applicant acquire the LURs.

Table 6.1   Land use rights transfer fees and government revenue

	Area of land sales (ha)	LURs fee (million yuan)	Government revenue (million yuan)	LURs fees as a % of government revenue
1993	57338	42078	434900	9.7
1995	43092	38752	624220	6.2
2000	48633	59558	1339523	4.4
2005	163200	588382	3164929	18.6
2006	232500	807764	3876020	20.8
2007	234961	1221672	5132178	23.8
2008	165860	1025980	6133035	16.7
2009	209000	1591020	6851830	23.2
2010	291500	3010893	8310151	36.2

Sources: China Statistics Yearbook (1990–2012), China Land Resources Statistics Yearbook (1995–2012).

In China, in most cases, the LURs assignment fee is a lump-sum premium collected by local governments through negotiation, auction or tender in the primary market. Table 6.1 shows that land revenues contributed to approximately 9.7 per cent and 36.2 per cent of the government revenue in 1993 and 2010, respectively. Another noticeable phenomenon is the growth of LURs fees generated by units of land. Compared with 1993, government revenue from every square metre of supplied land was 14.2 times greater in 2010, which can be attributed to the infrastructure investment and the favourable macroeconomic environment. This will be further discussed at the local level in Chapter 7.

The LURs assignment fee can be recharged in the following situations:

1. Planning parameters modification. In order to alter planning parameters attached to the contract, land users have to apply for permission from the land and planning departments. If these departments approve their applications, they will require a new land use contract and an additional premium for the modification of parameters, based on a valuation of the potential increase of land value after the parameters change.
2. Land lease expiration. According to the 1990 Provision, when their land leases expire, land users have to repay a LURs reassignment fee based on an updated land valuation. So far there has been no lease approaching its expiration in China, therefore the outcome has not been tested.

The LURs assignment fee has proved to be an effective tool to recover the investment in infrastructure investment. Its implementation, however, was not without problems. Firstly, local officials have become highly motivated to maximize local revenues for their own interests due to decentralization and the re-emergence of localism (Zhu, 1999a). Since the LURs assignment fee as a lump-sum premium has substantially increased local revenue and generated a market-driven property industry, which is one of main industries supporting the local economy in many cities, local governments are tempted to lease as much land as possible within their tenure. According to the Ministry of Land and Resources (MLR, 2005), 4735 development zones all over the country, excluding Hong Kong, Macao and the Inner Mongolia Autonomous Municipality, were withdrawn until June 2004. The planned land area of these development zones is 24 100 km^2, which is more than two-thirds of the existing built-up area of cities all over the country. Data from local levels can reaffirm this statement. Guangzhou leased land of 264.7 km^2 from 1986 to 1997 for development, almost amounting to the built-up city area in 1998 (266.8 km^2) (Guangzhou Urban Planning Bureau, 2000).

Secondly, local economic growth and city image have been key criteria to assess the performance of local top officials, and local governments have been committed to gross domestic product (GDP) growth since the economic reform. Excessive land leasing has caused serious anxiety concerning sustainable development. Given the scarce land resources and high population density in China, oversupply of land has exacerbated the shortage of cultivated land and brought the twin challenges of where to find enough land and how to raise public funds for future urban development.

Thirdly, although a lump-sum fee has provided a strong incentive for local governments, it cannot be a sustaining tool of capturing land value increment generated by public actions. As Table 6.1 shows, land value has dramatically increased since the urban land reform. The government, however, can only recover the investment from the newly leased land. Part of the land value increment has gone into the pockets of sitting occupiers as unearned interest.

Last but not least, a lump-sum premium for a long period has been a huge burden for enterprises, particularly industrial enterprises. In order to promote local industrial development, land at a low price has usually been used as a tool to attract industrial investment, leading to a substantial loss of land revenue. Zhao's (2007) research based on a survey of the MLR shows that in 31 provinces the average cost for industrial land was 120 yuan/m^2, but the average selling price was only 91 yuan/m^2 in 2005.

Therefore, the MLR issued a benchmark price for industrial land leasing to prevent further loss of land revenue.

Generally speaking, the lump-sum LURs fee has acted as a political short-term priority, and pressures on public finances take precedence over the longer-term economic development objectives. Realizing the weakness of a lump-sum LURs fee, some Chinese scholars propose that an annual rent plus a property tax system should be introduced to reduce the amount of LURs fees and guarantee sustainable land revenues for future governments (Dai, 1999; Wang, 2001). In this regard, Hong Kong's experience can be instructive. Besides a lump-sum land premium, the Hong Kong government levies a rate on owner-occupied properties based on their 'rateable value'. The rateable value is the annual rent that property owners might reasonably expect if they let their property in the open market. The government sets the level of rate annually, depending on its financial needs (Hong, 1995).

The introduction of an annual rent system, however, has many potential difficulties in China. The high assessment cost and the required expertise may be beyond the Chinese government's current capacity. Considering possible impacts of the introduction of annual rent on the existing LURs granting system, the Chinese government has been very cautious about the introduction of annual rents in metropolitan cities. Wang (2001) argues that the annual rent system is more suitable for industrial and commercial land use that has a relatively high profit return, but may not be beneficial for residential land with relatively low liquidity and return. Moreover, the uncertainty of annual rent may impinge on the transactions in the housing market.

6.1.2   Real Estate Taxation

According to Bird (2004), taxes on land and real estate have an important potential role to play in funding urban needs, for two key reasons. Firstly, real property is immovable when it is taxed. Secondly, there is a connection between the type of services funded at the local level and the benefit to property values.

Real estate taxes were first created in the People's Republic of China (PRC) in January 1950 when the State Council promulgated the Principles of Taxation and Finance. In practice, real estate tax started in Chinese cities in August 1951 when the State Council issued the Urban Real Estate Tax Ordinances. In 1973, in order to simplify the tax system, urban real estate tax was categorized into industrial and commercial taxes. Thereafter, in many cities 'real estate tax' was virtually non-existent. After the economic reform, the Chinese government restored the real estate tax and separated property and land use taxes. In October 1986, the State Council promulgated the Provision for Real Estate Taxes (Song et al., 1999). Since then real estate taxes have been implemented all over the country.

It has been argued that the real estate tax has been the most complicated one in the Chinese taxation system (Tan, 1999; Gao, 2003). Driven by the incentives to raise revenue, local governments have levied a number of land taxes and charged various kinds of fees to developers and housing purchasers. Tong and Qu's (2003) research reveals that the numbers of land taxes and fees in Beijing, Wuhan and Guangzhou were increased to 72, 72 and 58 from 15, 12 and 6, respectively, during the period of 1986–1996. *Inter alia*, the average number of taxes has been relatively stable, at around 13, implying the desire of local governments to charge apparently widespread fees to open up local revenue, whereas part of the taxes go into central and provincial governments' pockets. Generally speaking, Chinese real estate taxes can be categorized into four groups, as follows.

Tax on LURs acquirement
Farmland Requisition Tax The farmland requisition tax has been levied since 1987 in order to protect farmland. It is levied on a range of 1 to 10 yuan per square metre of acquired farmland. The less farmland a city has, the higher the tax rate is levied. The land for public use and developed by overseas enterprises is exempt from this tax (State Council of China, Provisional Regulations on Farmland Requisition Tax, 1/4/1987).

Tax on holding
Real Estate Tax The real estate tax started in 1986. Its base ranges from 70 per cent to 90 per cent of the original value of the building, depending on local situations, and the tax rate is 1.2 per cent per annum. It is mainly levied on buildings of commercial, industrial and office use. Houses for residential use are exempt from the building tax (State Council of China, Provisional Regulations on Real Estate Tax, 1/10/1986).

Land use Tax The land use tax was implemented in 1988, and is calculated based on the amount of land area. It varies across cities and by locations within a city by grade of land (see Table 6.2). Furthermore, widespread 'exemptions' have been granted: for example, land for government offices, military use and public use. The tax rate is incredibly low, merely reflecting land ownership rather than functioning as economic leverage to guide resource allocation (Ding, 2003).

Table 6.2   Land use tax rate in China

Tax rate	Levied from
0.5–10 yuan/m²	Large cities with a non-agricultural population larger than 500 000
0.4–8 yuan/m²	Medium cities with a non-agricultural population between 200 000 and 500 000
0.3–6 yuan/m²	Small cities with a non-agricultural population less than 200 000
0.2–4 yuan/m²	Towns and industrial districts

Source: State Council of China, Provisional Regulations on Urban Land Use Taxes, 27/9/1986.

Tax on transactions
Contract tax   A contract tax is levied for both sellers and purchasers when property is transferred. It started in 1997. The tax rate ranges from 3 to 5 per cent of the selling price of the transferred LURs or property in different cities.

Stamp duty   A stamp duty is levied for purchasers when property is transferred. It started in 1988. The tax rate ranges from 0.03 to 0.05 per cent of the selling price of the transferred LURs/property in different cities.

Land capital gains tax   The land capital gains tax was introduced in 1994 to cool down the overheated real estate market and capture surplus land value. It is levied at a four-level progressive rate when the land or property is transferred, and is paid by the original land user (see Table 6.3). The State Tax Bureau, however, temporarily exempted the individual household from this tax to promote the resale housing market in 1999 (http://politics. people.com.cn/GB/1027/3384596.html, accessed 22/11/2005). With the booming real estate market, some cities reintroduced land capital gains tax several years ago. For instance, Shanghai started to levy land capital gains tax for the transfer of houses with the holding period not more than five years (http://finance.sina.com.cn/chanjing/b/20070715/14223786433. shtml, accessed 26/5/2014).

   Theoretically a land capital gains tax has certain advantages in forestalling land speculation and capturing surplus land value. In practice, however, it has been difficult to implement. Firstly, in view of the complexity of the land and building costs, the calculation of Appreciation Value has been very problematic, which has made the administrative cost of land capital gains tax very high. Secondly, the levy of a land

Table 6.3   The progressive rate of land capital gains tax in China

Level	Tax base	Tax rate (%)
1	The proportion of AV* which is less than 50% of land and building cost	30
2	The proportion of AV* which is between 50% and 100% of land and building cost	40
3	The proportion of AV* which is between 100% and 200% of land and building cost	50
4	The proportion of AV* which is above 200% of land and building cost	60

Note: * AV, appreciation value = resale price of property – land and building costs (including relevant taxes and fees).

capital gains tax is very unpopular in an emerging land market, particularly when the real estate market is not active. After the Provisional Regulations on Land Capital Gains Tax were released in 1994, the real estate market cooled down. Moreover, the land capital gains tax is shared between the central government (75 per cent) and local government (25 per cent), therefore many local governments such as Shenzhen, Guangzhou, Nanjing and Shanghai abolished this tax without seeking permission from the central government. With the real estate market upturn since the start of this century, some cities, such as Guangzhou and Shenzhen, introduced this tax again in 2005, adopting a flat rate of 20 per cent of the Appreciation Value. Individual houses used for more than five years, however, can be exempt from this tax (Guangzhou and Shenzhen Local Tax Bureaus, 2005). Beijing and Shanghai also adopted similar policies.

Other taxes
There are several other types of relevant real estate taxes, including domestic enterprise income tax, overseas enterprise income tax, agriculture tax, urban maintenance and construction tax, and the individual income tax. The complexity and rigidity of the current real estate taxation system has received widespread criticism in China (Tan, 1999; Gao, 2003; Tong and Qu, 2003; Zhang, 2003; Hua, 2013). The criticism focuses on three problems. Firstly, many real estate taxes are not based on the market value of land and property, but on the plot or property size, or the original value, and thus cannot reflect the dynamic market value of land and property or act as economic leverage. The importance of real estate taxation is to reallocate social welfare through income redistribution and reduce unearned

income for landowners owing to the population growth and infrastructure investments made by the community. Real estate taxes in China, however, cannot achieve these goals. Urban residents are exempt from real estate tax and land use tax, leading to the failure of the objective of alleviating income disparity. Furthermore, this taxation system may produce injustice, particularly when some users pay high taxes and enjoy public service with low quality, but others enjoy public service with high quality and pay lower taxes (Ding, 2003). Secondly, the levy of current real estate taxes focuses on the transaction of land and property, instead of the holding of land or property, which indirectly encourages speculation because the cost of holding a property is very low (Zhang, 2003). Thirdly, the cost of government departments in assessing and collecting miscellaneous taxes is high, and developers are also often confused with the variety of tax types and rates. Real estate taxation reform is therefore imperative, according to the State Council of China (Economic Information Daily, 24/10/2005).

Recently many Chinese scholars and officials have proposed the introduction of a property tax based on periodical valuation to replace the real estate tax, land use tax and land capital gains tax, in order to make the taxation system more adaptive and curb speculation on the ground that a property tax will increase the cost of holding property (Zhou, 2004; Hua, 2013). Furthermore, it has been argued that the introduction of a property tax could reduce the amount of the LURs assignment fee and thus lower rising housing prices and increase housing affordability (Zhang, 2003). The Third Plenum of the 16th Congress of the Chinese Communist Party held in October 2003 states: 'in order to initiate urban real estate taxation and fee-charging system reform, property tax will be introduced at an appropriate time, meanwhile some taxes will be abolished'.

The introduction of a property tax, however, has been controversial. Although some scholars hold that the average housing price would decrease by 10 to 20 per cent and that speculation in the real estate market could be curbed (Zhou, 2004), others are suspicious of the influence of property tax (Zhang, 2003). Moreover, the assessment of property value requires a good valuation system; something not easy to achieve in the rapidly changing conditions of developing countries, and particularly difficult in a country like China where property rights in land are not clearly defined and the existing taxation system is far from market value-based (Li, 1995). Other concerns include potential negative effects on the real estate market, the resistance from a large percentage of households with more than one property, the high time and administrative cost in evaluation and collection, and the lack of a computerized plot-by-plot cadastre system (Zhang, 2003). Starting from 28 January 2011, Shanghai and Chongqing initiated the long-awaited trial property tax in order to cool off the red-hot housing market. Nevertheless, the levy of property tax only targets rather limited households and has exerted little impact on the housing market. Shanghai sets a property tax rate at 0.4 to 0.6 per cent, and only newly bought second and second-plus homes of permanent residents in Shanghai are taxed if the average floor area per family member of all homes, including the existing ones, is more than 60 m^2. Chongqing taxes all villas as well as new apartments priced at least twice the average price of all newly built homes in the southwestern city. The annual tax rates are 0.5 per cent of the transaction prices for villas and apartments priced less than three times the average price, 1 per cent for those priced three to four times the average, and 1.2 per cent for those priced more than four times the average (*China Daily*, 28/1/2011). In either Shanghai or Chongqing, those households which already owned more than two apartments but do not buy new ones do not have to pay any property tax, which has a very limited influence on the real estate market.

Generally speaking, in view of the great needs for urban development expenditures in the future, and the likelihood that the role of land and property taxation as a source of local finance will increase over time, it is important to ensure that the future development of urban land and property tax systems takes into account the need not only to be politically acceptable but also to be administratively and economically feasible (Bird, 2004).

6.1.3 Land Banking

Under the LURs system, land banking is expected to be a relatively efficient way to address betterment and compensation. Realizing the importance of land banking for enhancing government intervention, circumscribing land speculation and recouping betterment, Shanghai established China's first land banking agency in 1996, and Hangzhou city set up its land banking centre in 1997, which has been regarded as the most successful among Chinese cities in terms of raising public funds. In 2001, the State Council issued a notice which encourages local governments to learn from the experiences of the Hangzhou Land Banking Center and establish a land banking system. To date, more than 3000 cities and counties have set up their own land banking organizations (Tian and Ma, 2009).

Currently, the source of land for banking can be divided into two types:

1. The requisition of farmland. The farmland within the boundary designated by a city master plan is a major source of land for banks. Usually the farmland will retain its rural land use until it is expropriated by the government for development.

2. The change of urban land use. Besides farmland, some urban land can be included in the land bank. This includes:
    *   land which is taken back for public benefit;
    *   land which has been vacant for a certain period;[1]
    *   administratively allocated land which is no longer in use, for example the land of bankrupt state-owned enterprises (SOEs);
    *   land whose leasehold is expired, where the land user does not apply for the extension of the lease or where their application is not approved.

Usually the land in the bank will be sold through auction or tender several years or just after the municipalities acquire the land, depending on the market demand. From August 1997 when the Land Banking Center was established, to 2003, Hangzhou acquired land of more than 667 ha, leased land of 260 ha, and received a revenue of more than 5 billion yuan by the end of 2003, of which only 45 per cent is for land costs such as compensation, land servicing and land administration, showing the huge benefit of land banking (http://www.lifeweek.com. cn/2004-10-19/000539901.shtml, accessed 27/11/2004).

Since land banking is still at the embryonic stage, there has been no corresponding legislation and sophisticated financial framework in China. Which land and how it can be acquired for the purpose of land banking is mainly within the discretion of local authorities.[2] The majority of funds for land banking are from bank loans. The potential risk associated with the unpredictable land market and non-transparency of the government in purchasing, selling and developing land, however, has not been paid enough attention. This will augment the hidden risks in land purchasing and developmental loans (Chen and Berrell, 2004).

Initially, land banking was proposed for stabilizing housing prices and enhancing the ability of government to control land supply. Ironically, it has been criticized for resulting in the rise of average housing prices within the last several years (Liu, 2003). The national average land price increased by 10 per cent within the first half of 2002 when the nation-wide land banking system was introduced. The average housing price of Hangzhou was around 2700 yuan/m^2 of building area in 1997, but it jumped to 5565 yuan/m^2 in 2004, and then rocketed to 25840 yuan/m^2 in 2010 (http://house.focus.cn, accessed 17/11/2012). It has been argued that the increasing monopolization by the government and complete implementation of auction or tender in profitable land supply have resulted in the rise of land prices, leading to a considerable increase in housing prices, thus making house prices unaffordable for many households.

Through the introduction of land banking, SOEs have been forbidden to sell their land for development, and local authorities have become the sole land suppliers. As a consequence, more local revenues have been raised. Meanwhile, developers' profits are not squeezed because of rising housing prices. In Hangzhou, local revenue from land banking has been increasing at a rate of 56 per cent per year since 1997 (http://house.focus.cn, accessed 18/10/2008). With regard to enlarging revenue, business-oriented local authorities and developers have been in the same growth coalition (Zhu, 1999a). With growing housing prices and the lack of sufficient provision of affordable housing, medium- and low-income households have suffered financial difficulties in purchasing houses. No land banking agencies the author visited in China have listed the improvement of housing affordability as an objective of land banking. This has long been regarded as one of the key objectives in developed countries such as Sweden, the Netherlands and Singapore. Furthermore, excessive reliance on bank loans has put local authorities at great financial risk. Although a land bank can prosper in a flourishing real estate market, it is vulnerable to an emerging market characterized by instability. Finally, a legal framework has not been established to regulate land banking, and this has weakened the statutory power of land banking in practice. This legal framework should:

- explain the legislative power of government in acquiring land for banking;
- indicate the purposes of land banking;
- illustrate what types of land can be acquired for land banking;
- specify the compensation standard for land requisition.

6.1.4 Planning Obligations

The provision of urban infrastructure and public facilities is a lengthy process involving financing, construction and maintenance. With the rapid urbanization process since the 1980s, China's cities have not kept pace with the new demand for public facilities and urban infrastructure that had long been ignored in the pre-reform period. Meanwhile, local governments have realized that land equipped with infrastructure is a major tool to attract foreign investment. The importance of infrastructure-led development has become more apparent after the 1988 urban land reform. Urban infrastructure is considered to be a good form of government investment because it can increase revenue from land leasing (Wu, 1999). The huge cost of infrastructure construction, however, frustrates many local governments with limited local revenue. In 1985, a new earmarked tax, the urban maintenance and construction tax, was launched nationwide and collected by local governments to invest in public facilities. Any company or individual who is subject to capital gains tax or income tax must pay urban maintenance and construction tax at a rate of 7 per cent of the sum of capital gains tax and income tax in the city, or 5 per cent in the county and town (State Council of China, the Provisional Regulations on Urban Maintenance and Construction Tax, 8/2/1985).

A single tax, however, has not been enough to fund expensive infrastructure construction. In order to reduce their financial burden, many local governments started to require developers to build public facilities as a condition for the receipt of planning permission. Similar to exactions in the USA and planning gains in the UK, developers are asked to pay rental in kind, that is, building on-site or off-site infrastructure or social projects which would otherwise be local government responsibilities. Developers are responsible not only for the costs of compulsory land acquisition, relocation and compensation to sitting tenants, and infrastructure and accessory facilities that are to be built within the development area, but also for other infrastructure projects such as greenery maintenance, connection of access roads and substation installation near the development site. These projects are carried out as a payment to local government for using the land (Zhu, 1999b).

In July 1993, the Ministry of Housing and Urban–Rural Development (MOHURD) issued the Criteria of Planning and Design in Urban Residential Areas (hereafter the 1993 Criteria), where Chapter 6 lists the required public facilities to be built in residential areas. These public facilities can be divided into two types: (1) non-profitable facilities, for example school sites, open space, parking spaces, and cultural and medical facilities; and (2) for-profit facilities such as supermarkets, bookstores, hairdressers and bank branches, which are categorized as public facilities due to the legacy of the planned economy where all of these facilities were provided by the government. The number and area of public facilities vary according to the size of the site: that is, the larger the site, the greater the amount of facilities provided. In practice, local authorities usually refer to the 1993 Criteria, calculate the area of different types of facilities, and attach the planning obligations requirement in the Land Use Planning Permit (LUPP).

The 1993 Criteria do not say who should be responsible for the provision of public facilities, and many local authorities attribute this responsibility to the developers. The regulation on the provision of these facilities varies from city to city. For instance, according to the stipulations of the Guangzhou Municipal Government, developers have to provide land for these facilities, and complete their construction. The building cost of some facilities, such as schools and medical facilities, can be refunded by the government. Others, such as cultural facilities and a community office (a local government agency), have to be financed by the developers. As soon as the construction is finished, these facilities are devolved upon relevant organizations; for instance, schools are transferred to the Education Department, and medical facilities are transferred to the Health Department. Developers can retain some commercial facilities to manage themselves, or simply sell them (Tongji University, 2003).

The implementation of planning obligations has been very problematic in China. Firstly, the 1993 Criteria mainly borrow ideas from the scheme under the planned economy, and the categorization of public facilities includes miscellaneous for-profit facilities. Simply requiring developers to provide all these facilities has incited resistance from developers. Very often the construction of these facilities lags far behind that of residential buildings, which causes great inconvenience for the residents (Tongji University, 2003). The substitution of cash payment for the provision of public facilities has been considered by some local authorities, yet they are hesitant due to the difficulty of assessing impact fees, and more responsibilities of government departments after the abolition of planning obligations.[3] Secondly, the equity issue is controversial. Because of the lack of clear regulations and uniform standards, planning obligations vary from developer to developer. Sometimes developers have to provide oversized improvements, but are not entitled to reimbursement for facilities in excess of those needed by their development. Sometimes developers provide fewer facilities than their development needs; therefore the burden is transferred to the community. Thirdly, the negotiation in planning obligations has bred corruption. Which and how many public facilities should be provided in a project largely depend on the discretion of local officials. A very flexible land use planning system subject to bargaining inevitably brings about rent-seeking, and prevalent rent-seeking makes the land market the commons (Zhu, 2004a). According to the author's interviews and observations, many corruption cases have arisen through secret agreements between local officials and developers, and bribes are paid in exchange for the shrinking planning obligations. Last but not least, another problem is ambiguity of property rights in these facilities. The property rights of some facilities, such as school sites and medical services, are clearly transferred to government organizations. But for other facilities such as open spaces and parking spaces, the property rights are not well defined. In theory, these facilities belong to the whole community. In reality, however, these spaces are often occupied by developers and then converted to other uses, or are mortgaged by developers in the name of their own property. Thus far, there has not been any regulation on the property rights of these facilities, and the ambiguity of property rights in community facilities has led to litigation in China (http://www.dzwww.com/fangchan/lsrx/ t20020924_159159.htm, accessed 2/3/2006).

6.2   COMPENSATION SCHEMES

In China, compensation is only available when land or property is compulsorily purchased. Usually city expansion is facilitated by the conversion of rural land into urban land. Moreover, a large-scale urban redevelopment programme requires the transfer of LURs from original users to the state or developers. In either situation, compensation and relocation issues are considerable. However, there is limited room for negotiation on compensation terms; the affected collectives and individuals have to comply (World Bank, 1993). Moreover, no compensation is payable for the loss of value, whether this loss is caused by public actions or not. Local authorities' wide discretion has generated great uncertainty in the real estate market because there is no corresponding policy that can internalize the externalities caused by government. Several worsenment cases without compensation will be discussed in Chapter 7.

6.2.1   Land Requisition Approach

In China, compulsory land requisition started to accommodate state construction in the early 1950s, and was codified in the 1986 Land Management Law. After the 1988 urban land reform, rapid city growth has been accompanied by the requisition of a large amount of rural land and the involvement of the private sector. Nevertheless, not until 1998 was land requisition manifested in Article 58 of the 1998 Land Management Law, which lists the situations where the government can retrieve the LURs compulsorily:

1. When the government acquires land for public benefits.
2. When the government implements city plans and regenerates old districts.
3. When the land lease expires, the original land user does not apply for a renewal or extension of the lease, or their application is rejected.
4. When government departments or enterprises with administratively allocated LURs are abolished or relocated.
5. When airports, railways, highways and mines are discarded.

Under the situation in points 1 and 2, compensation should be paid to the original land users.

There have been two approaches to managing land requisition in China. Under the first approach, the prospective new land user directly negotiates with the affected farmers or sitting tenants. This approach is widely adopted in market-economy countries in order to settle various compensation issues concerning land requisition. Very soon this approach was found to be too time-consuming and expensive to accommodate rapid city growth, particularly when the prospective land user is a private developer. Many local authorities therefore switched their strategies. Under the new approach, local governments take full responsibilities in land requisition, either for public purposes or for private development projects. Usually the Land Resources Bureau or its affiliated agency is responsible for land requisition on behalf of the prospective land user. Its duties include negotiating with existing users about compensation issues and arranging resettlement according to rules and policies. Owing to the extensive and intensive participation of government in relocation and compensation schemes, the average requisition time and financial cost have been greatly reduced, which has accelerated city growth. This approach, however, has incurred much criticism on the ground that government has abused the power of 'compulsory purchase' for profitable use, which shall be discussed below.

6.2.2 Compensation Standard

The compensation standard has been very controversial in China. Actually it is a 'dual' standard according to relevant Chinese legislation. The compensation for farmland requisition is not based on market price; instead, the state provides a compensation package including a resettlement fee, housing compensation, compensation for the loss of crops, and so forth. Article 47 of the 1998 Land Management Law states that the compensation consists of three parts: land compensation, relocation compensation and property compensation. Land compensation is calculated as 6–10 times the average annual output in the previous three years of the farmland, and relocation compensation is based on the size of the affected household. The property compensation standard is set down by local governments, and it covers a range of collectively owned and privately owned structures or other farming facilities, including fishponds, water irrigation projects and buildings. Compensation is paid to the collectives or individuals who own the property. If the total compensation is not enough for affected farmers to maintain their previous living standard, local governments can increase the compensation standard, but the total maximum compensation should be 30 times the average annual output of the farmland in the previous three years.

For relocation and compensation in the redevelopment project, the 2001 Regulation for Urban Demolition and Relocation (hereafter the 2001 Regulation) and the 2011 Regulation for Urban Demolition and Relocation (hereafter the 2011 Regulation) illustrate existing market value as the compensation standard. In reality, the actual amount of compensation is negotiated between the compensating agency and the sitting tenant. Besides cash compensation, compensation in kind has been frequently used, for example on-site and off-site replacement of demolished buildings. Generally speaking, on-site relocation is very popular among affected occupants, but it makes a project financially challenging. Under the on-site relocation scheme, households receive housing space at least as large as they used to own. Usually there is a big difference between the values of old and new structures, therefore the higher on-site replacement, the less profitable the project will be. In some situations, for instance, when the residential land has been acquired for open space or public facilities, on-site relocation is unavailable. While more and more redevelopment projects proceed, less and less on-site relocation has been adopted. Instead cash compensation and off-site relocation have been prevalent. Off-site relocation has been a mechanism to facilitate redevelopment through encouraging households to move to outlying areas to obtain more space.

Recently, besides cash compensation to dispossessed farmers, many cities have promised farmers a monthly pension payment if they reach retirement age. For example, in Chengdu, the capital city of the inland province of Sichuan, local government has committed to provide a monthly pension of 300 yuan to male dispossessed farmers over 60 years of age and female dispossessed farmers over 50 years of age (Cao et al., 2008). However, under the current land compensation scheme, the fair market value of the land and the negative impacts of land acquisitions on farmers' livelihood have not been sufficiently considered by the government. The dispossessed farmers are largely excluded from sharing the land value appreciation resulting from land development and urban growth in China (Zhu and Roy, 2007).

Meanwhile, it is necessary to state that the compensation standard for dispossessed farmers has been a 'dual' one. On the one hand, compensation for farmers in most areas of rural China has been significantly underestimated; however, on the other hand, the compensation for the villagers in the *chengzhongcun*[4] and peripheral villages has been astonishingly high. According to the *Yangcheng Evening News* (8 April 2008), 33 households in a village of Luohu District, Shenzhen city were allocated more than 1300 apartments with floor space of 65000 m^2 as the compensation in a redevelopment project, and the average asset value of each household reached nearly 100 million yuan. They thus have become the de facto 'landlord' and benefited from enormous unearned interest. Based on the data of the Ministry of Finance, the compensation for land acquisition, compensation and other relevant expenses was 71.2 per cent of total LURs fees in 2011 (http://news.95191.com/detail/21696.html, accessed 12/10/2013), which has resulted in the serious debt crisis of local government in China. Moreover, the large inequality in land value capture has been regarded as one of the major reasons of income disparity and social unrest (Hua, 2013).

6.2.3 Implementing Compensation Schemes: Problems and Debate

Driven by the strong incentives of GDP growth and creating a new urban image, development-oriented local authorities tend to lower compensation standards,[5] either in farmland requisition or in urban redevelopment. Generally speaking, throughout the country standards for compensation are not well defined (Han, 2000). The 1998 Land Management Law has left much leeway for local authorities to formulate their own compensation standards. In many cases the lives of affected farmers were much worse after losing their land because they did not receive enough compensation to maintain their standards of living in the future. According to a rough estimation in the Yangtze River Delta (YRD), the average compensation standard for farmland was 375000–450000 yuan per hectare, and the average LURs assignment fee was 2100000–5250000 yuan per hectare in 2002. The former figure is only around one-tenth of the latter. According to *China Youth Daily* (3/14/2009) by 2020 the number of farmers who have lost their land because of land requisition will be around 100 million in China; however, their social security support has not been established (http://www.cqvip.com/QK/88775X/200904/29943852.html, accessed 29/5/2014). The lack of sufficient compensation for farmland requisition has resulted in social unrest in some rural areas, which has caught wide attention from the central government. In 2006, China reported a total of 17900 cases of 'massive rural incidents', in which a total of 385000 farmers protested against the government. Approximately 80 per cent of these incidents were related to illegal acquisitions (Cao et al., 2008).

In 2007, the Property Law of the People's Republic of China was promulgated and came into effect on 1 October 2007. It has been regarded as the first piece of legislation in the People's Republic of China to cover an individual's right to own private assets. The law covers all three property types within the People's Republic of China, which are state, collective and private. These are defined in Chapter 5 of the law. Article 42 stipulates that the state can only compulsorily acquire land or property owned by a collective, individual and *danwei* for the public use. This imposes constraints on the abuse of compulsory purchase power. The 2011 Regulation confirms this principle.

Given the highly speculative nature of land markets, the principle of 'existing market value' as a compensation standard itself is tenable. As stated in Chapter 4, many developed countries, such as the Netherlands, Sweden, the UK and Singapore, use existing market value as their compensation standard. This issue has never been a purely financial one in reality. Under some circumstances where great hardship may be caused by relocation and compensation at the current market value, extra welfare should be provided to ensure social stability. In China, farmers and urban residents living in dilapidated areas are often in the medium- or low-income class. Due to historical reasons, the size of demolished houses is very small in the city centre. Under such circumstances, the compensation based on existing market value may not be enough for the affected households to find affordable housing in other areas of the city. Although an '*Anju*' project (commercially built subsidized affordable housing for the middle- and low-income group) was launched in 30 medium-to-large cities in 1994, the housing price of the *Anju* project units has been beyond the capability of low-income families. A survey conducted in Beijing, Shanghai, Guangzhou, Chongqing and Wuhan in 2004 by the Economic Assessment Center of the China National Statistics Bureau reveals that only 24.35 per cent of households could afford *anju* houses with an average price of 2000 to 4500 yuan/m². Moreover, *anju* houses are inaccessible to many qualified households due to their limited number. The proportion of investment of *anju* houses in national real estate investment decreased from 10.9 per cent in 1998 to 3.1 per cent in 2009, implying further weakening housing affordability for middle- and low-income families (Report of China Real Estate Market Operation, 2009). Realizing the serious problems caused by high housing prices, the central government initiated an Affordable Housing Programme and required all local governments to finish a certain number of affordable houses each year.

The problems caused by the low compensation standard are becoming so nationwide that the central government needs to take them into account seriously. According to the MOHURD, half of development was from redevelopment projects in 2004, and the large scale of redevelopment generated numerous complaints against low compensation standards. Within the first half of 2004, the MOHURD received 18 620 complaints about low compensation, while 18 071 were received in the whole year of 2003 (http://news.xinhuanet.com/house/2004-07/05/content_1571678. htm, accessed 5/7/2004). In March 2004 the Constitution was amended concerning land requisition. Clause 3 of Article 10, 'The government can requisition land for public benefits according to relative legislation', was amended as: 'The government can requisition the land for public benefits according to legislation after the payment of compensation'. The amendment has been regarded as a relative advance in addressing the benefits of affected groups, although the government was very cautious not to use the terms of 'just compensation' or 'fair compensation'.

Compulsory purchase has been equally hotly debated in China. Many scholars argue that the government has abused the power of compulsory purchase in acquiring land (Xie et al., 2002; Bao and Hu, 2003). Although the 1998 Land Management Law, the 2007 Property Law and 2011 Regulation require that the use of this power should be based on 'public benefits' or 'the city plan', in reality many local governments are actively involved in assisting private development, and this has incurred a plethora of criticism. Compared with their counterparts in Western Europe where compulsory purchase can only be used after a municipality has tried and been unable to reach an agreement with a landowner for a voluntary purchase, China's local governments are participating in urban development in an entrepreneurial way because of their alliance with developers.

It appears that the Chinese government fears that compensation for hardship may incur indefinite liabilities and unnecessary delays or prohibitive expenses, which would stunt efficient development, and cause many valuable schemes to be stifled at their inception, particularly under the current circumstances of large-scale redevelopment and insufficient public funds. The worries of the government about high compensation are not without foundation. During rapid city expansion and increasing competition among cities, local governments fear that high compensation may drive land costs up and cause investors to flinch at the prohibitive cost. Realizing the potential problems of high compensation, the World Bank (1993) warned that Chinese local governments should consider taking complete control of the suburban land requisition process, expropriating rural land for all urban conversion purposes, including those that promote economic development, in a transparent manner, for there is no effective income tax system in place to capture part of any 'windfall gains' obtained by the rural communities. Compensation rules should be transparent, as well as equitable. Compensation amounts, but not the requisition itself, could be subject to appeal before regulatory bodies.

Local governments appear to be in line with the World Bank's view of taking full responsibility in suburban land requisition, not only in farmland requisition, but also in land requisition for redevelopment, in order to speed up city growth and regeneration at low cost. Given the uniqueness of the state land ownership under the LURs system, theoretically the state is empowered to compulsorily acquire any land under the legislation. The land requisition process and compensation decision, however, are made behind closed doors. Very often the affected households do not know that they will be relocated until the final decision has been made, and there is very little possibility for them to challenge this decision. In order to reduce resistance from affected households, the purpose of land requisition is often portrayed as being for a 'public purpose' by the notice from the government, even when it is obviously for a private purpose. According to the survey carried out by the South China Net in five provinces and cities in 2003, the frequently used excuses for land requisition were 'open space construction' or 'infrastructure construction', but many projects turned out to be commercial facilities or commodity houses. The lack of prior notice and public hearing, or simply false notice, is one of main reasons for confrontation and tension between affected tenants and local government.

The extensive application of the compulsory purchase power, on the one hand, speeds up city growth and renewal of old districts, while on the other hand the low compensation standard and the lack of restriction on this power encourage local authorities to occupy more land than they need (Bao and Hu, 2003). Partly owing to the low compensation cost, a large amount of requisitioned land has not been developed. A survey in ten provinces in 2003 shows that around 43 per cent of expropriated cultivated land has long been vacant, exacerbating the shortage of cultivated land (http://www.house2008.com/article.asp?articleid=6048, accessed 29/3/2004).

Finally, the lack of participation of an independent land valuation agency and the judicial system in solving disputes over compensation has created an institutional vacuum. The land valuation agencies are subject to the examination of the government, and thus they hope to build up good relationships with government. Judicial institutions, which guarantee a high degree of predictability in Western-style legal systems, are lacking or undeveloped in the PRC (Kent, 2004). According to Article 16 of the 2001 Regulation, the courts do not directly hear appeals of relocation and compensation cases because the designated local government agencies are empowered to make decisions in this area. Only after the appellant is dissatisfied with the decision of government agency can they file a lawsuit. However, the demolition can proceed without their consent, regardless of the result of the adjudication. Some scholars argue that this is an illegal police power and a deprivation of citizens' litigation rights (Liu, 2003). Local courts are empowered to hear the cases of demolition and compensation directly, yet they are of lower authority than the local party committee, which causes power and *guanxi*[6] to affect the court rulings significantly (Cao, 2003). Therefore, adjudication usually favours government and developers who are often in the same coalition with regard to city growth, while affected land users are left in an unfavourable position without equitable bargaining power (Xie et al., 2002). This is obviously detrimental to the credibility of the judiciary system.

6.3   THE ROLE OF THE STATE IN THE LAND MARKET

In the economic reform of China, the state has been playing a critical and active role. There is no exception in the land market. As the agent of the state, local government becomes a de facto landowner, which provides it with incentives to maximize its own revenue and minimize the cost of city growth. The role of the state in the land market, therefore, is essential to understand current betterment and compensation policies.

6.3.1   Stakeholders in the Land Market and the Central–Local Relationship

In the land market, there have been various stakeholders – central government, local government, developers, and farmers and city residents – and their relationships have a significant impact on the city development of China (Figure 6.1). In most cases, their interests have been contradictory: for instance, developers are inclined to lower the compensation standard to achieve the maximum profit margin, while the farmers and city residents claim compensation as high as possible. Local government, which is highly dependent on land financing, prefers a low compensation standard and a high land selling price. In the land market of China, due to the

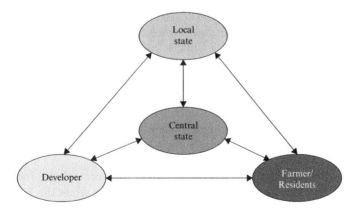

Figure 6.1   Key stakeholders in the land development of China

strong state control legacy, the central–local relationship has been playing the dominant role in the land development of China.

The objectives of land development of the central state and the local state have obviously diverged. While land leasing has become a major source of local revenue, the rapid shrinkage of farmland has been a major source of social instability and food insecurity, both of which concern the central government. Meanwhile, forced eviction and inadequate compensation during land expropriation are the main causes of social unrest. According to the *China Daily* (6/11/2010), about 65 per cent of mass protests in rural areas are triggered by land disputes. In contrast to the central government, local governments have been mostly concerned with land revenue, although social stability is equally important for them. However, food security and farmland preservation are not on their agenda. Therefore, local governments tend to enlarge city size through the acquisition of farmland.

Moreover, the fiscal relationship between central and local government has experienced dramatic changes since the opening reform. In the early 1980s, in order to make localities fiscally self-sufficient, and reduce the fiscal burden on central government, the central government established a tax responsibility system. All municipalities, prefectures, counties and townships were required to submit only a portion of their local revenues to the upper levels and retain most of the remainder. Local governments thus became the independent fiscal entities that have responsibilities in local expenditure and autonomy in retaining their revenue (Oi, 1992). The fiscal relationship between the central and local governments, however, was reconfigured in 1994. The tax sharing system successfully transferred revenue from local governments to the central government, but it failed to adjust expenditure responsibilities for local governments (Cai, 2011). According to Ye and Wu (2014), from 1980 to 2010, the central government controlled over 51 per cent of the national fiscal revenues while it covered less than 20 per cent of the expenditures. Local governments had to be responsible for over 80 per cent of the fiscal expenditures with less than 50 per cent of the revenue, despite some intergovernmental transfers from the central government (Figure 6.2). Therefore, local government has to resort to extra-budgetary revenue to supplement inadequate government funding, and land revenue has been a powerful tool to fill the gap between revenue and expenditure.

Meanwhile, the share of land revenue between central and local government has experienced frequent changes. In 1988 when the Land Use Rights system was established, the State Council required 40 per cent of land revenue to go to central government, and 60 per cent to be left in

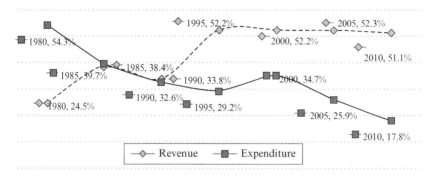

Source: Ye and Wu (2014).

Figure 6.2   Central government's revenue and expenditure as a proportion of the national total, 1980–2010

local government. In order to foster the burgeoning local land market, the Ministry of Financing issued an interim measure to reduce the share of central government to 5 per cent in 1990. In 1994 when the tax sharing system was launched, all land revenue went to the local coffers, and the land revenue thus became the 'second revenue' of local government. Motivated by the enlarging land revenue, local governments have been committed to land expansion, leading to the significant loss of farmland (see Table 5.1). In order to inhibit the impulsion of local government in land expansion, the 1998 Land Management Law adjusted the share of local government land revenue to 70 per cent, and the remaining 30 per cent was collected by the central government. Since 2004, the central government has started to place restrictions on the expenditure of land revenue of local government. A total of 45 per cent of local land revenue has to be used for: construction of affordable houses (10 per cent), education investment (10 per cent), construction of irrigation projects (10 per cent) and farmland reclamation (15 per cent) (http://www.mlr. gov.cn/, accessed 11/10/2013).

6.3.2   The Local Developmental State

Liew (1995) attributes the success of the Chinese gradualist economic reform to strong government and the participation of cadres in business. Wu (2002) notes that local governments have strong incentives to develop their own business activities in order to increase local revenue sources, and the close relationship between the governing and the governed in economic activities at the local level forms a basis for entrepreneurial endeavour. Under the development-oriented approach, local governments are committed to GDP growth and to improving their city's image, which have been used as the main means of evaluating the performance of both the leadership and local officials (Chen and Berrell, 2004). Zhu (2004b) asserts that with decentralization, China's local governments have become economic interest groups with their own policy agendas, and thus the 'local developmental state' has emerged.

Local officials are addicted to real estate development, not only because real estate has opened up local revenue and spurred economic growth, but also because large-scale real estate development has created a new modern city image which is regarded as the biggest achievement of mayors. Under a booming real estate economy driven by both the actual demand and the desires of local officials, many investors see real estate development as an opportunity for quick returns and high profits. An investigation by *China Industrial and Commercial Times* (31/8/2005) found that in 2005 the profit margin of many real estate development companies was higher than 30 per cent in Shanghai, much higher than the profit margin of other industries such as manufacturing, which is usually less than 10 per cent. Driven by the thirst for profit and economic growth, local governments and enterprises form a coalition. Gradualist urban land reforms have been employed as a tool to nurture the local property industry operating under new market conditions and to protect local enterprises from harsh market discipline (Zhu, 2004b).

This coalition, on the one hand, contributes to the rapid growth of the real estate industry; on the other hand, it incurs wide criticism. Wang (2003) states that governments have been extensively involved in the market, either through establishing public–private partnership or through setting up quasi-public companies. This extensive participation, however, exacerbates the already considerable lack of transparency in local fiscal matters, reducing the effectiveness of budgetary procedures, creating considerable opportunities for both waste and corruption, distracting government officials from their primary task of providing public services, and hindering market reform. Zhu (2004b) asserts that, driven by growth performance and constrained by fiscal deficiency, the local development state becomes myopic: pursuing quantitative rather than qualitative and sustainable growth.

6.3.3   Local Plans as a Main Tool of Intervening in Land Markets

With rapid and large-scale city construction, local government needs to enhance its control over urban development. Local plans thus become a major tool to serve its purpose. Urban planning as a discipline has achieved unprecedented growth since the 1988 urban land reform. The 1990 City Planning Act introduced a two-tier planning system to China: the city master plan and the site development control plan. Medium-sized and large cities must prepare district plans based on the master plan. The amended 2008 Urban and Rural Act confirmed this planning-making system.

City master plan

A city master plan is prepared by the planning department. It forecasts the size of a built-up city's area and population for 20 years, designates areas for various types of land uses, such as residential, commercial, industrial and farmland within the city planning boundary designated by the municipal government, and arranges trunk infrastructure and city-wide social amenities. A city master plan has a significant impact on the real estate market, particularly since the arrangement of infrastructure facilities can change the land values of certain areas. The formulation of a city master plan, however, is very physically orientated, and seldom takes social and financial factors into account. According to the World Bank (1993: 98):

> new or amended master plans prove only that the Design Institutes in charge, reporting to the local Urban Planning Bureaux, continue to be dominated by architect-planners with little access to 'feedback' based on systematic monitoring of relevant small-area demographic and economic indicators, and these agencies still show little apparent concern about the economic cost or consequences of the actions outlined in the plans.

Moreover, the examination and approval of a city master plan usually takes nearly a decade.[7] When the plan is approved, it is almost a one-decade-old legally binding document and not adaptable to current land use and density issues. The existing master plan has no phasing related to the implementation of its policies. It is more like a physical design than a comprehensive plan. Due to its lack of financial considerations, the implementation of a city master plan has proved problematic. In practice, the economy operates with few constraints imposed by city master plans. For instance, the open space designated in the master plan is often eroded by construction, and the type of land use of areas is often changed to accommodate new investment.

Under the 2008 Act, cities with populations of more than 200 000 are required to prepare district plans, which should be consistent with the master plan. District plans are prepared by the municipal government and specify purposes for land use and infrastructure facilities on a more detailed scale.

Site development control plan
Theoretically, the approved city master plan and district plan set up the framework of the site development plan. The site development control plan is prepared by either the municipal or the district government. Its framework borrows some ideas from the US zoning system, but it is not a statutory plan. The site development control plan identifies eight main planning parameters plot by plot:

1. Permitted land use type.
2. Maximum plot ratio.
3. Maximum building height.
4. Maximum plot coverage ratio (footprint area divided by the plot size).
5. Minimum open space ratio.
6. The location of the entrance.
7. Minimum car parking standard.
8. Public facilities contribution.

The site development control plan is essential in defining the development rights of a piece of land, and therefore forms the basis of planning management. The planning parameters stipulated by the site development control plan are attached to the LUPP. Among these parameters, permitted land use type and plot ratio are the most important factors in determining land value.

Similar to the development plans in the UK, the approved site development control plan in China does not guarantee that a development proposal consistent with the plan can automatically be granted planning permission. Local authorities have wide discretion in deciding whether planning permission can be granted and what planning parameters can be imposed, even though these granting parameters are inconsistent with the approved site development control plan. The preparation of a site development control plan, like that of a city master plan, is very design-based, and designers (whose education in urban planning is largely affected by the former Soviet Union system, and are thus trained to operate in the planned economy) seldom take financial and market factors into consideration. Thus it is not unusual that the site development control plan is frequently violated when planning permission is granted. As the site development control plan is not statutory, it is not unlawful to deviate from the approved plan. The wide discretionary power of local authorities has left much room for developers to manoeuvre and pay bribes to planning officials to obtain favourable planning parameters. Furthermore, there are frequent discrepancies between what is required by planning permissions and their attached parameters, and the completed development.

A common punitive measure for the violation of planning permission is a financial penalty; however, throughout the country there is no well-defined penalty standard, and the penalty largely depends on the discretion of local planning departments. Under such circumstances, bribes and personal relations play critical roles in paying reduced penalties.

6.3.4   Trade-off between Efficiency and Equity

Often there is a trade-off between efficiency and equity in economic relations. In many societies, attempts in pursuit of equity tend to impair efficiency, and vice versa. Nowadays, while most developed countries have achieved impressive economic and social welfare, absolute social equity has never existed. On the other hand, excessive stress on equity can lead to the loss of incentives and economic standstill. The failure of command economies serves as an example. Too much stress on efficiency and neglect of equity, however, leaves the society vulnerable to social instability. The trade-off relationship between efficiency and equity, therefore, requires a process of optimization (Qian, 1999).

At the early stage of China's economic reform when the resources were limited and people were poor, the slogan of 'Prioritizing economic efficiency and considering equity' (*Xiaolv youxian jiangu gongping*) was regarded as pragmatic, and thus acceptable to society. Limited resources were employed to spur economic growth and build infrastructure facilities, and much less were invested in alleviating income disparity. The housing commodification in 1984 and land marketization in 1988 have substantially contributed to city development and wealth accumulation in China. With great support from government, a property industry has been established within a short time period, and the marketization process has been accelerated.

After nearly three decades of economic reform, income disparity in China has been worsening. Statistics from the United Nations Development Programme show that the Gini coefficient, a statistical measure of inequality in which zero expresses complete equality while one expresses complete inequality, was 0.474 in China in 2012 (China Statistics Yearbook, 2013). The serious wealth gap in China has surpassed the reasonable limit (the internationally recognized alarm level of the Gini coefficient is 0.4). Twenty per cent of China's population living at the poverty level accounted for only 4.7 per cent of the total income or consumption; 20 per cent of China's population living at the affluence level accounted for 50 per cent of the total income or consumption (*People's Daily*, 21/9/2005). Since the economic reform, the state has been converting itself from an economic producer and socialist welfare provider to an advocate for growth, with progressive reforms that are gradually phasing out socialist welfarism (Zhu, 1999b). In the land market, local governments often emphasize the interests of developers who can serve their objectives of GDP growth, whereas the interests of low-income households and adversely affected groups are neglected. The low compensation standard and the lack of compensation for the loss of value are conspicuous in contemporary China.

Nevertheless, it is one-sided to blame market-oriented reform for income disparity. The excessive addiction to equity can lead to inefficient resource allocation and economic standstill, as has been proved by the command economy. Therefore, in China the market-oriented reforms were more driven by bottom-up popular aspirations than by top-down political decisions (Zhu, 1999b). Nowadays it is accepted in China that only development can solve many problems, including inequality. This does not necessarily mean that the current situation of priority over efficiency should continue, but more efforts and measures should be adopted to alleviate the income disparity, without seriously affecting the incentives of local governments or individuals (Wang, 1999).

Efficiency and equity are not mutually exclusive. On the one hand, efficiency is a precondition of equity. Without social wealth, equity is illusive, although economic growth does not necessarily lead to equitable distribution of wealth, which depends on governance. On the other hand, equity is an important institutional guarantee of long-term economic efficiency. The World Bank's (2007) *World Development Report 2006 on Equity and Development* argues that greater equity is a key ingredient of long-term prosperity. With more than two decades' priority over economic growth, now it is time for the Chinese government to redress the exacerbating social inequalities; otherwise society will be prone to high crime rates and unrest. The Shanwei incident, which happened in December 2005, reflects the serious confrontations between local government and affected land users.[8] Other unreported riots over low compensation and hardship are believed to be widespread (*BBC News*, 17/1/2006). Striking a balance between long-term economic growth and social equity is a very challenging task facing the Chinese government.

6.4 OBSTACLES TO ADDRESSING BETTERMENT AND COMPENSATION

Cheung (1982) identifies two major obstacles to institutional change: (1) the cost of obtaining correct information about other institutional arrangements; and (2) the cost of persuading or forcing the privileged group to acquiesce. These costs can be very high and impinge on institutional change. In China, failure to adequately address betterment and compensation can be attributed to these costs, and the privileged group, mainly the officials, have an incentive to distort information and shape the rules of the game to their own competitive advantage.

6.4.1 Non-existence, Inconsistency and Non-disclosure of Information

The availability of property information is one of the conditions for an efficient property market. In most developed countries, property information is readily available from various sources such as real estate agents, local authorities, the land title office and the press. In Mainland China, it is very difficult to obtain such information. Property information is mainly controlled by government departments. The formerly closed nature of China still has a strong influence on the release of information (Chan, 1999). There are two reasons for this phenomenon. Firstly, the departments concerned do not know which data can be released. Although the open door policy has been implemented for years, there are no clear-cut guidelines as to which information can be disclosed. In this situation, officials are very cautious about responding to requests for information. Secondly, public access to real estate information is restricted. In general, information is available to the parties of a transaction only after careful scrutiny of their identities, or through their connections with personnel working in the departments concerned. Finally, records have not been well maintained, and thus information cannot be readily retrieved. Even researchers funded by government departments have difficulties in obtaining accurate and systematic information.

Cadastral maps and their topographic base maps may provide a source of fundamental physical information, and other important information includes thematic topics such as land use, land values, demography and social conditions. Such information, when overlaid onto the topographic database, provides a comprehensive geographic information system (GIS), and is an invaluable resource for land management (World Bank, 1993). Unfortunately, under the current land management scheme of China, the fragmentation of authorities in record-keeping leads to relevant documents being assembled and filed by different agencies, reporting different sets of rights and obligations. Urban planning, land resources and housing departments are all involved in land use management. Planning permissions and their attached parameters are recorded by the planning department, and land-use and real estate transaction data, such as LURs fees and property transaction prices, are recorded by land resources and housing departments. In some cities another authority, the Construction

Committee, is involved in collecting exaction fees from developers. Each agency embraces its particular area of responsibility and attempts to develop its own independent GIS. Likewise, the registration of property is complex and fragmented. A property has to be registered with two separate government departments: the Land Resources Bureau and the Property Management Department. Separate title documents are issued respectively by these two departments in respect of the land and the structures. Overlapping of work and the lack of information sharing are bound to occur and cause delay and a waste of resources (Chan, 1999).

The lack of a mechanism to rapidly access data has hindered the development of land markets. 'Secrecy and land market development are simply incompatible' (World Bank, 1993: 91). For instance, the non-disclosure of real estate information to the public has led to many frauds committed by developers selling property. The exaggeration and concealing of transaction information on property are frequently used developer strategies to bid up property prices.[9] The government exercises little supervision over the dealings of developers, and the lack of public access to property information has provided developers with many opportunities to report false information to consumers. As a corollary, the price mechanism is distorted, leading to much speculation in the real estate market.

6.4.2   Uncertainties of Property Rights in Land

The gradualist reform is characterized by the gradual and informal reformation of property rights. It is different from the conventional wisdom, which regards stabilization, liberalization, privatization and democratization as conditions for successful transition. One serious problem undermining private incentives, however, has been insecure property rights (Qian, 1999). Li (1996) argues that ambiguous property rights appear when there are no pre-agreed and binding rules as to who will be in control in various *ex post* contingencies, so that owners have to fight for control in every circumstance. In the absence of a clearly defined legal system, the property rights in land, either *ex ante* or *ex post*, are ambiguous and have been left open to be captured by different parties under the LURs system. The uncertainties of property rights in land include the following.

The informal development rights of *danwei* in land markets
Under the planned economy, Chinese governments provided their employees with low-rent housing as an in-kind supplement to a low salary. Since the housing commodification programme of 1982, state-owned housing was gradually sold to employees who work for government departments or SOEs at low prices. The welfare housing allocation was abolished in

2000 as a result of housing reform, but the *danwei* still retain some privileges to construct houses for their employees on their allocated land. Zhu (2002) argues that the ambiguous property rights over land assets between the principal (the state) and the agent (local governments and *danwei*), have incurred short-term profit maximization at the expense of long-run urban development, and resources have been hastily converted into assets of the agents. As the agent of the state, the *danwei* landholders do not need to pay the LURs fees, and they use land to establish joint ventures and build estates with developers. Usually developers invest in building structures, and return a certain amount of floor space to the *danwei* as a condition of receiving free LURs. Although the *danwei* is not permitted to transfer the LURs, through cooperation with developers *danwei* land users can capitalize the allocated land. Moreover, houses owned by the employees of *danwei* can be sold in the real estate market. It is evident that *danwei* land users have been actively seeking to maximize their interests within the ambiguous property rights framework. As the agents of local developmental states, *danwei* have become the *de facto* landowners. Driven by the incentive to capitalize land rents, *danwei* land users are often motivated to rush through ill-considered development projects, rather than to maximize land value by waiting for the best timing and opportunity (Zhu, 2005). As a consequence, some land assets have been dissipated.

The informal development rights of collective land in the city
In China, collective ownership and state ownership in land coexist. According to the 1998 Land Management Law, all urban land belongs to the state, while land in rural districts and villages belongs to collectives. Collective land belongs to various farmers' economic units such as farmers' co-operative societies or village committees. Besides, Article 43 stipulates that: 'Any individual or work unit requiring the use of state land must apply for planning permission to the relevant government departments. The construction of village-enterprises, farmers' housing, and village public facilities in collective land, however, can be exempt from this application'. The 1998 Land Management Law, therefore, manifests a double-track system in both land ownership and land use management.

While the establishment of the LURs system in 1988 has allowed the leasing, transferring and selling of urban land for different periods of time, in rural areas collective ownership has allocated farmers plots of land for cultivating and building their own houses (this land is called *zhaijidi*). The collective land can be inherited, but it cannot be converted to urban use without going through the legal process. Through strictly demarcating a line between urban land and collective land, the Chinese government has created a dual land management system. The double-track land use system is uniformly implemented all over the country. In view of the huge income disparity between the urban and rural areas, the free use of collective land is clearly beneficial to farmers. In the rural areas where population density is very low and externality is trivial, the use of collective land has not generated conspicuous problems.

In the city area, particularly in the fast-growing cities where farmland acquisition is massive, the value of collective land has greatly increased, but throughout China there has never been a clear regulation of development rights in collective land at the periphery of the city. This ambiguity is one of main reasons why compensation issues are so contentious and prevalent in China now. The contradiction of legal rights and economic rights is as noticeable for collective land as in other areas in the land market, and the ambiguity over collective land should be blamed for the abundant unauthorized construction and transaction at the city periphery (Tian, 1998).

Lack of clear regulation as to what will happen and who should own the improvements on the land when a lease expires

The lack of this regulation has drawn keen attention from many scholars. By around 2030[10] when some leases will approach their expiration, this issue will attract much wider concern. Some countries and cities with a public land leasehold system have different institutional arrangements for the expiration of a lease. For example, in Canberra, provided that the land is not required by either the territory or the Commonwealth for public purposes, towards the end of the lease the government will grant a new residential lease to the person holding the old residential lease, without requiring payment. This gives the lessee continuing security of tenure. In Hong Kong, land lessees have been able to apply for a renewal of their leases within the last 20 years, thus providing land users with incentives to continue to invest and redevelop their properties. In Mainland China, however, the 1990 Provisions state that the LURs and improvements will be withdrawn by the government without any compensation, and land users have to pay the newly assessed LURs fee if they want to renew their leases. Considering the extensiveness of land leases in China, it is likely to be very difficult for the government to retrieve the LURs and improvements without compensation. Since the first leases will expire in the near future, this issue is in need of clarification.

The above-listed issues do not exhaust uncertainties of property rights in land under the LURs system. Other problems, such as the vague rules of law and weak enforcement of law, further contribute to uncertainties of property rights in land and result in the waste of resources. The gradual reform, however, is characterized by the gradual establishment of well-defined property rights, and interests of agents are not disappear-ing immediately, but gradually declining to reduce the resistance from them and avoid the country being trapped in political chaos. Li (1996) argues that ambiguous property rights are a response to high transaction costs and high uncertainties in the emerging market place. Therefore, the clarification of property rights will not be a 'shock therapy' process, which characterizes reform in the former Soviet Union and Eastern European countries. Rather, the reform of ambiguous property rights in land in China will likely be a gradual and incremental process under the LURs system.

6.4.3   Incompetent Governance in Land Management

Corruption in land management
Wide discretion and a lack of transparency are almost certain to lead to corruption. Corruption is seen as China's biggest political and economic challenge in the twenty-first century. Scholars estimate that the cost of corruption is between 13 and 16 per cent of China's GDP, a conservative range.[11] Among the issues that arouse many complaints from the public, corruption in land management has given rise to most widespread concern. According to the MLR and National Inspection Bureau, lawbreaking cases in land management numbered 5 490 000 and involved a land area of 122 000 hectares, and 3433 violators were warned, but only 363 were convicted from 1999 to 2002 (http://www/people.com.cn/GB/2014899. html, accessed 27/10/2004). In 2011, 37 000 illegal land cases were reported from January to September, involving a land area of 16 400 ha, and 16 000 cases were convicted (http://gb.cri.cn/27824/2011/10/25/5311s3413548. htm, accessed 22/10/2013). Compared with the widespread corruption in land management, only a small proportion – 10.6 per cent – of government officials charged with corruption were convicted, implying that corruption is a low-risk activity in China, which has encouraged officials to take the risk of demanding or receiving bribes.

Motivated by the high profit return, some developers pay bribes to government officials to obtain land at low prices and with favourable planning parameters. The ambiguity of property rights in land has left much leeway for government officials to take bribes. The recent most common corruption in land management is the grant of higher plot ratios. As noted earlier, the plot ratio is critical for the land value. With higher plot ratios, developers can build more floor space and earn more money without paying extra LURs fees. It is also not unusual for developers to pay bribes to be exempt from, or reduce their responsibilities for, building public facilities. Before the MLR 2002 No. 11 Circular, when negotiation was the main means of land leasing, local officials had plenty of discretion to decide the land price in most Chinese cities. Some real estate developers obtained their LURs at very low prices, because of their *guanxi* with government; but others, particularly newcomers, had to pay a much higher price for land in similar locations and of similar size. This land transaction system has resulted in prevalent land speculation. In Beijing, for example, parcels of land are often sold and/or transferred several times before the construction begins (*China Business Weekly*, 4/8/2004).

Corruption in land management is reflected not only in personnel taking bribes, but also in government agencies pursuing organizational self-interests at the expense of social benefits, a practice which is somewhat institutionalized and not regarded as corruption in China. Either at the state or the local level, officials are keen to compete for power and financial benefits. Many government agencies require land in good locations for the construction of housing for their employees, and require more compensation when their land is acquired for redevelopment. The more powerful the agency, the more land it requires, and the more bargaining power it will have in redevelopment (Zhu, 2002).

Insufficient expertise in land management

Assessing and addressing betterment and compensation requires technology such as a powerful computer-based GIS, and methods for planning land use and property valuation. These technologies have been applied to land management around the world, and they include statistical analysis and decision-support models, such as interactive multiple goal programming (IMGP), and computer simulation models for econometric analysis and impact analysis. These critical technologies that are widely used in developed countries, however, are not frequently used in China. Even where the technology and information are already available, they are not optimally used because of ineffective information storage, retrieval or sharing, as discussed earlier. In Mainland China, decision-makers and planners apply descriptive analysis much more frequently than scientific analysis in the project assessment. Usually top officials make the decision and the relevant research institute collects information to substantiate it without any questioning, and the cost–benefit analysis is seldom applied in decision-making. The dominant methods employed by planners and property assessors are still characterized by the legacy of the planned economy; for example, urban planning is design-oriented, instead of being driven by comprehensive social and economic analysis, resulting in many discrepancies between the planning and actual market performance. The decision-makers therefore prefer their own judgments to the analysis of the planners and assessors in many cases.[12]

Moreover, land management involves multiple administrative agencies, as discussed in Chapter 5. It is common for different sectors to have sector-specific initiatives in their development strategies. There are overlaps, gaps and even contradictions among different policies, leading to the confusion of plan implementation.

Weak law enforcement
'When legal institutions are weak or incomplete, property rights are informal' (Weimer, 1997: 3). Although impressive new legislation has been enacted over the past two decades, law enforcement has not been satisfactory in China. According to United Nations statistics, currently China has 2.5 billion yuan in unenforced court rulings (http://www.unchina.org/goals/html/obj10_law.shtml, accessed 10/12/2005). There are many loopholes in existing laws and regulations, which allow malpractice and mismanagement to thrive (Wang et al., 2004); for example, the lack of clear definitions of 'public interest' in acquiring land has led to the abuse of compulsory purchase power for profitable development. The widespread network of *guanxi* makes law enforcement difficult, since the *guanxi* network can substantially reduce the speed and effectiveness of law enforcement agencies, and thus raise transaction costs in the land market. It is difficult to build trust outside of the *guanxi* network (Cao, 2003).

The intricate central–local relationship is also a reason for weak law enforcement. Since the economic reform, the central–local relationship has experienced decentralization and re-centralization. In the 1980s and the early 1990s, in order to promote local economic development, the central government adopted a strategy of decentralization, and local governments were permitted to retain certain 'extra-budgetary revenue' and thus gained much autonomy to decide their own affairs. This decentralization provided a strong incentive for local economies. Nevertheless, it also resulted in the weakening influence of central government, and strong localism. In 1994, the central government launched a path-breaking measure to counter the trend of fiscal decline. This measure introduced a clear distinction between national and local taxes and established a national tax bureau and local tax bureaux, each responsible for its own tax collections (Qian, 2000). As for issues of land management, central government required that land supply above a certain area has to be approved by the State Council, and 30 per cent of LURs fees have to go to the central government (10 per cent before 1998) according to the amended 1998 Land Management Law. Local governments, however, still can enjoy much freedom in local affairs. Although land is owned by the state, in practice, local governments are de facto agents of the state in land management, and thus it is not difficult to understand why local governments often ignore national policies to maximize local interests.

Local government is often the culprit of land law violation. According to *The 21st Century China Economy* (19/1/2005), 80 to 90 per cent of land law violation cases since 2000 have been caused by local governments, and most of them are about the land supply beyond their jurisdiction. Few local officials, however, have been reprimanded. Punishment by administrative and party discipline, including warnings, serious warnings and loss of office, are often used to replace criminal prosecution, particularly when officials violate the law but do not receive bribes directly.

SUMMARY

Theoretically, the LURs system can provide many tools to capture land value increments and compensate worsenment. The LURs assignment fee has been a powerful scheme to collect land rent and invest in urban construction; however, given the local governments' desire to open up local revenue within their terms through land leasing, sustainable development becomes problematic. Local governments tend to lease as much land as they can, and this will certainly cause difficulties for future governments in finding sufficient land for urban development. The real estate taxation system has inherited much from the planned economy, and the levy of real estate taxes is not related to the market value of a property, which results in the failure of real estate taxes to curb speculation and alleviate income disparity. Under the LURs system, land banking is supposed to be an effective tool to capture betterment and stabilize housing prices. Under China's current institutional arrangements, however, land banking has been applied as a means of increasing local revenue by growth-led local governments. Ironically, land banking has been regarded as leading to a rise in housing prices. Like planning gains in the UK and exactions in the USA, planning obligations are equally contentious in China, not only because they raise the problem of equity, but also because they are one of the sources of corruption in land management.

Under the current compensation scheme of the LURs system, the most controversial issues are compulsory purchase power and compensation standards. The government's excessive intervention in land requisition and its failure to establish a fair compensation scheme has incurred a great amount of criticism, and the wide discretion and development-oriented approach adopted by local authorities can be blamed for it.

Therefore, although the marketization of land has achieved dramatic progress since the urban land reform, betterment and compensation schemes are characterized by some legacies of the command economy and strong government intervention. The coexistence of the introduction of market elements and the retention of old administrative measures reflects the characteristics of the gradual approach of economic reform in China.

Clearly, the inability of the government to adequately deal with betterment and worsenment will lead to uncertainty in real estate markets and the weakening fiscal capability of governments to provide public goods, therefore impinging on long-term urban development. Information with little publicity and a lack of transparency has allowed avoidable contradictions and problems to recur, and resulted in corruption and fraud. Moreover, the gradual reform approach is characterized by the lack of a comprehensive reform package to activate the market mechanism in all aspects of the macroeconomy that intermittently affects urban land markets (Li, 1999), thus generating ambiguity in property rights in land and uncertainty in land markets. Incremental land reforms have also been used as an instrument of positive intervention by local governments in the peculiar Chinese political structure to further their own interests. Widespread corruption and weak law enforcement make clarification of property rights in land difficult, therefore there is a long way to go before China can launch further institutional reform in the land market. In Chapter 7, some empirical evidence from Guangzhou illustrates to what extent betterment and worsenment issues have influenced the real estate market.

NOTES

1. In many cities, developers are required to complete a certain proportion of their construction within two years after they obtain the planning permission from the government. Failure to conform to either requirement can render the developer liable to forfeiture of the plot without compensation.
2. Under the 'trial and error' approach adopted by the Chinese economic reform, usually the new policy or policy change is firstly implemented in some cities. If the result is as good as expected, the new policy will be spread all over the country.
3. Source: Interviews with local officials in Guangzhou and Shenzhen from September to December 2005.
4. Literally *chengzhongcun* is 'villages encircled by cities'; please refer to Chapter 8, section 8.3.2 for detailed information.
5. There may be some exceptions under some situations where a portion of value of LURs may be offered as an incentive to encourage existing land users to relocate themselves quicker in order to achieve more speedily goals of urban redevelopment or environmental protection (Xie et al., 2002).
6. '*Guanxi*' may be the most frequently used word in the current social life of Mainland China. '*Guanxi*' means personal connections, particularly with government agencies and officials.
7. According to the 1990 City Planning Act, the master plans of all provincial capital cities and cities with more than 1 million of population have to be approved by the city, province congresses and State Council.

8.   In December 2005, villagers in Dongzhou, Shanwei city, said that as many as 30 people died when paramilitary police opened fire during demonstrations against the seizure of land for a power plant.
9.   Very often developers hire people as false housing purchasers when the property is sold at the beginning. False contracts between developers and the pseudo purchasers are signed showing a much higher price than the market price of the property to bid up the housing price.
10. The shortest leasehold is 40 years for commercial and office use under the LURs system. Therefore, the commercial and office leases issued in the late 1980s will expire by around 2030.
11. Angang Hu (2002) identifies at least ten categories of economic losses caused by corruption which equalled 13.2 to 16.8 per cent of China's GDP in the late 1990s.
12. Source: interviews with employees in local planning departments and land resource departments in Shanghai and Guangzhou in October 2004.

7. Assessing and addressing betterment and compensation in Guangzhou: empirical evidence

In China, constrained by the lack of accurate and adequate data, the evaluation of betterment and worsenment is very difficult either at the municipal level or at the project level. This chapter seeks to fill this gap by adopting a case study approach at two levels: municipal level and project level. The adoption of this two-level case study approach is based on the different activities of the main stakeholders – the government, the developer and the individual – in betterment and compensation schemes. To elaborate, the municipal government is responsible for providing public facilities, and charging fees and taxes for using public facilities. However, it is not possible to allocate the government's costs in an individual project. Therefore, it is easier to identify the costs and financial benefits of government at the municipal level rather than at the project level. At the project level, the quantification of betterment and worsenment can be easier than that at the municipal level, and some assessment methods, such as repeat-sales and hedonic regression, have been developed over the last few decades to identify impacts of government actions, for example, the construction of infrastructure facilities on the real estate market.

7.1 CASE SELECTION AND DATA SOURCE

7.1.1 Two Levels of Case Studies

Two levels of case studies are deployed in this research.

A city-level case study
Carrying out a national survey in terms of betterment and compensation is very difficult because of the vastness of China, and the diversity of land market structure and land management mechanisms in different cities, thus it is impractical to conduct a nationwide analysis of betterment and

compensation. Under such circumstances a pilot case can be chosen to evaluate betterment and compensation approaches. Yin (1994) suggests several criteria, such as convenience, access and geographic proximity, for selecting the final case in the case study design. Another possibility is that the pilot site represents the most complicated of real cases, so that nearly all data collection issues will be encountered at this site.

In this research, Guangzhou is selected as a city-level case study based on the following reasons:

- Guangzhou is the economic centre in the South China, and one of fastest-growing cities in China.
- It is one of the cities which took the lead in establishing the land use rights (LURs) system and introducing the auction and tender system of land.
- The land market of Guangzhou is relatively sophisticated and stable compared with the rest of China. Its land management mechanism is to some extent typical in big cities.
- The accessibility of data and the author's acquaintance with the city are also reasons for selection.

The study scope, however, will not be limited in Guangzhou, in order to avoid the danger caused by a lack of generalization of the overall study. Data from Beijing and Shanghai, which are the capital city and the biggest city of China, respectively, and some other Chinese cities, will also be collected to supplement the illustration.

Project-level case studies
At the project level, the Guangzhou Metro Line 2 (ML2) and Inner Ring Road (IRR) are selected as case studies to evaluate betterment and worsenment. The ML2 was announced in 1998, and completed in 2003. The construction of the ML2 has triggered the booming real estate development along the metro line. According to real estate agents, the prices of commodity housing adjacent to metro stations have been greatly increased, indicating a change of land value and betterment for the sitting occupants and developers. The IRR was announced in 1998 and completed in 2000. It has been built to resolve the serious traffic congestion in the old city, and its major part is elevated. The value of property along the elevated road has decreased significantly due to the noise, pollution and visual disfiguration of the elevated road. The IRR is therefore a project involving worsenment.

Guangzhou is selected as a case study to illustrate the performance of land markets since the 1988 land reform. This selection is based on the

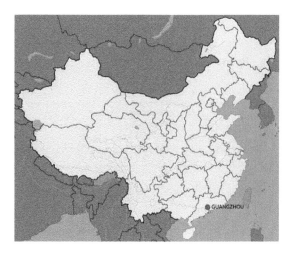

Source: Edited according to *China Atlas* (2002).

Figure 7.1   The location of Guangzhou in China

economic situation of the city and the size of the land market. Guangzhou is at the centre of the Pearl River Delta (PRD), one of the most prosperous economic zones in China, and it has the third-biggest urban economy in China. It is the 'Southern Gateway' of China (Figure 7.1), and one of the fastest-growing cities in the country. It has been considered to be one step ahead of the rest of China in economic reforms and development because of its proximity to Hong Kong (Vogel, 1989; Figure 7.2). Moreover, Guangzhou took the lead in piloting the sale of LURs in 1988 and introducing the auction and tender system of land in the mid- and late 1990s.

Guangzhou stretches over 7434 square kilometres and its population reached 12.7 million in 2010. Guangzhou has been growing very fast since the economic reform, in terms of both economic performance and built-up area. From 1980 to 2010, the average annual gross domestic product (GDP) growth rate reached 14.2 per cent. Meanwhile, the central built-up area more than doubled in size (Table 7.1, Figure 7.3). In 2000, two county-level cities, Panyu and Huadu county, were transformed into districts of Guangzhou, and the data of the central built-up area after 2004 thus includes the area of Panyu and Huadu. In 2010, the central built-up area reached 952 km^2, including the two new districts.

Source: Wu (1998).

Figure 7.2   The location of Guangzhou in the Pearl River Delta

Table 7.1   City expansion of Guangzhou since 1980

Year	1980	2000	2004
Central built-up area (km²)	136	298	350.8
Population (million)	5	7	10.2

Source: Guangzhou Urban Planning Bureau.

7.1.2 Data Collection

Official statistics and reports from the statistics bureaux, ministries, departments of land, real estate and planning, laws, ordinances and regulations are collected at three levels. One is the national and provincial level, and the focus is on the constitutional decisions, legal framework and policy analysis to provide a clear political and economic background. The second is the municipal level. Data is mainly collected from Guangzhou. Some data from Beijing, Shanghai, and other cities is also included to illustrate betterment and compensation policies in China. The choice of localities depends on their geographical spread and data availability. The third is the project level, and the transactional data is prepared to conduct the regression analysis.

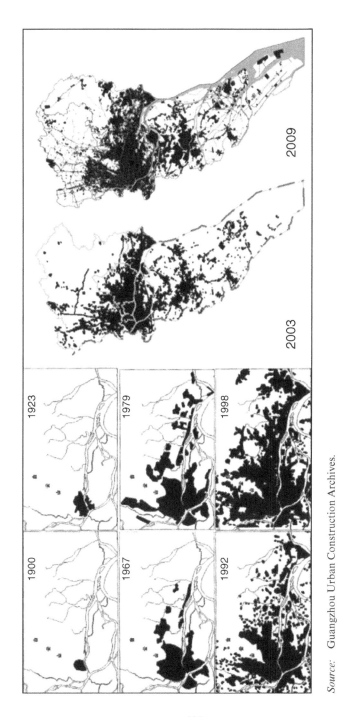

Source: Guangzhou Urban Construction Archives.

Figure 7.3 Rapid city expansion of Guangzhou since 1900

Webb et al. (1966) suggest that social scientists are likely to exhibit greater confidence in their findings when there is more than one method of investigation. Denzin (1970: 310) advocates an approach of 'multiple observers, theoretical perspectives, sources of data and methodologies'. Therefore, another type of data, from secondary sources such as unpublished monographs, statistics, documents from government agencies, reports of research institutes, press and newspapers, academic journals and books are heavily used to be an important supplement to official data, for they illustrate the problems of the land market from different aspects.

The author, however, met unexpected problems during the data collection process. One was the unavailability of data; for example, a plot-by-plot cadastre is not complete, and transactional data is not always registered and incorporated into a computerized system. The data of real estate taxes is distributed among different departments, and therefore very difficult to collect. Sometimes the data from different resources is inconsistent and requires much time and effort to discern which is more reliable. More importantly, much data, which is published in developed countries, has been kept secret in China. The government agencies usually do not provide data, and the author had to seek help from government employees. Resorting to the help of realtors and government employees, the author has collected some data to conduct the analysis. Although the author's working experience and network facilitated the data collection in Guangzhou, data collection was very difficult in Shanghai. Even with help from alumni, the required relevant data could not be gathered. Hence the author had to give up the comparative study between Guangzhou and Shanghai.

Personal interview is another effective and efficient way to obtain relevant information and remedy the deficiency of data collection. Unstructured personal interviews have been extensively applied, and people including government officials, planners, developers and realtors from Guangzhou, Shanghai, Shenzhen and Beijing were interviewed. Questions were designed in order to identify many issues such as current policies of addressing betterment and compensation, their merits and shortcomings, and to seek answers about what evaluation framework can be adopted to assess betterment and compensation. These interviews proved to be very helpful in identifying evaluation framework and data sources.

7.2 MUNICIPAL-LEVEL CASE STUDY: ASSESSING AND ADDRESSING BETTERMENT AND COMPENSATION IN GUANGZHOU

7.2.1 Criteria for Evaluation

Thus far there have been very few studies to gauge the extent to which the state has captured surplus land value and compensated worsenment at the municipal level, under either the freehold or the leasehold system. The main reasons are the scale of the analysis, the unaccounted spillover effects and the existence of many intervening variables (Banister and Berechman, 2000).

Among the few studies that evaluate the betterment capture, Yeh (1994) adopts several indices, including total land premium,[1] percentage of land premium in total revenue, total land-related expenditure, and percentage of land premium in total land expenditure, in order to evaluate the Hong Kong government's land value capture. He concludes that the total revenue from land sales accounted for 55 per cent of the total land-related expenditure in Hong Kong from 1974 to 1990. Hong (1995) argues that the percentage of land revenues in the total government budget is not an adequate indicator to reflect the ability of the government to capture future surplus land value. He proposes the proportion of public infrastructure expenditure financed by the captured value as another indicator, on the ground that the 'sustainability' of public infrastructure investment may lead to property value increases, and therefore the state should be able to recapture most of the land value increments generated by its projects, and the captured land value should pay a large part of infrastructure expenditures.

In Mainland China, the revenue generated from land, including both land leasing income and real estate taxes, composes one of the main sources of urban infrastructure investment. Therefore, several indicators, such as the contribution of land revenues to local revenue, their percentage to urban infrastructure investment and the revenue generated by unit land area, are selected to estimate to what extent the government has captured land value increments.

7.2.2 Real Estate Investment and the Local Economy

Although local GDP has been growing, real estate investment has experienced peaks and troughs owing to national policy adjustments in China. Since the late 1980s, Guangzhou has experienced four phases: emergence in the late 1980s, stagnation in 1990, an upsurge in the early 1990s, and

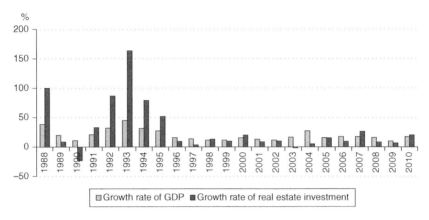

Source: Guangzhou Statistics Yearbook (1993–2011).

*Figure 7.4   A comparison between the GDP growth and the real estate
            investment growth in Guangzhou*

relative stability after 1995 (Figure 7.4). Compared with the national real
estate market (Figure 5.3), Guangzhou's real estate market has not been
experiencing the upturn phase, which is characterized by the real estate
heat in the Yangtze River Delta (YRD) since 2000. Real estate investment
dropped in 2003, which has been attributed to the high cumulative vacant
floor space of commodity houses in 2002 (93363000 m²; Construction
Committee of Guangzhou). During the cyclic downturn, the developers
reduced investment in 2003. After 2003, the real estate investment went
up again.

7.2.3   Land Revenue and Government Revenue

In China, land revenue consists of two major parts: LURs fees and real
estate taxes. The former are lump-sum fees collected from land leasing;
and real estate taxes include the urban land use tax, real estate tax, sales
tax on real estate development companies, construction tax, education-
affiliated tax and real estate transfer tax. In Guangzhou LURs fees were
not levied until 1992. Therefore, the following statistics begin from 1992.
Figure 7.5 reveals that the land revenue has been growing fast, particularly
after 2005. In 2008, land revenue went down due to the global financial
crisis, but it substantially rose in 2009 due to the stimulation of the 'Four
Trillion Plan'. Table 7.2 shows that land revenue has been an increasingly
important proportion of Guangzhou's government revenue since the early
1990s. Its contribution to government revenue ranges from 22 per cent

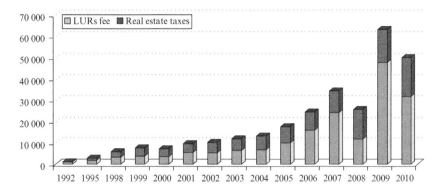

Sources: Guangzhou Statistics Yearbook (1993–2011), GZLRB.

Figure 7.5   Growth of land revenue in Guangzhou (million yuan)

Table 7.2   Contribution of land revenue to government revenue of Guangzhou

Year	Land revenue as % of government revenue	Land area supplied for profitable use (km²)	Revenue per m² of land (million yuan/km²)
1992	24.1	11.4	98.52
1995	24	5.72	129.2
1998	36.5	51.79	66.09
2000	38.8	12.06	305.97
2003	34.5	12.12	544.31
2005	32.2	17.78	575.93
2006	36.5	13.02	1215.59
2007	39.7	28.02	866.45
2008	29.3	10.98	1097.54
2009	47.3	12.49	3837.23
2010	36.5	11.13	2867.48

Sources: Guangzhou Statistics Yearbook (1993–2011), GZLRB.

in 1993 to 47.3 per cent in 2009. As a whole, the Guangzhou municipal government received 35.1 per cent of government revenue from LURs fees and real estate taxes from 1992 to 2010. Under the land financing regime, the municipal government has shown more and more reliance on land leasing.

Table 7.2 also presents another key indicator, the change in LURs fees per km² of supplied land. Since the land for infrastructure and public facilities is exempt from LURs fees, it is not included in the area of supplied land. The revenue per km² of land supply for profitable use increased dramatically in Guangzhou during the early 1990s. The municipal government was willing to lease more land in pursuit of its objective of increasing local revenue, while responding to the increasing land demand. The combination of market forces and the government's willingness to lease more land resulted in an oversupply of land from 1992 to 1995. The oversupply of land in turn led to a decrease in land prices, contrary to the government's expectations of maximizing land revenue. For instance, the LURs fee per km² of land decreased from 98.52 million yuan in 1992 to 39 million yuan in 1993. According to statistics of the Guangdong Land Society (1996: 47), the average land price per square metre was 524 yuan in Guangzhou in 1993, only one-sixth of the benchmark price designated by the municipal government, implying that the land was leased to developers at very low prices, and that leasing income which should have gone to the government and the community accrued to developers. In the late 1990s, the negotiation process for acquiring land was abolished in Guangzhou, and thereafter land prices grew substantially, except in 1998 when most land was leased for a science park at a very low price to attract high-tech enterprises. By 2010, the LURs fees per km² of land reached 29.1 times that in 1992.

7.2.4 Land Revenue and Urban Infrastructure Investment

Infrastructure expenditure is regarded as one of the key factors spurring economic growth and land value increase. It includes spending on roads, rail, airports, open spaces, schools and other public facilities. As infrastructure expenditure composes a large portion of government budgets and can lead to the increase of land prices, the government has legitimacy in recouping part of land value increments generated by its investment.

Urban investment in infrastructure rapidly increased during the period of 1992–1999, and then remained relatively stable (Figure 7.6). The upsurge in the late 1990s was derived, firstly, from the needs of a fast-growing city; and secondly, was reinforced by the adjustment of macro-financial policy to encourage the massive investment in infrastructure. Under the tutelage of Premier Zhu Rongji, China engaged in a quite massive Keynesian-type stimulus of public sector spending from 1998 to 2000, in order to successfully counter the deflation caused by insufficient consumption demand.

During the early 1990s, land revenue played a key role in funding the construction of infrastructure facilities. The percentage of land revenue to

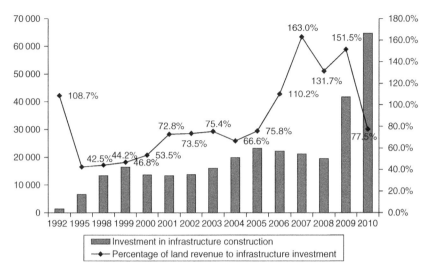

Source: 'Fifty years of Guangzhou', Guangzhou Statistics Yearbook (2000–2011).

Figure 7.6 *Percentage of land revenue to urban infrastructure investment of Guangzhou*

infrastructure investment ranged from 38 per cent in 1993 to 163 per cent in 2007, and the annual average percentage was 90.5 per cent from 1992 to 2010, which means that if all land revenue was used for the infrastructure construction, it would fund around 90.5 per cent of infrastructure investment from 1992 to 2010.

7.2.5 Compensation

It is very difficult to gauge worsenment and compensation at the municipal level, due to the lack of data and available methods. Therefore, this research mainly examines compensation policy from a descriptive perspective, and examines worsenment from several cases.

Compensation for land acquisition
With the rapid city expansion, more than 100000 households were relocated, and 4 million square metres of buildings were demolished in Guangzhou from 1997 to 2002. Nationwide problems such as a low level of compensation and the abuse of compulsory purchase power in acquiring land for profitable use were equally prevalent in Guangzhou. Under the pressure of more and more complaints, the Guangzhou municipal

government amended its compensation standard. On 1 January 2004, the Measures for the Control of Urban Relocation and Compensation of Guangzhou (hereafter, the 2004 Measures) came into effect. Realizing that the low compensation for old buildings[2] had led to hardship for existing tenants, the 2004 Measures increased the compensation standard based on the existing market value by 20 per cent in the designated urban area, mostly in the old city centre. Even so, there is still a lack of sufficiently detailed published materials to illustrate compensation standards, and the assessment of the existing market value of affected properties is controversial, mostly because the assessment agency is either government-affiliated or subject to the examination of government. Furthermore, the affected party has to seek arbitration from the government before they can apply to appeal against the awarded compensation.[3] Therefore, the government has great discretion in deciding whether, and how much, to pay affected parties.

Worsenment
There has been no compensation for the loss of value in Guangzhou, even though worsenment is caused by government action such as the construction of infrastructure facilities and the change of planning parameters. This has drawn more and more attention recently.

Neither the 2011 Regulation nor the 2004 Measures makes any stipulation as to how to compensate the adjusted LURs, which usually involves developers rather than individual households. For instance, in the middle of 2004, the Guangzhou municipal government amended planning parameters in certain areas of the city, and required all land plots that had not been developed to decrease their plot ratio by 20 per cent without compensation, on the ground that the traffic was overcrowded in that area. When their LURs are required to change, many developers choose negotiation with government to obtain relatively favourable planning parameters, instead of appealing against the government, considering that a good relationship with government is critical for their development projects. Some developers, however, were not satisfied with government decisions, and filed suits against the government. The Ersha Island case is one of the most important recent influential cases (Box 7.1).

As people have become more aware of their property rights, more conflicts between public facilities construction and private interests have emerged, leading to many complaints against government. Lijiang Garden serves as an example (Box 7.2). Under the growth-led approach, however, the pattern of lack of prior notice and zero compensation for worsenment remains, and appears not to be on the immediate agenda of government.

BOX 7.1 ERSHA ISLAND CASE

Hanxian International Ltd acquired the LURs of one plot in Ersha Island in 1999. According to the approved development plan, this site could be developed for commercial use. On 23 April 2001, the Guangzhou municipal government issued a notice and required this plot to be converted into open space after paying compensation to the developer. The reason for the adjustment is that the previous government was preoccupied with real estate development during the early 1990s and ignored improvement of the urban living environment, leading to the undersupply of open space.

The debate focuses on the compensation amount. Hanxian asked for compensation, including the LURs fee reimbursement and the loss incurred by the delay of the project, or alternatively, to acquire the LURs of another plot with similar location and size, but the municipal government rejected its application for another plot, because according to current regulations, the LURs for profitable use can only be acquired through auction or tender. Moreover, the municipal government could only pay back the LURs fee, instead of the LURs fee plus the loss entailed by the adjustment. Hanxian brought an action against the municipal government, and so far no agreement on the compensation has been reached.

Note: ■ Commercial land   ■ Land for public facilities
      Land for open space   Residential land
      ○ Hanxian Lot

The Master Plan of Ersha Island, 1987

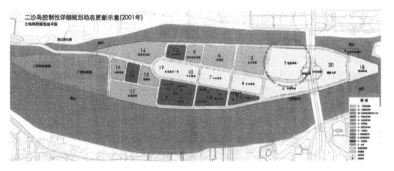

Note: ▨ Land for open space   ▨ Residential land
          ▮ Land for public facilities
          ○Hanxian Lot

The amended Master Plan of Ersha Island, 2001

BOX 7.2   LIJIANG GARDEN EVENT

Lijiang Garden is located in the west of Nanpu Island, in the Panyu district of Guangzhou, and is well known for its beautiful living environment. It was awarded 'Best Human Habitat' by the United Nations in 2000.

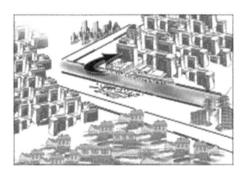

In December 2002, a trunk road 40 metres wide, dividing Lijiang Garden into two parts, was built without informing affected residents. The resale data shows that the price of affected property decreased around one-third because of the construction of this road. On 12 May 2003, 41 households in Lijiang Garden filed a 'taking' suit against the Guangzhou Urban Planning Bureau, but lost the case. The court pointed out that the construction of the road was for the public interest, and had been approved by the municipal government.

7.3 PROJECT-LEVEL CASE STUDIES: ASSESSING IMPACTS OF THE ML2 AND IRR

Compared with the assessment at the municipal level, the evaluation of betterment and compensation at the project level can be more quantitative. The following presents some empirical evidence of betterment and worsenment, taking two project-level case studies in Guangzhou (Tian, 2007).

7.3.1 Selecting Samples for Case Studies

The major objective in conducting case studies was to examine the extent of betterment and worsenment generated by government actions. In this research, two projects, the ML2 and the IRR, were selected to conduct the evaluation of government activities on property value changes.

The ML2 was announced in 1998, in order to promote development of the south of the city through launching a transit-oriented development (TOD) strategy. Its construction began in 2001. The ML2 includes 20 metro stations, and its whole length is 23.265 km. Its total cost was estimated to be 9.5 billion yuan. Its first section was put into operation in June 2003 (Figures 7.7 and 7.8). Although there is a lack of published statistics, based on the interviews and observations of the author, the price of commodity houses adjacent to metro stations, whether new or second-hand,[4]

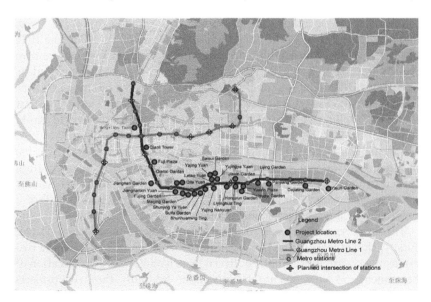

Figure 7.7   Project locations along the Guangzhou Metro Line 2

Figure 7.8   Residential projects along the Metro Line 2

have been greatly increased, indicating a change of land values and betterment for the occupants and developers.

The IRR is the other example (Figures 7.9 and 7.10). It also was announced in 1998 and the construction was finished in 2000. The IRR has been one of the largest infrastructure projects in Guangzhou to resolve serious traffic congestion in the old districts. It is 26.7 km long, and its major part, 20.26 km long, is elevated. The demolished building area was 393 000 m², and the relocated residents numbered 20 000. The project cost around 7.7 billion yuan, and was partly sponsored by the World Bank. Land prices along the IRR were considerably affected: while the value of some land was increased thanks to improvement of accessibility, the value of other land was reduced due to noise, pollution and view disfiguration caused by the elevated road. In other words, the project bestowed benefits on some groups and imposed costs on others. The IRR is therefore a project involving both worsenment and betterment.

There are several reasons why these two projects have been selected. Firstly, the impacts of the construction of the ML2 and IRR on the real estate market are substantial, not trivial, which makes the quantification of betterment and worsenment relatively easier. Secondly, these two projects involve both betterment and worsenment, which makes them typical of government actions that have effects on land value. Thirdly, the investment

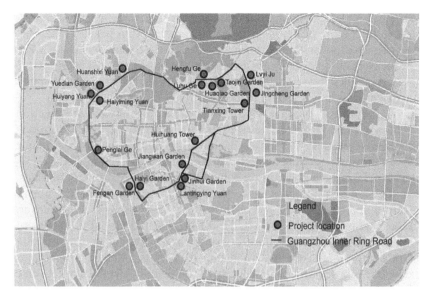

Figure 7.9   Project locations along the Guangzhou Inner Ring Road

Figure 7.10   Residential projects along the Guangzhou Inner Ring Road

in these two projects is huge, but the municipal government has not considered value capture or hardship compensation, and thus has not made any *ex post* evaluation on these two projects. As a consequence, it has not taken any measures to internalize the betterment or worsenment. Therefore, the research on these two projects is expected to draw some attention owing to their significance for the land market of Guangzhou city.

Next, residential projects whose value was affected by the construction of the ML2 and IRR were selected. The selection of residential projects was from the author's careful consideration and discussion with some developers and government staff. Certainly the construction of the infrastructure facilities has effects on commercial and office property markets, but the transactional data of commercial and office markets is not as plentiful and readily available as those of residential projects. Moreover, in the catchment area of the ML2 and IRR, the majority of development is residential projects. Welfare housing, though permitted for resale at market value and covering a substantial part of affected property, is excluded because the original sales price could not reflect the market value of the property and land. Therefore, the samples focus on the commodity houses that were mostly built after 1990. The author spent one week visiting all commodity residential projects along the ML2 and IRR, and marked them on the map. The samples of the ML2 are limited to within walking distance (less than 15 minutes) of metro stations, and those of the IRR to within the residential projects which, or part of which, directly face the elevated road.

7.3.2 Data Collection

Since the mid-1990s the Guangzhou Municipal Real Estate Transaction Center (RETC) has been recording the transactional information on commodity buildings. Unfortunately the transaction data is not open to the public. Furthermore, the registration systems for sales of new houses and second-hand houses are separate; in other words, the historical record of one dwelling unit is not available in the RETC. With the help of RETC employees, the author collected the information of average selling price (ASP, in yuan/m^2) of all residential projects for the first transaction between the developer and the house purchasers. The ASP of a project is calculated by the developer and registered by the Land Resources Bureau. The calculation equation is:

$$\text{ASP} = \frac{\sum f_i P_i}{\sum f_i} \qquad (7.1)$$

where:
f_i = floor space of the ith apartment
P_i = selling price per square metre floor space of the ith apartment.

However, ASP alone is not enough to carry out the analysis. The information on resale housing information is critical for analysis. Interviewing realtors has been an effective way to collect information on real estate transaction, but not all realtors are willing to release the transaction information because they regard them as commercial secrets. Therefore not enough information can be collected merely from realtors, and other sources have to be explored. For instance, real estate magazines such as *Real Estate Information* and *Real Estate Weekly* publish periodical advertisements on property sales. The Internet has also proved to be a useful tool in gathering information; http://house.gznet.com is a popular Internet website, and many residents who want to resell their houses post information, including the floor space and expected price, on this website. Although these prices are asking prices, not transaction prices, they help to zero in on the actual transaction price. For example, if the seller overestimates the price of their apartment, and nobody is interested in this price, they have to ask for a lower price until somebody is interested and a transaction happens. Therefore, the last price they ask before the information of their apartment disappears can be regarded as closest to the transaction price. Through utilizing multiple sources, the author collected data on 397 dwelling units along the ML2 and 184 dwelling units along the IRR (Table 7.3).

Among the samples of the ML2 project, 60.71 per cent are transaction prices, and the remaining 39.29 per cent are asking prices; among the samples of the IRR project, 72.18 per cent are transaction prices, and 27.72 per cent are asking prices. Since the asking price is always higher than or equal to the transaction price, the impacts of the ML2 and IRR may be slightly overestimated.

Table 7.3   Property information source

Source	Dwelling units along the ML2	Dwelling units along the IRR
RETC	169/42.57 %	95/51.63 %
Realtors	72/18.14 %	38/20.65 %
Internet and media	156/39.29 %	51/27.72 %
Total	397	184

Note: % means the proportion of dwelling unit information from different sources in total units.

7.3.3 Estimating the Land Value Changes: Repeat-Sales Model and Hedonic Regression

While it is impossible to exclude all the external factors affecting housing price, two alternative approaches, the repeat-sales approach and hedonic regression, are used to examine the consistency.

Repeat-sales model
The repeat-sales model assumes that the characteristics of any given property, such as the living area, surrounding public facilities and open space, do not change as time goes by. Therefore, a comparison of several transaction prices of one unit can illustrate the impact of an event such as the construction of metro lines (see Chapter 4, equations 4.2 and 4.3). In developed countries such as the UK and the USA, it is usual for one house or apartment to be transferred several times during its physical life. In China, however, since the real estate market emerged less than two decades ago, it is much less common for one house or apartment to have been transferred several times. A distinctive feature of the Chinese housing market is the dominant share of newly built houses. Usually developers purchase the LURs, build dwellings, and sell the finished houses to individual occupants. A property development takes the form of one or several blocks of apartments with similar building quality standards, built together or in several stages on the same site. They may share certain facilities such as a garage area, a garden or a swimming pool. Recently the resale market has been emerging and becoming more significant. Statistics from the Guangzhou Land Resources Bureau show that the resale of houses only constituted 6.1 per cent of all transactions in the housing market from 1992 to 1998, but the share jumped to 32 per cent in 2001 and 43 per cent in 2004.

The assumption that housing characteristics are constant over time is the basis of the repeat-sales model. However, under the LURs system of China, the change in building age has a significant effect on property value, which cannot be neglected. Under the land freehold system, costs related to land are usually not depreciable. Under the LURs system, however, the residential leasehold is 70 years maximum. When the lease expires, the government will repossess the land and the on-site improvements.[5] Therefore the land is depreciable and its recovery period is 70 years. Moreover, decoration has certain impacts on house price in China. In Guangzhou, many developers sell housing with decoration, and the most common standard for the decoration is 500 yuan per square metre of floor space.[6] The physical life of decorations varies according to the quality of materials and maintenance, but its economic life is usually regarded as five years. In other words, new purchasers are not willing to pay for decorations more than five years old.[7] In order to make the evaluation manageable, we assume that the decoration cost of all dwelling units is 500 yuan/m², and the recovery period of decorations is five years.

According to interviews with realtors and developers in Guangzhou, new properties depreciate faster in value in their early years, and depreciate more slowly in value as they age. Thus depreciation is accelerated rather than straight-line at the early stage. The quantification of this acceleration speed, however, is very complicated and beyond the scope of this research. The trade-off strategy to achieve both manageability and precision in this research, therefore, is to make an assumption: that is, the recovery period of decoration cost (500 yuan/m²) is five years; and the recovery period of other costs, the selling price minus the decoration cost, is 70 years. Both have been assumed to depreciate on a linear basis. Given the characteristic of the accelerating speed in the early stage, the introduction of the decoration cost can somewhat offset the bias of the assumption of straight-line depreciation.

Since the assumption of a standard repeat-sales model cannot be supported under the LURs, its application should be modified. In this research, all samples have been transferred only twice, and building age is incorporated into the equation in order to take the land depreciation into account. Then a new equation can be obtained as follows:

$$P_2 (1 + r)^{N-n} = P_1 (1 + r)^N \tag{7.2}$$

where:
P_1 = the first transaction price
P_2 = the second transaction price
N = the lease period, in years; 70 for residential projects in Guangzhou
n = the period from the purchase to resale, in years.

In equation (7.2), the decoration cost should be deducted from the transaction price because its recovery period is different from that of land. To make the transaction prices comparable, decoration cost is deducted from both P1 and P2. For simplification, the depreciation of decoration cost is set as 100 yuan/m² per year. For instance, the first transaction price of one unit in Fujing Garden was 4342 yuan/m² in 2001, and its resale price was 4332 yuan/m² in 2004. Both of these prices include decoration. In order to exclude the impacts of decoration cost, the first transaction price is adjusted to 4342 − 500 = 3842 yuan/m², and the second transaction price is adjusted to 4331 − [(5 − 3)*100] = 4131 yuan/m², where 5 is the economic life of decoration. Since the decoration age is three years, the remaining economic life of decoration is two years, so the remaining decoration value is 200 yuan/m². The adjusted prices are regarded as P1 and P2 respectively. Taking the natural log of equation (7.2) yields:

$$(70 - n) \, LN(1 + r) = LN(P_1/P_2) + 70LN(1 + r) \qquad (7.3)$$

According to equation (7.3), the cumulative appreciation index $(1 + r)$ of all samples is estimated. Tables 7.4 and 7.5 reveal the average index of all samples in every project, and then this index is compared with the general house price index. The RETC publishes the general housing index of the whole city on its website (http://g4c.laho.gov.cn/). The house price index of the base year, 2004, is set as 1, and indexes in other years are

Table 7.4   Comparison between cumulative appreciation index of projects along the ML2 and general house price index

	Project name	Site area (M²)	Sample size	n (Year)	Cumulative appreciation index	General house price index
1	Fujing Garden	16712	32	3	1.0244701	0.962943
2	Qianxi Garden	38088	14	2	1.1909488	0.974498
3	Shunjing Ya Yuan	41976	19	5	1.0821106	1.039473
4	Liyinghua Ting	21629	23	2	1.4543943	0.974498
5	Yujing Nanyuan	48340	27	4	1.0119574	0.994776
6	Yajing Yuan	13543	21	6	1.1540565	1.101137
7	Dajiating Garden	27300	8	4	1.0034635	0.994776
8	Yujingya Yuan	42837	33	4	1.1632653	0.994776
9	Yuexin Plaza	21827	15	7	1.1222505	1.095322
10	Qile Yuan	34976	45	4	1.2552536	0.994776
11	Jiaxin Garden	20654	12	4	0.9989458	0.994776
12	Meijing Garden	20654	5	4	0.997915	0.994776
13	Shunhuaming Ting	7872	8	3	1.0243029	0.962943
14	Hongyun Garden	42000	16	6	1.0017486	1.101137
15	Jiangnan Garden	43583	28	6	1.1945004	1.101137
16	Huayi Garden	4590	16	7	1.009764	1.095322
17	Hengxinyu Yuan	9901	6	2	0.9969842	0.974498
18	Letao Yuan	18728	11	4	1.107208	0.994776
19	Lijing Garden	2854	4	6	1.1188361	1.101137
20	Suifa Garden	1426	5	7	1.109771	1.095322

Sources: data from RETC, realtors, Internet and media.

Table 7.5   Comparison between cumulative appreciation index of projects along the IRR and general house price index

	Project name	Site area (M²)	Sample size	n (year)	Cumulative appreciation index	General house price index
1	Haiyi Garden	31536	11	4	0.9664953	0.994776
2	Huanshixi Yuan	35396	13	3	0.9935311	0.962943
3	Huiyang Yuan	21000	8	3	0.9368553	0.962943
4	Hengfu Ge	7800	16	8	0.9047301	1.057269
5	Jingcheng Garden	49961	17	5	0.9447005	1.039473
6	Taojin Garden	31254	22	6	0.9349163	1.101137
7	Huaqiao Garden	13284	19	8	0.9233265	1.057269
8	Tianxing Tower	–	5	7	0.9420996	1.095322
9	Yuedian Garden	–	6	6	0.9494336	1.101137
10	Luhu Ge	8536	7	7	0.9949264	1.095322
11	Jinhui Garden	30738	9	6	0.9663796	1.101137
12	Jiangwan Garden	150941	18	7	0.9397078	1.095322
13	Fengan Garden	6711	6	6	0.9563755	1.101137
14	Lvyi Ju	5505	5	4	0.9699037	0.994776
15	Haiyiming Yuan	9463	9	4	0.8433674	0.994776

Sources: data from RETC, realtors, Internet and media.

converted into the comparable value. For example, the average cumulative appreciation index of the Fujing sample is 1.02447 within three years, and the general house price index in 2001 is 0.962943, compared with 2004, indicating that the construction of the ML2 has a positive impact on property value.

Table 7.4 and Figure 7.11 show that the appreciation indexes of two projects, Hongyun Garden and Huayi Garden, are less than the general house price index, and the appreciation indexes of the other 18 projects are higher than the general house price index. This indicates that the construction of the ML2 has induced a property value increase for most residential projects. Likewise, Table 7.4 and Figure 7.12 compare the cumulative appreciation indexes of residential projects along the IRR with the general house price index. The result reveals that the appreciation index of all samples, except Huanshi Xiyuan, is much lower than the general house price index, which implies a significant value reduction induced by the construction of the IRR.

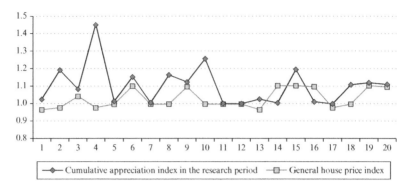

Figure 7.11   Comparison between cumulative appreciation index of projects along the ML2 and general house price index

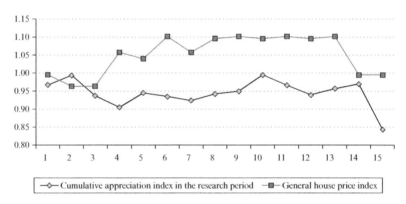

Figure 7.12   Comparison between cumulative appreciation index of projects along the IRR and general house price index

Hedonic regression

The hedonic regression methodology has the advantage of being able to quantify price changes relative to specific events such as the construction of infrastructure facilities. Compared with the repeat-sales model, hedonic regression can select the samples that are completed after the construction of the infrastructure through the introduction of a dummy variable, the construction dummy, and therefore more data can be utilized. The hedonic regression requires much more information including the physical and neighbourhood characteristics of samples. Constrained by the lack of sufficiently detailed data, it has proved very difficult to apply hedonic regression to analyse the effect of the IRR. In the hedonic regression analysis of the IRR, whether the apartment faces the elevated road is the most important independent variable, but the transactional data registration does not provide information on the location of the apartment in the project. In other words, whether the apartment faces the elevated road is unknown. Therefore the hedonic regression can be only used for the analysis of the impact of the ML2.

The hedonic model assumes that property value is a function of a set of locational and property-specific characteristics, where property price is the dependent variable and the vector of physical and neighbourhood characteristics are independent variables. The following function can be estimated:

$$P = \beta_0 + \beta_1(X_1) + \beta_2(X_2) + \ldots + \beta_i(X_i) \tag{7.4}$$

where:
P = house selling price
X_i = physical characteristics of house
β is the coefficient which needs to be estimated according to the variables of the sample. The explanatory variables are defined as follows.

Building characteristics
X_1 = floor space: the floor space of an apartment has a significant influence on property value in Guangzhou.
X_2 = building age: as mentioned above, building age is an important determinant for property price under the land use rights system where the residential land leasehold is usually 70 years.
X_3 = building height: usually the high-rise residential building (more than 12 storeys with lifts) costs 300 to 500 yuan per square metre of floor space more than the medium-rise residential building (usually six or fewer storeys without lifts). The building height dummy is set as 1 in the case of a high-rise building, otherwise 0.

There are other variables that have influences on property values, for example, the orientation and number of storeys of the dwelling. Unfortunately this information is not readily available in the current registration system.

Land use density
X_4 = plot size: usually a larger plot can provide more facilities and a better living environment, compared with a small site.
X_5 = overall floor space: it is the sum of all dwelling units in one project. The more floor space, the more households and facilities in the project.

Surrounding facilities   There are two groups of variables reflecting the quality of surrounding facilities.

X_6 = public facilities, including shops, education facilities, open space and so on have certain effects on the property value. In general, the more facilities, the higher the property value. The level of public facilities is set as a dummy variable. It is 1 if there are shopping areas and education facilities within the radius of 1000 metres of the project, otherwise 0.

X_7 = adjacent bus stations: this is also a key indicator of property value. In general, a developed bus network can increase accessibility and have benign effects on property values. It is set as a dummy variable. The value is 1 if the walking distance to the bus station is less than 500 metres, otherwise 0.

There are other variables of neighbourhood quality such as the views from a dwelling unit, noise and pollution level that can influence property value, but unfortunately that information is not available.

Accessibility and effects of the ML2

The primary purpose of this study is to isolate the effects of the ML2 on values of residential properties within the walking distance of metro stations. There are two variables measuring accessibility in this model.

X_8 = walking time distance to the closest metro station. The accessibility of a property to public transport is a critical factor affecting property value.

X_9 = construction dummy. Some scholars use an announcement dummy instead of a construction dummy to measure effects of transit in developed countries (Gatzlaff and Smith, 1993). In China, however, because of the volatility of policies, the announcement only has weak influences on the real estate market, but construction shows a much stronger signal. Therefore the construction dummy is set as 1 if after 2001, otherwise 0.

The data of the dependent variable, *P*, includes the transactional information before and in 2004. To make the data comparable, 2004 is used as a current base year, and all transaction prices happening before 2004 are converted into the present value of 2004.

A total of 371 dwelling units in 26 projects along the ML2 were selected to conduct the linear regression analysis. The dwelling units in one project share some characteristics: for example, surrounding public facilities and the same walking distance to metro stations.[8] A stepwise regression process, which adds significant variables and removes insignificant variables while constantly recalculating the model, was used to achieve an adjusted R-square value of 0.838 with an F-value of 214. Two variables, X_4, plot size and X_7, adjacent bus stations, are insignificant. The analysis result is presented in Table 7.6.

Table 7.6 Summary of regression estimates and heteroscedasticity test

Variables			Unstandardized Coefficients	Standard error	t	Sig.
	X_0	(Constant)	−17852.024	15205.301 (17741.83)	−1.174 (−1.006)	.241 (0.315)
Building characteristics	X_1	Floor space	4138.218	117.202 (181.032)	35.308 (22.859)	.000
	X_2	Building age	−9989.823	2312.399 (2565.635)	−4.320 (−3.894)	.000
	X_3	Building height (1 if high-rise, otherwise 0)	25805.770	6765.806 (7391.957)	2.814 (3.491)	.000
Land use density	X_4	Lot size	−0.016852	0.072785 (0.057402)	−0.232 (−0.294)	.817 (.769)
	X_5	Overall floor space (1000M^2)	77.818	0.262 (0.258)	2.944 (3.014)	.003
Surrounding facilities	X_6	Public facilities (1 if convenient, otherwise 0)	30075.488	12396.102 (14312.39)	2.426 (2.101)	.016
	X_7	Bus stations (1 if convenient, otherwise 0)	−4972.910	10653.14 (9901.596)	−0.467 (−0.502)	.641 (.616)
Accessibility & the effect of the ML2	X_8	Walking time distance to metro stations	−5449.233	1022.564 (1336.466)	−5.329 (−4.077345)	.000
	X_9	Construction dummy (1 if after 2003, otherwise 0)	68447.460	12233.763 (12969.18)	5.595 (5.278)	.000

Summary of statistics: No. of observations = 371; Adjusted R square = 0.838; F statistics = 213.8 (0.000)

Note: The adjusted values of White's heteroscedasticity consistency are presented in parentheses. Others remain the same.

The regression coefficients in the hedonic model represent changes in the dependent variable attributable to changes in the explanatory variable. Variables X_8 and X_9 capture the effect of the ML2 on the value of properties proximate to metro stations. The regression coefficient of X_8 shows that further walking distance results in lower property price. Controlling for other factors, every one-minute increase in walking time was associated with a 5449 yuan decrease in the mean price of sampled dwelling units. The regression coefficient of X_9 means that the construction of the ML2 had a positive impact on property value. Because of the construction of the ML2, the mean price of sampled dwelling units increased to 68447 yuan, all else being equal. Both of these coefficients are statistically significant.

Table 7.8 also reveals that another five variables – X_1 (floor space), X_2 (building age), X_3 (building height), X_4 (overall floor space) and X_6 (public facilities) – are statistically significant in explaining the house price. For every square metre increase in the mean floor space of a dwelling unit, the property value increased by 4138 yuan, all else being equal. The negative parameter of building age is consistent with the observation, that the older the building, the less valuable it is, and the increase of one year in the building age could lead to the decrease of 9990 yuan in property value. The coefficient of the building height dummy means that a dwelling unit in a high-rise building had a 25805 yuan premium added to it, compared to a dwelling unit in a medium-rise building. The land use variable, the overall floor space, has a coefficient of 77.8, which means that every 1000 square metre increase in overall floor space of a residential project could result in a property value increase of 77.8 yuan. This small number means that only a substantial increase of overall floor space can exert influence on the mean property price. The positive parameter of public facilities reveals that a dwelling unit with convenient surrounding public facilities was 30075 yuan higher in price than a dwelling unit without them, if all other conditions are equal.

Two variables, X_2 (plot size) and X_7 (adjacent bus stations), are not statistically significant in this model, which may be explained as overall floor space can more precisely illustrate the scale of a residential project, and the bus network is quite developed in Guangzhou, therefore there is no significant difference in the bus service among residential projects near metro stations.

Due to the existence of potential heteroscedasticity and bias, a heteroscedasticity test is needed. Table 7.6 lists the result of a heteroscedasticity test, which shows that all coefficients remain unchanged after White's heteroscedasticity consistency test, and only the standard errors, t value and the significance levels of variables that are not statistically insignificant are slightly changed. This reveals that the hedonic analysis is robust, and the estimation result is reliable.

The application of repeat-sales and hedonic regression models has shown that the construction of the ML2 and IRR has a significant influence on property values. Although the construction of the IRR caused hardship for some land users, there are social, environmental and distributional issues as well as changes in property values for both the ML2 and the IRR. A comprehensive research methodology in conducting cost–benefit analysis is necessary for analysing other benefits and costs generated by these projects.

7.3.4 Implications of Addressing Betterment and Compensation in Transport Projects

Usually demands for transport infrastructure investment have been very high and also unmet in the fast-growing cities of developing countries. Investment in infrastructure facilities can lead to soaring land prices. It is therefore reasonable for the government to recover surplus land value generated by its investment, and to recover at least part of its cost, if not all, for further investment. On the other hand, construction of transport facilities does not necessarily yield benefits. Land users may be adversely affected by being located very close to a transport station or along a transit line. Nuisances include noise, air pollution and increased automobile traffic from users. Evaluation of impacts of transit infrastructure on property values can assess the degree of positive or negative consequences of transit investments, and thus is critical for internalizing externalities of public transit investment. Furthermore, the added value of the transit can open up opportunities for new forms of creative financing such as in-advance requisition of land near transport facilities and increasing property tax rates (Cervero and Duncan, 2001), thus alleviating the deficiencies in cost recovery of fast-growing cities in developing countries.

In spite of the dramatic influences of the ML2 and IRR on the property market of Guangzhou, the municipal government has not taken any measures to capture the betterment or compensate the worsenment caused by these transit projects. The result is that while some enjoy the unearned benefits, others have to bear the costs. As a consequence, the inability of the government to address betterment and worsenment can lead to several problems that are worthy of attention. The first problem is that the inability to recover the surplus land value may weaken the fiscal capability of governments to provide public services. If users are not charged for services provided, large benefits may accrue to adjoining landholders, and thus cause the government to lose the opportunity to gain the revenue that should have gone into public coffers. The second is that the failure to compensate the hardship caused by government actions may lead to uncertainty in the land market, therefore acting as a restraint on the long-term land market development. Most transport infrastructure has been funded through the public sector, and there should be some means by which the added value of the transit can be captured through development taxes or other forms of exactions; otherwise there will always be a 'free-rider' problem (Banister and Lichfield, 1995). Value capture stands as a potential source of revenue to help pay off the debt on transport invest-ments (Cervero and Duncan, 2001). On the other hand, compensation for hardship can help the government refrain from hasty decisions reached because it knows it does not need to pay. Through the introduction of policies that can internalize these externalities, a fairer and more efficient land market can be achieved.

SUMMARY

Since the urban land reform, Guangzhou has been taking one of the leading roles in the land market of China. Its experiences in addressing betterment and compensation are, to some extent, typical in Chinese cities. In this research, Guangzhou was selected as a case study to evaluate to what extent the government has captured betterment and compensated worsenment at both the municipal and the project levels. Given the inadequate and imperfect data, an exhaustive investigation into how development effects can be isolated and measured has been very difficult.

At the municipal level, some indicators and assessment methods were employed to obtain a rough understanding of the extent of land value capture and compensation standard. Through applying several indicators, this research found that the Guangzhou municipal govern-ment obtained 35.1 per cent of local revenue from land leasing and real estate taxes, and funded 90.5 per cent of urban infrastructure facilities construction from 1992 to 2010 from these sources. However, there is no compensation scheme for loss of value generated by government activities.

At the project level, the ML2 and IRR were selected as case studies. The above analysis reveals that these two transport projects had significant impacts on residential property values in Guangzhou. Through the repeat-sales and hedonic regression analysis of the ML2, strong evidence was found that the construction of the ML2 had positive impacts on values of residential properties within walking distance of metro stations. This finding is consistent with the observation that in a dense city where public transport is dominant, the construction of a metro line can have a substantial influence on the property market. The application of the repeat-sales model shows that construction of the IRR induced value reduction in samples which face the elevated road. Nevertheless, because of the short time period between the operation of the ML2 (2003) and the IRR (2000), and the research base year 2004, further impacts of the ML2 and IRR have not appeared. This requires future research. The IRR has been a controversial project not only because it caused hardship to some property owners, but also because it is mainly targeted for the use of private cars, rather than public transport. There is also criticism that the elevated road encircling the old city has damaged the historical heritage of Guangzhou, a city with a history of more than 2100 years, and caused displacement of around 20 000 residents.

Unfortunately, the government did not take possible impacts of these projects on land users into account during its *ex ante* research, neither did it take any *ex post* measure to internalize these externalities. In order to explain and understand the current attitude of the government toward betterment and compensation, the trajectory of institutional arrangements and evolution of property rights in the land market of Guangzhou needs to be examined.

NOTES

1. There are two main types of payments for land leasing in Hong Kong. One is a one-off payment at the time of granting the lease, called the premium, and the other is an annual rent, called the Crown rent. In order to obtain a Crown lease, the lessee pays a premium in a lump sum on the date of the lease, or in special cases by instalments over a number of years after the date of the lease, and an annual Crown rent.
2. For historical reasons, old buildings in the old districts of the city usually have little floor space and are crowded with low-income households. The existing value of these buildings is often very low because of their small size and old age. Very often the relocated households cannot afford a new apartment with the compensation assessed on the existing value.
3. Some scholars argue that this is a deprivation of citizens' right of appeal (*China Youth Daily*, 13/8/2005).
4. The biggest realtor agency in Guangzhou stated that the average resale price of some residential buildings along the ML2 had been increased by 200 yuan per square metre of building area within one year after the completion of the ML2, an increase of 5–10 per cent, but it did not provide detailed information.
5. Land users are permitted to apply for renewal of their leases before the lease expires, after paying the reassessed LURs fee, provided that their land will not be converted into other uses.
6. The decoration usually includes appliances in the kitchen and bathroom, wall painting and carpeting in Guangzhou.

7. Sources: *Real Estate Information*, *Real Estate Weekly* and consulting with developers and realtors.
8. Strictly speaking, dwelling units in the same project do not necessarily have the same walking time to the metro stations. Nevertheless, the plot size of selected residential projects is not large enough to generate substantially different distances to metro stations, therefore all dwelling units in one project are assumed to share the same walking distance.

8. Institutional evolution in the land market of Guangzhou

Betterment and worsenment are derived from externalities, and the internalization of externalities requires the clarification of property rights in land. To understand the government's responses to betterment and compensation, an analytic framework of institutional changes and property rights to identify the associated problems and costs is needed. As North (1990b) states, institutional change is critical for societal and economic evolution and exhibits the characteristics of path-dependence; it paves the way societies evolve through time and hence is the key to understanding historical change. Latham (2002: 219–220) claims:

> Contemporary China has to be understood not only in terms of the radical economic changes and social transformations that have taken place over the last two decades of reform, but also in terms of what has not changed . . . Even when present practices are radically new, one needs to place them in terms of what came before them and what has persisted from that past.

In order to understand the current mechanism of addressing betterment and compensation, it is necessary to probe into the evolution of institutional changes and to explore the role of property rights in the land market. This chapter represents such an attempt, taking the land market of Guangzhou as an example.

8.1 EVOLUTION OF LAND ADMINISTRATIVE FRAMEWORK

Since 1949, the land administration of Guangzhou has experienced several changes. When the People's Republic of China (PRC) was established, the Public Facilities Bureau was set up to manage construction and land issues. In 1950, it was renamed as the Infrastructure Construction Commission. In 1953 the Infrastructure Construction Commission and the Financing Commission were merged into the City Construction Commission, to be responsible for city construction, land allocation and urban planning.

In 1977, the Urban Planning Bureau (GZUPB) was established to prepare city master plans and detailed plans, to allocate land for construction, and to examine and approve building applications. City plans at various levels provided some guidance to city development, but did not show much concern for arable land protection. The rapid farmland loss in the early 1980s aroused great concern on the part of the central government, and the State Land Administration Bureau (upgraded as the Ministry of Land Resources in 1997) was set up to administer arable land use and land registration in 1986, followed by the enactment of the Land Management Law.

Correspondingly, land resources departments were established in local governments. In Guangzhou, the Land Resources Bureau (GZLRB) was set up in 1986 to manage farmland and accommodate urban land reform. Its main responsibilities include land-use rights (LURs), leasing and land registration. Some functions of the GZUPB such as land allocation were transferred to the GZLRB. In 1992, the GZLRB was enlarged to be responsible for real estate market management and was renamed the Land Resources and Real Estate Bureau (for convenience it is still abbreviated as GZLRB). Therefore, the Land Resources and Real Estate Bureau has become the main department of land and real estate management. The GZUPB, however, still plays a critical role in defining the development rights of the land. Moreover, the Construction Commission is involved in land requisitions for infrastructure and public facilities (see Figure 8.1).

The evolution of the land management scheme has revealed the increasing importance of land issues in Guangzhou. Since its establishment in 1986, the GZLRB has been placing more emphasis on land policy formulation and management improvement, which is quite different from the construction-oriented approach of the Construction Commission and the GZUPB that is used to manage land issues.

Lack of coordination, however, still exists; for example, these departments build their own information systems separately and do not share with each other, and the LURs are defined by both the GZUPB and GZLRB: land development rights are defined by the Urban Planning Bureau (UPB) through planning control parameters, but the LURs fee payments and the registration and transfer of LURs are under the control of the Land Resources Bureau (LRB). The unwillingness to share information and the sectoral interests often lead to conflicts in land-use management.

The most common conflict in land management is between the LRB and UPB, as both sectors pursue their own interests and struggle for more power. Sectoral interests originate from the legacy of a centrally planned economy, under which jobs and pay were closely related to the type of work that was assigned to the sector. As a result, the UPB proposes

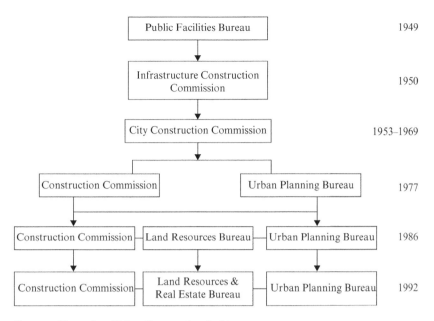

Source: Guangzhou Urban Construction Archives.

Figure 8.1   Evolution of the land administration mechanism in Guangzhou

city plans as land use management tools, and the LRB seeks to use the overall land use plan to exercise control of arable land and its conversion into developable land (Cao, 2003). The lack of coordination leads to inconsistent plans, confusion and chaos in the land management, and creates opportunities for developers to capture land value increments. For example, some developers obtain planning parameters through the revision in the UPB, but do not pay fees for amended parameters to the LRB.

Realizing that overlapping functions of various departments have prolonged the examination and approval process of LURs application and led to conflicts of organizational interests, the Guangzhou municipal government set up a panel in 1998, composed of the deputy mayor, the heads of GZLRB, GZUPB and the Construction Commission, in order to formulate land use policies, approve the LURs applications, and prepare land supply plans. The heads of the Planning and Economic Development Commission, Finance Bureau and Environmental Protection Commission also need to attend the panel meeting to air their opinions. The panel meetings have been held regularly according to LURs applications and market demands. The conflicts among different organizations are usually dealt with by the panel meeting led by the deputy mayor.

8.2   FORMAL RULES AND REGULATIONS IN THE LAND MARKET

8.2.1   Land Supply Policies

In the primary land market, the government is the sole land supplier. Since LURs fees are a major tool to capture surplus land value, the municipal government has been greatly motivated to supply as much land as possible to increase local revenue. An oversupply of land, however, may lower land prices and reduce the land revenue. Therefore, the municipal government must strike a balance between the supply area and revenue collection.

In 1987, Guangzhou launched LURs reform, which allowed developers to acquire LURs with cash or in-kind contributions. During this period most developers were state-owned enterprises that acquired LURs at the expense of providing public facilities, instead of direct cash payment. In 1989, the Guangzhou municipal government promulgated the Interim Measures of LURs Leasing in Guangzhou, and the Measures of Managing Overseas Investment in the Real Estate Market, which further illustrate the land leasing management mechanism. From 1987 to 1990, land with an area of 1200 hectares was leased for various uses, and most of them were designated as residential and industrial uses.

Despite the early interest of Guangzhou in the LURs reform (Guangzhou launched its land reform in 1987, which is earlier than the amendment of the Constitution in 1988), it was not until 1992 that Deng Xiaoping emphasized that economic reform must continue in China, after his well-known southern tour to the Shenzhen Special Economic Zone. The Pearl River Delta (PRD), including Guangzhou and Shenzhen, suddenly became enthusiastic about real estate development. Driven by the incentive to open up local revenue and the overheated demand for land development, the Guangzhou municipal government leased much more land than there was real demand for, leading to the oversupply and high vacancy rate of land and commodity houses (Figure 8.2).

Land supply means: negotiation, auction and tender
Before 1997, negotiation was the dominant way of acquiring developable land, and the land price varied largely from developer to developer. In November 1997, the Guangzhou municipal government required all urban land to be acquired through tender or auction, except that used for public services, public housing, government agencies and defence, in order to reduce the oversupply of urban land, curb land speculation and nurture the land market. Guangzhou took the lead in the comprehensive

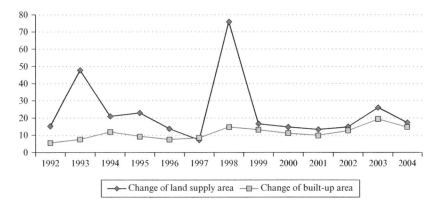

Sources: GZUPB, GZLRB.

Figure 8.2   Comparison of changes of land supply and actual built-up area of Guangzhou (km²)

Table 8.1   Land auction and tender in Guangzhou

Year	Number of LURs sales	Land area (ha)	Floor space (m²)	Asking price (million yuan)	Transaction price (million yuan)
1997	1	0.39	31 552	88.0	88.0
1998	7	10.12	399 378	540.0	564.0
1999	5	5.77	217 241	–	272.9
2000	7	41.66	1 009 623	1245.1	1387.5
2003	11	23.3	812 031	2082.5	2107.6
2004	4	11.8	366 756	804.7	867.3
2007	135	966.09	–	–	–
2008	154	763	–	–	–
2009	188	1482.46	–	–	–
2010	210	1165.29	–	–	–
2011	185	820.22	–	–	–

Source: Guangzhou Land Development Center.

introduction of auction and tender in the land market of China, where nationwide auction and tender was implemented in 2004.

Table 8.1 shows the land area leased by auction and tender in Guangzhou since 1998. Compared with negotiation, auction and tender can reflect market price more precisely and reduce leeway for corruption, thereby providing more certainty on the land supply side. In 1993, when negotiation was the major means of land supply, the average land price was 524 yuan/m² in Guangzhou; however, the average price of land through auction and tender was 5328 yuan/m² from 1997 to 2004, indicating a large difference in prices between the artificial allocation and the market mechanism. From 1997 to 1999, the auction of two pieces of land failed because the asking prices were higher than developers' expectations. Since 2000 all auctions and tenders have been successful, and the municipal government has become more experienced and responsive to market needs. After 2004, the data of Panyu and Huadu district was included in the statistics of the Guangzhou Urban Planning Bureau, and the real estate market was more flourishing: the figure of LURs sales through auction and tender grew dramatically and the peak was 2009 when the area of LURs sales reached 14.82 km².

Land supply and demand
Figure 8.2 presents the changes in land supply and built-up area from 1992 to 2004.The latter means the actual land demand.[1] It can be seen that there was a dramatic oversupply of land from 1992 to 1995. The sharp increase of land supply in 1998 was attributed to the promulgation of the amended 1998 Land Management Law. The 1998 law requires that any basic agricultural land,[2] any cultivated land exceeding 500 *mu* (Chinese unit, 1 *mu* = 1/15 ha), or any other land exceeding 100 *mu* must be approved by the State Council (Article 45, 1998), and 30 per cent of income from LURs fees must go to the central government (Article 55, 1998). Many local governments thus leased much land for infrastructure and high-tech uses to increase the land stock so as to avoid future application for approval from the State Council, even if this land could not be developed within the near future. For instance, the Guangzhou municipal government leased around 37 km² of land for Guangzhou Science Park in 1998. The land supply, however, has been approaching the actual demand since 1999.

Land supply structure
Another noticeable phenomenon is the change in the land supply structure. Figure 8.3 compares changes in residential land supply and total land supply, and illustrates the dramatic changes of policies in residential land supply. In 1992, the residential land supply accounted for 51.72 per cent of total land supply. Its proportion in total land supply dropped to 12.27 per cent in 1998 due to the adoption of the Land Management Law, and jumped to 17.94 per cent in 2004. In 2008, the local government leased more residential land to stimulate the real estate market, and the proportion of residential land reached 25.09 per cent. In 2009 and 2010,

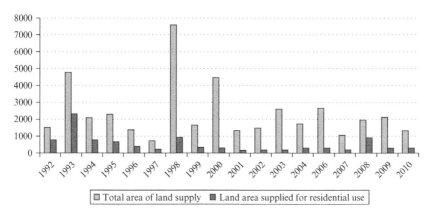

Sources: GZUPB, GZLRB.

Figure 8.3   *Comparison of residential land supply and total land supply in Guangzhou (ha)*

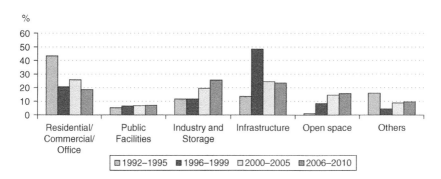

Note: 'Others' includes mainly land for military use, religious use and construction in the rural area.

Sources: GZUPB, GZLRB.

Figure 8.4   *Changes in the land supply structure in Guangzhou*

this figure was 7.61 per cent and 12.71 per cent, respectively. In total, the residential land supply accounted for 18.75 per cent of the overall land supply from 1992 to 2010.

Figure 8.4 compares the proportion of land for various uses in total supplied land in four periods, namely, 1992–1995, 1996–1999, 2000–2005 and 2006–2010. From 1992 to 1995, most land was supplied for residential, commercial, and office use to increase land revenue, and land supplied for infrastructure was obviously inadequate. After 1995, due to national policy adjustment to cool down the real estate market and the aggrava-tion of urban problems incurred by the lack of infrastructure facilities, in particular transportation facilities, local government had to adjust their land supply policies. As a result, the Guangzhou municipal government reduced the land supply for profitable use and increased land supply for infrastructure, open space and high-tech from 1996 to 1999. Since 2000, with the revival of the real estate market, the proportion of land for prof-itable use increased slightly, and the proportion of infrastructure went down, owing to a substantial supply of land for infrastructure in the earlier period. Meanwhile, the proportion of the total land supply for indus-trial, storage and open space increased, mainly because the Guangzhou municipal government put its emphasis on economic development into the port industry and designated much land for ecological corridors in 2003. During the period of 2006–2010, the proportion of residential land decreased to some extent, and meanwhile the proportion of industry and storage land went up.

Land supply and housing affordability
With tightening land supply policies and the abolition of negotiation for profitable-use land supply, the Guangzhou municipal government has been more responsive to market demands. The improvement of land man-agement has somewhat squeezed the 'bubbles' in the real estate market, and the greater housing affordability serves as an example (Figure 8.5). The average new commodity house price reached its peak in 1994, and then it began to decline and remained relatively stable after 1995. In 2004, the average housing price went up due to the influence of the real estate

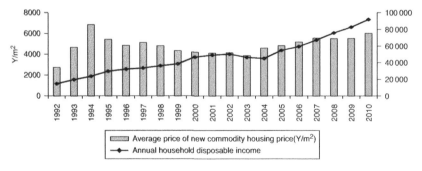

Source: Guangzhou Statistics Yearbook (1993–2011).

Figure 8.5   House price changes and housing affordability in Guangzhou

market heat of the Yangtze River Delta, resulting in a slight decrease of housing affordability. Since then, house prices have increased steadily. Compared with the growth in house prices, household disposable income has been increasing more rapidly and housing affordability has improved dramatically. A key indicator of housing affordability, the ratio of house price to annual household disposable income, was highest in 1994, which means that houses were most unaffordable in 1994. However, housing became increasingly affordable after 1994. After 2004, the growth rate of household disposable income overtook that of house prices, indicating the improvement of housing affordability.

8.2.2 Planning Control

Planning control is one of the main tools to minimize externalities and uncertainty; however, planning control itself can be a source of externality, and an overflexible planning control system without accountability can generate uncertainty. Under the transitional economy, the trade-off between certainty and flexibility has been a very difficult task. Rigidity does not serve the fast-growing cities, whereas flexibility encourages rent-seeking and corrupts the market in the absence of supervision (Zhu, 1999b).

Planning control framework
The GZUPB is responsible for planning issues throughout Guangzhou, and it has branches in all districts and counties. The UPB is in charge not only of city plan preparation, but also of monitoring the adherence of development projects to planning requirements. The UPB adopts various plans to guide and control development. The regional development strategy and plans are used to ensure city plans are consistent with central guidance for land use. Under the guidance of regional development strategies and plans, according to the 1996 Provisions for City Planning of Guangzhou, city plans are divided into four levels: city master plan, district plan, site development plan and detailed construction plan (Figure 8.6). Master plans and district plans are macro-level plans. Site development plans define planning parameters of every piece of land, such as land use type, maximum plot ratio (of building to land), maximum building coverage ratio, minimum open space ratio, maximum building height, minimum car parking space and provision of public facilities. Therefore they have become the most important tool for land use management. The detailed construction plan is prepared before physical construction on a plot, and it provides a site design plan, including the layout of buildings, open space, roads and underground pipelines, under the planning parameters provided by the GZUPB.[3] In some development areas

Source: Based on Xu and Ng (1998: 48).

Figure 8.6   Hierachy of planning in Guangzhou city

with great local significance, such as the city centre and historical areas, the GZUPB is also in charge of preparing for urban design, which adds extra control elements such as building style and open space atmosphere, besides planning parameters required in the site development control plan.

Planning dilemma in fast-growing Guangzhou: certainty and flexibility
A major study emphasis of planning control is the degree of certainty and flexibility provided by the planning system (Wakeford, 1990; Tang et al., 2000). Planning control can reduce externalities, and thus provides some certainty to the land users for investing in the land. On the other hand, there are obvious benefits for the government in maintaining flexibility to deal with unforeseeable circumstances. Similar to the discretionary planning system of the UK, planning control is not regulatory in China. The

land use plan does not guarantee an application consistent with the plan will be approved automatically.

Planning certainty can be obtained when the same decision would be given to similar development applications (Tang et al., 2000). Planning control decisions in China, however, have been made with regard to ambiguous criteria. Article 4 of the 1996 Provisions for City Planning in Guangzhou requires that preparation and implementation of city plans should abide by the following principles:

- be consistent with the development strategies of Guangdong Province and the PRD;
- designate reasonable land use density and population density;
- guarantee the needs of public safety, public health, urban traffic and landscape;
- protect and improve the city ecological environment, and increase open space in the city.

All of these criteria seem too ambiguous to be implemented. In reality, physical and environmental amenity factors remain the key criteria for planning decision-making, and social and economic effects have only been given intuitive considerations, rather than systematic analysis. The approved site development control plan can be a guideline for planning parameters decisions for a specific piece of land, but not always. The decision on planning parameters is subject to wide discretion by planning officers. The developer frequently bargains with the planning officer to obtain favourable planning parameters, usually for higher density, more floor space or less public facilities contribution. All decisions are made behind closed doors, therefore decision-making of development control is basically a black-box process. With the lack of internalizing the externalities due to planning parameter changes, this planning control system has invited rent-seeking and caused some uncertainty in the land market (Zhu, 2005).

Table 8.2 discloses the discrepancy between planning parameters and completed construction in Guangzhou. From 1997 to 2004, unauthorized space amounted to 8.19 per cent of total completed floor space. The most frequently adopted measure against illegal construction is financial punishment. The penalty for illegal space was 186.08 million yuan from 1997 to 2004, and the average penalty was only 35.42 yuan/m^2 of floor space, which was a very slight penalty for the developer.[4] Some developers realize that with the low penalty, unauthorized floor space can make profits, and this indirectly encourages serious violation of planning controls. Only a small proportion of illegal space, 4.62 per cent, was demolished as a

Table 8.2   The deviation from planning control in Guangzhou

Year	Number of illegal cases	Illegal floor space				Proportion of illegal space in completed commodity space
		(M²)	% of demolished space	% of space with penalty	% of space exempt from penalty	
1997	426	228 836	11.10	88.90	0	3.49
2000	285	1 448 449	2.91	96.48	0.61	16.80
2002	100	974 088	0.20	99.80	0	9.00
2003	240	421 062	0.00	99.53	0.47	3.70
2004	136	316 224	0.01	98.19	1.80	3.34
2006	1920	–	–	–	–	–
2007	2076	–	–	–	–	–
2008	1148	–	–	–	–	–
2009	877	–	–	–	–	–
2010	867	–	–	–	–	–

Source: GZUPB.

punishment. Meanwhile 5.36 per cent of illegal space was exempt from any penalty, which was mainly attributed to the good connections of these developers with government departments, or simply because the violator itself was a government-affiliated agency.[5] After 2005, the illegal cases significantly increased, and this is because data for Panyu and Huadu districts were included. In these areas, illegal cases are more prevalent compared with the central area due to slacker planning control.

While the planning department usually makes favourable planning decisions for developers who have *guanxi* with the government, there is a lack of compensation for those whose development rights have been adversely affected by government actions. For instance, there is no compensation for the partition of a piece of land or the decrease of the plot ratio allowed. With the consensus of the primary importance of *guanxi* with government departments, there have been very few cases in which developers have sued the planning authority against unfair planning parameters or planning application rejections in Guangzhou. The lack of financial accountability in planning decisions enhances the discretion of local government and exacerbates the uncertainty in the land market.

In order to curb corruption in development control and increase planning certainty and transparency, the Guangdong provincial government promulgated the Provisions for Site Development Control Plan Management of Guangdong Province in March 2005. This requires that site development control plans have to be displayed for at least 20 days before their final approval, and any amendment of the approved site development control plan has to go through the legal process. Meanwhile, the Guangzhou municipal government has been considering the introduction of a statutory land use plan. Traditional planning is very aesthetically and physically oriented, and has great difficulties in accommodating social and economic change. The legalization of this kind of site development control plan can generate unexpected consequences. In an adjacent city, Shenzhen, which firstly introduced the statutory land use plan in China in 1998, the implementation of the plan has been contentious. Zou and Chen (2003) conducted a sample survey of 87 cases where land users applied for the amendment of planning parameters from 2001 to 2002, and only 15 per cent of applications were rejected by the planning department. They conclude that constrained by many factors, such as the lack of social and economic consideration of statutory land use plans, pressures from powerful land users and top officials, and unforeseeable circumstances during the transitional period, the statutory land use plan has frequently been challenged by land users, leading to dilemmas for the planning authority, very often amending the plans approved by itself. In spite of many problems, Shenzhen city has been successful in publishing site development control plans and increasing planning transparency. Further success of the statutory land use plan, however, requires further political reform and a marketization process with a nationwide scope.

8.3 INFORMAL PROPERTY RIGHTS IN LAND

An implicit assumption of many New Institutional Economics theories about the evolution of property rights is that a society experiences transition from open access to exclusive communal property, then to exclusive individual property, minimizing the transaction costs (Omura, 2004). In an imperfect world, however, the transaction cost of establishing a well-defined property rights scheme may be astronomically expensive or be vulnerable to the resistance of existing land users. In China, many rights outside the formal property rights framework, such as township village enterprises, are regarded as providing incentives to economic development (Qian, 1999; Ho and Lin, 2003), with the tacit approval and participation of the government at the cadre level. Under the 'trial and error' reform approach adopted by the Chinese government, informal property rights, following customs and norms, may play significant roles.

The incomplete reform of property rights has led to the coexistence of the planned economy legacy and newly introduced market mechanisms.

In order to reduce resistance from sitting land users, the municipal government retains the informal property rights of some sitting land users. Through forgoing a part of betterment, the Guangzhou municipal government achieved miraculous growth in the 1990s. The long-term cost of this strategy, however, has been substantial and beyond the consideration of policy-makers.

8.3.1   Informal LURs of *Danwei*

Zhu (2005) divides the land reform into three periods since the 1978 economic reform: Period I (1978–1987) when land allocation was free; Period II (1988–1992) when greenfield land sites were developed extensively under the new regime of land commoditization; and Period III (1993–present) when brownfield land sites were brought into the land market by *danwei* land users. Under the large scale of urban redevelopment, with the lack of central regulation, *danwei* land users have invented various methods to convert their land to profitable use. Factory relocation and exchange of land between users are common, and *danwei* may become partners with third parties, involved in businesses that are unconnected to their function (Wu, 2002).

As the principal agent of governments, *danwei* has been granted many privileges through either financial subsidy or the state's implicit approval of their activities. The enjoyment of these privileges has led to the emergence of cellular communities. To foster the personalized mode of control, these communities have erected walls encircling their activity spaces, thus a city consists of many walled regions (Tang, 2000). Because of the complex relationship between segmented bureaucracies, land authorities find it difficult to control the land use of *danwei* in the same way as other land in the city, resulting in dualism in the land market.

The informal LURs of *danwei* have been reflected in two aspects in Guangzhou. Firstly, government-affiliated agencies can be granted LURs free of charge for the construction of housing for their employees, although acquiring free land has become more and more difficult. In spite of the abolition of welfare housing allocation in 2000, a *danwei* is permitted to build houses on the allocated land (these houses are called *danwei jizi* housing in China), and then sell them to its employees at the price of building cost, which is much lower than market price, but higher than the price of welfare houses with direct government subsidy. Since these houses can be transferred at market prices in the real estate market, land assets have gone into the pockets of *danwei* employees. Usually the higher the authority is, the more land with better location it can claim. Despite the lack of official statistics on *danwei jizi* houses, a survey carried out in

January 2002 shows that 19 per cent of households lived in *danwei jizi* houses among 1232 households in Guangzhou, and this percentage was 30 and 21 per cent in Beijing and Shanghai respectively (*Beijing Youth Daily*, 13/2/2002).

Secondly, redevelopment of factories within the city proper has released much land to the market, thus alleviating the bottleneck of stringent greenfield land supply policy since 1998. Before the urban land reform, much land within the city built-up areas was occupied by state-owned enterprises (SOEs). Land for industrial use was 90 km², accounting for 45 per cent of the city built-up area of Guangzhou in 1994.[6] According to Zheng (2001), among the 336 factories of Guangzhou, 8.04 per cent of factories were located in the city centre, and 43.16 per cent in the city proper in 1995 (Table 8.3 and Figure 8.7). The dramatic difference between the benchmark prices (BMP) of industrial, commercial and residential land indicates that the industrial land in the city area has huge potential to be redeveloped.

The mixed industrial and residential use in the city area caused many problems such as air pollution and noise, which brought increasing complaints about the environment quality. Meanwhile, constrained by the difficulty in enlarging land area for production and burdened with redundant workers, many factories found that profit-making possibilities from production were quite small. Realizing that land assets of the factories in the city area could be an important incentive to relocate factories, the Guangzhou municipal government started the large-scale relocation of factories in the city proper in 1996. To foster the relocation of industrial land, the government promulgated some

Table 8.3   Locations of factories in Guangzhou in 1995

Location	Number of factories	Proportion in total factories (%)	BMP of commercial land (yuan/m²)	BMP of residential land (yuan/m²)	BMP of industrial land (yuan/m²)
City centre	27	8.04	5580*	2880*	1980
City proper	145	43.16	3870*	2250*	1170
Suburb	142	42.26	2880*	1350*	775
Exurb	22	6.55	1440*	900*	595
Total	336	100	–	–	–

Note: * means the price for floor space, instead of land area.

Sources: Guangzhou Urban Planning and Survey Institute, GZLRB.

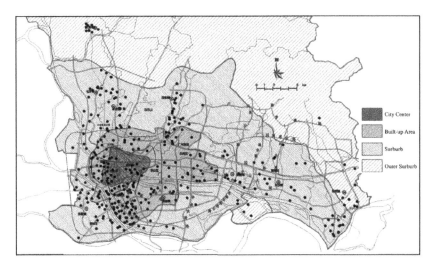

Source: Zheng (2001: 106).

Figure 8.7   Distribution of 336 factories in the built-up area of Guangzhou in 1995

preferential measures. For instance, the developer could obtain a 36 per cent discount in the LURs fee and exemption of certain fees for the redevelopment of industrial land. Compared with expensive and time-consuming residential land redevelopment, the relocation cost of industrial land is much lower and timing is more prompt, owing to its lower density. Moreover, the developer only needed to reach an agreement with the governing body of the factory to carry out the redevelopment before 1997.[7] With strong support from the government, many developers found that the involvement in the redevelopment of industrial land could be very profitable, and the active participation in industrial land relocation opened up opportunities for developers' growth. For instance, the R&F Property Group was established with only ten employees in 1993, but became the biggest developer in Guangzhou, with nearly 10 000 employees in 2004, through actively participating in industrial land redevelopment. To date the R&F Property Group has finished development of more than 3 million square metres of property floor space, and more than 60 per cent of its acquired land was from industrial land redevelopment.

With the large scale of industrial land redevelopment, more and more industrial land has been converted into residential or commercial use. According to a rough calculation by Zheng (2001), due to the preferential

LURs fee policy, the Guangzhou municipal government has forgone LURs leasing revenue of 8 to 10 billion yuan since 1988, most of which has been captured by the developers and *danwei* land users. Within the same period, the LURs fee income was only 40.5 billion yuan in Guangzhou. Zhu (2004a) terms informal LURs of *danwei* as land development rights (LDR), and defines an LDR thus: 'what a sitting *danwei* can claim, based on its land use right, to redevelop the site occupied by itself and, if necessary, neighbouring sites occupied by other *danwei* land users or residents'. With the underpriced LDRs, land assets which should have gone to the government have been taken by developers and *danwei* land users, and the hasty decision to capitalize the rents of *danwei* land often leads to suboptimal land resources use.

8.3.2   The *Chengzhongcun* Land

Emergence of *chengzhongcun*
Over the last two decades, China has witnessed rapid urban growth. With the surplus rural labour unleashed by the de-collectivization programme in 1978, the rapid industrialization and a continuing large income disparity between rural and urban residents, the massive rural–urban migration has been overwhelming since 1980 (Liu et al., 2003). With the accelerating urbanization and city expansion, a number of villages that used to be located on the periphery of the city have been engulfed by urban development. When these villages are faced by urban development, local governments adopt two different approaches (Figure 8.8). One is the Shanghai and Beijing model, where all land in villages, including both farming and residential land, is directly converted into urban land after paying compensation to farmers; and the other is the Guangzhou model, where part of the land in villages, mainly cultivated land, is converted into urban use, but the residential land is retained to reduce the compensation and time cost, leading to the emergence of *chengzhongcun* (literally: 'villages encircled by the cities') in the inner city. Some other cities in Guangdong province, such as Shenzhen and Zhuhai, have also adopted this approach. Under this approach, farming land can be requisitioned for urban use, but farmers can maintain their status as farmers and the right to live on their individual plots (called *zhaijidi*) so that local governments do not need to pay compensation for their relocation. As an incentive for farmers to give up their farmland to urban use, 8 to 12 per cent of the requisitioned farmland area can be returned to village committees as so-called economic development land (EDL). EDL can be used for profitable purposes operated by villagers themselves, or simply be rented out to developers with some shares held by the village committee, but the ownership of EDL

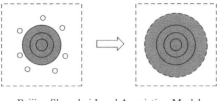

Beijing Shanghai Land Acquistion Model

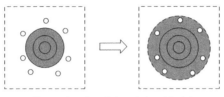

Guangzhou Land Acquistion Model

Source: Tian (2008).

*Figure 8.8   A schematic illustration of two different farmland requisition
approaches*

cannot be transferred or traded. Therefore, the residents of *chengzhongcun*
can enjoy the benefits of both individual *zhaijidi* and EDL (Tian, 2008).

With the massive number of immigrants in the city, farmers on these
chengzhongcuns have discovered that building rental housing can be more
lucrative than growing cabbages. Nominally agricultural parcels under
the administrative control of village committees are now being utilized
for the construction of high-density rental accommodation (Leaf, 1998).
The retention of collective land ownership in these villages, on the one
hand, has made low-rent affordable housing available for migrants; on the
other hand, it has exposed urban villages to many social, economic and
environmental problems.

With the implementation of EDL policy, Guangzhou has been the city
with most *chengzhongcuns* in China. According to an aerial map of 1998,
the land area of 120 villages in Guangzhou was 30.1 km^2, which covered
11.6 per cent of the total built-up area. The population in *chengzhongcuns* (including tenants and villagers) was 1.2 million, accounting for 30
per cent of total population in the built-up area. The number of villages
increased to 139 by the end of 2001, and these villages have been scattered
throughout the city built-up area (Figure 8.9). With the soaring land price
generated by city expansion and government investment, urban land has
become an increasingly scarce resource. The increase of land value in
chengzhongcuns has provided farmers with dramatic incentives to develop

Source: GZUPB.

Figure 8.9   Chengzhongcun in the built-up area of Guangzhou, 2001

their land for profitable uses. Since the 1998 Land Management Law and other relevant legislation do not strictly regulate the use of collective land, and local governments do not have direct jurisdiction in collective land use management as they do for urban land, much leeway has been left for village committees to maximize indigenous villagers' benefits.

Social and economic characteristics of *chengzhongcun*

In *chengzhongcun*, the villagers' residency status has been converted to a non-agricultural status. However, inherited old methods in the administrative systems and operating mechanisms within the *chengzhongcun* still remain, leading to the coexistence of the urban administration and rural administration in the city built-up areas. The villagers in *chengzhongcun* can have certain privileges such as *zhaijidi* land, and permission to have two children, compared with urban residents. Therefore, they are reluctant to be converted to urban residents.

Investigation has shown that usually there are more migrants than indigenous residents in *chengzhongcun*. For example, the ratio of migrants to indigenous residents in five *chengzhongcun* located in the city center was 4.4:1 in 2000 (Tian, 2008). Moreover, *chengzhongcun* in Guangzhou display the characteristic of heterogeneous migrant settlements in terms of occupation and native places. Meanwhile, the collective economy in *chengzhongcuns* has been prosperous. According to Tian's survey (2008), the agricultural economy almost disappeared in these villages, and services such as wholesale markets, hostels, and other commercial uses have dominated the village economy.

As the central city of the south of China, Guangzhou has attracted a large floating population. In 2010, the floating population of Guangzhou reached 7.2 million (*Guangzhou Daily*, 31/3/2011), and most of them are rural-to-urban migrants. However, the migrants are often excluded from the urban housing market in terms of affordability and eligibility, and the long-standing neglect of local governments for their housing demand makes affordable housing more difficult for them to access. Lack of access to subsidized housing has made migrants' housing conditions the poorest in the city.

In *chengzhongcun* has become the most popular place for low-income migrants. In 2001, around 80 per cent of the 1.2 Guangzhou million migrant workers lived in the 85 000 rental houses or temporary houses in *chengzhongcun*, and the average rent for houses in *chengzhongcun* only ranged from one-fifth to one-half of the rent for authorized urban houses within similar locations but of much better quality (Guangzhou Urban Planning and Survey Institute, 2003).

Given the limited land resource and high population density, land use regulations are usually stringent in urban areas, and violation can incur a heavy financial punishment. Compared with urban land, farmers' self-help houses are much less regulated. The construction of houses is only subject to the approval of the village committee, instead of the city planning department. The lack of regulations and management has led to chaotic land use and slum-like settlement in *chengzhongcun*. Overlapping residential, industrial and commercial uses of land, mixed new and old apartments, crowded buildings: all of these have created an anomaly in the city environment (Figure 8.10). The weakness of control has also led to environmental and security problems in these *chengzhongcuns*. Houses with five or six floors are no longer uncommon; some houses have eight or nine floors without lifts. There is hardly any space between the houses, only narrow dark alleyways. They are described as 'houses extending their hands to each other' or 'houses in the act of kissing' (Figure 8.11). Fire engines cannot enter these *chengzhongcuns* because roads do not meet the basic requirements for transportation and fire control standards. The infrastructure facilities are accessible to residents, but their quality is very low. Electricity and telecommunication wires, as well as water and gas pipelines, are in disarray; sewers frequently become blocked up. Garbage is everywhere, creating dirty corners; open space and public services are

Figure 8.10   Chengzhongcun landscape in Guangzhou

Figure 8.11   Physical environment in chengzhongcun

extremely scarce; numerous barber and hairdresser shops and hostels are code words for sex trade premises in these villages. Drug abuse and crime are not unusual (Gransow, 2002). Around 75 per cent of criminal cases and 80 per cent of unauthorized buildings were reported from *chengzhongcun* in Guangzhou in 2003 (Guangzhou Public Security Bureau, 2004). In its adjacent city, Shenzhen, the situation was no better. Around 70 per cent of crimes and 90 per cent of unauthorized buildings were from *chengzhongcun* in 2003 (*People's Daily*, 26/10/2004).

Responses by the government

Although Zhang et al. (2003) argue that *chengzhongcun*, with little in the way of government resources and assistance, accommodate millions of rural migrants whose housing needs have been ignored by the government, owing to the social accessibility and affordability of *chengzhongcun* this booming informal housing and land market during the recent decade has led to significant negative impacts on urban development. Undoubtedly the rise of value of farmers' land on the periphery of the city originates from government investment in infrastructure and city expansion, but the land value increment has gone into the pockets of farmers by means of rent or other bonuses. Moreover, the expectation of high compensation of farmers in *chengzhongcun* has impinged on the government's participation in renovation of these slum-like villages. Other problems such as the dilapidated environment and the high crime rate are also prevalent in *chengzhongcun*. Finally, the informal construction in *chengzhongcun* has a substantial impact on the city's real estate market. In many *chengzhongcun*, village committees collect money from indigenous residents and build apartments for sale (*jizi* houses) with profits shared among the villagers. Since the sale of *jizi* houses is contrary to the national legislation that the collective land cannot be transferred, the buyers of *jizi* houses cannot be granted legal title. From 1990 to 1998, the floor space of *jizi* houses amounted to 12 million square metres in Guangzhou, while the total authorized completed floor space of commodity houses was 39 million square metres, indicating the considerable impact of informal housing on the urban housing market.

Pushed by the pressure from the urban public, the Guangzhou municipal government has planned to adopt a two-phase plan for the renewal of *chengzhongcun* in the inner city. The first phase is that policy-makers made efforts to break the old social networks in *chengzhongcun* and replace village committees with modern administrations like urban residents' communities; however, these efforts failed. The nominal transformation without reform of property rights in land has no influence on the social and economic identities of villagers, thus it is not helpful to initiate the institutional change of *chengzhongcun*. The second phase can be called a radical 'eliminating' approach. Under this approach, *chengzhongcun* will be demolished and reconstructed in the form of urban real estate development. The municipal government has tried to attract developers to participate in the renovation, but the vast demolition and negotiation costs make the developers baulk at the uncertainties. Furthermore, the abundant new construction after demolishing the old village buildings will exacerbate the problems of surplus supply in the real estate market. In view of this situation, the Guangzhou municipal government is not optimistic about the active participation of the private sector. The government itself, however, is unable to bear the enormous cost of renovation. A rough estimation shows that there were more than 30 million square metres of floor space in the 40 *chengzhongcun* in the inner city in 2001. The building structure costs alone were around 50–60 billion yuan, which was almost the sum total of local revenue of Guangzhou within the previous six to eight years (Li, 2004). *Chengzhongcun* remain a political hot potato for the Guangzhou municipal government.

Over the past few years, the rapid expansion of urban areas into the countryside has given rise to a wide variety of land-related problems. With the incomplete and non-tradable status of land use rights over collective land, the problem of land fragmentation remains highly intractable, and it is difficult for land markets to develop. Meanwhile, it has to be acknowledged that the existence of the dual land management system is reasonable in the vast poor rural area where the externality is low and land value is very low. The *chengzhongcun* of the inner city, however, are the other side of the coin and should not be treated equally to other rural areas of China. In the inner city where land value and externality increases substantially, the institutional discrepancy in land ownership, land management and residential registration systems within the city boundary has led to a series of problems.

The informal land market booms when the legality of transactions is unclear either because the law is vague or because they are not covered by existing laws (Ho and Lin, 2003). The ambiguous delineation of legal rights and the lack of systematic regulation in collective land have contributed to the booming informal land market in *chengzhongcun*. Although the informal housing market in *chengzhongcun* has provided low-cost accommodation for migrants who have difficulty in finding affordable housing under the institutional discrimination, it is dangerous to conclude that *chengzhongcun* should be an optimal way to house low-income migrants, for their contribution to housing affordability has been achieved at a huge cost of the dilapidated environment, security risk, unfair income distribution, government revenue loss and other social problems. Furthermore, informality in the *chengzhongcun* collective land market has made the emerging urban land market unfair and uncertain. Insecure property rights in land markets tend to induce short-term rather than long-term investments (Zhu, 2004a).

International experience has shown that enabling rather than simply eliminating slum settlements would be a better policy option for developing economies (United Nations Center for Human Settlements, 1996). The concept of the enabling approach involves providing existing slum settlements with better administration and services (Pugh, 1991). Nonetheless, different from slum settlements in other countries, *chengzhongcun* is controlled by the collective and indigenous residents, who have much more power than squatters, and have taken advantage of their land to seek rent. When legal rights remain poorly defined, the collective and villagers are motivated to maximize their economic rights in the informal markets, leading to the mushrooming negative externalities in *chengzhongcun*.

The property rights approach has been a controversial issue, and philosophers, political scientists and economists have not been able to agree whether collective property or private property is better, or how to justify property rights (Halia, 2007). New institutionalists realize that property rights involve not only economic and social relations, but also political performance. Property rights are the relative power of individuals to control valuable resources. Unfortunately, the New Institutionalists have been unable to develop an analytical framework of political and social meaning of property rights due to the inherent complexity of politics, the social situation and culture. As Cheung (1982) points out, economic theory is unable to specify the timing of change. The designing of institutions largely depends on an understanding of institutional change processes by decision-makers after considering their own specific political, economic, social and cultural contexts. Problems in *chengzhongcun* land seem very difficult to address without institutional changes, as the Guangzhou government did in its first phase plan. A simplistic property rights approach, however, cannot solve all problems. *Chengzhongcun* require a comprehensive analysis of combining their merits and problems from social, political and economic perspectives.

Overall, *chengzhongcun* are one of the outcomes of China's rapid urbanization and the dual institutions of land tenure overlapping in the urban area. The profound social and economic influences of the upheaval of these villages are worthy of much attention, and further research about them could be highly beneficial to China's urbanization process (Tian, 2008).

8.4   REFLECTIONS ON THE INSTITUTIONAL CHANGE IN THE LAND MARKET

China's economic reform has been regarded as deviating from mainstream economics, which regards well-defined property rights as the preconditions for economic growth. Blanchard and Fischer (1993) question why China has grown so fast in the absence of some necessary conditions. Many economists hold the view that without privatization, secure private property rights and democracy, there could not be genuine market incentives or political commitment to a market. The failure of reforms in some Eastern European countries and the former Soviet Union prior to 1990 has reinforced these views (Qian, 1999). The Chinese experience, however, has borne out that considerable growth is possible with sensible but imperfect institutions. Some transitional institutions can be more effective than the clear-cut institutions for a period of time because of the second-best principle: they can avoid the institutional vacuum when the old one is removed but the new one has not been established (Li, 1996; Qian, 1999).

Compared with overall economic reform, land reform was launched later. However, the real estate industry has achieved much faster growth than the general economic growth in China. Similar to the institutional arrangements in other areas, property rights are not precisely defined in the transitional land market. If we review the evolution of land markets, some lessons can be learned from the Chinese experience.

8.4.1 Government Incentive in the Land Market

Incentives are important for economic growth. Qian (1999) argues that reforming the government and providing it with incentives is as crucial as reforming the economy in the Chinese experience. Competition among localities can foster efficient resource use. Qian and Weignast (1997) assert that through linking local government expenditure with the revenue generated, to ensure that local governments face the financial consequences of their decisions, local governments must be self-financing. Meanwhile, they are allocated primary regulatory responsibility over the economy. Through decentralization local government gains more discretion and responsibilities over local economic and social affairs. The strict budget constraints on local governments have spurred them to be committed to local economic growth.In the land market, local governments are empowered to retain a large proportion of taxes and fees, and thus become de facto landowners. For instance, local government can retain 70 per cent of LURs fees (90 per cent before 1998) and a portion of real estate taxes, which has provided fiscal incentives for local government to pursue real estate growth. In Guangzhou, LURs fees and real estate taxes numbered 35.1 per cent of local revenue, and financed 90.5 per cent of urban infrastructure facilities construction from 1992 to 2010. The active participation of local governments has greatly boosted the land market and facilitated the construction of infrastructure facilities, which are essential for attracting investment in China. As Yang and Yang (2000) state, it would be very difficult for China to promote market-oriented reform if there were not active participation of local governments. The financial revenue from land leasing has provided local governments with incentives to regulate the land market according to local conditions, and capture surplus value through LURs fees and real estate taxes, in order to deliver public services.

Nevertheless, the financially motivated local governments incur many problems. Short-termism (the statutory term is five years) and rent-seeking are prevalent in local governments. On the one hand, local governments hastily lease much more land than there is actual demand for, to capture the short-run land revenue, and thus create problems of sustainable land supply. In order to pursue their organizational interests, government departments often impose miscellaneous fees on real estate developers. In Guangzhou, real estate developers needed to pay around 70 types of fees to complete construction and sales in 1996, which covered around 30 to 40 per cent of the total cost (Guangzhou Real Estate Association, 1997). Many developers complain that they never know the number and amount of various types of fees in advance, and these fees are finally borne by housing purchasers (*China Southern Daily*, 10/3/2006). The amendment of planning parameters without incurring financial accountability is also an example of the lack of rule of law. On the other hand, the neglect of hardship caused by government actions and low compensation standards exacerbates the inequity in the land market, and impinges on the long-run development of land markets. In this regard, local governments are predatory. Due to these increasing problems, there have been more and more appeals to re-examine the strategy of 'efficiency priority', enhance social welfare and curb the wide discretion of local governments (Wang, 1999; Kwan, 2003).

8.4.2   The Role of the Dual-Track System in the Land Market

China's gradual reform is characterized by the coexistence of the legacy of the planned economy and market mechanism, the formal and informal property rights. One might argue that the dual-track system would cause a distortion of resource allocation and impinge on growth. However, investment in the PRC has been increasing. According to Wang (2001: 87), 'the answer to this apparent puzzle lies in the efficacy of informal networks in China'. The dual-track system in China proves an effective tool in minimizing losers in the course of economic reform (Qian, 1999, 2000). Under this dual-track system, the market was first liberalized at the margin while planned prices were maintained and then phased out later.

Urban land reform in China has to work within the prevailing socialist ideology and strike a balance between the old and new systems. At the early stage of the land reform, in order to alleviate the resistance from the powerful *danwei* land users, they were allowed to retain some allocated land. Meanwhile, new LURs were sold to developers in the open market. With the further marketization process and the abolition of the welfare housing allocation scheme, *danwei* land users no longer enjoy the privilege of free land, and their employees have to purchase commodity houses in the market. Moreover, the negotiation as a main means of land supply was used to attract investment and promote local economic growth, and also provide land subsidies as a protective cushion to SOEs for their stable transition to fully fledged players in the competitive market. With the gradual phasing out of non-competitive SOEs, negotiation in the land supply was abolished. Instead, auction and tender have become the main tools of supplying land for profitable use throughout China.

Meanwhile, there is much criticism about the dual-track system of China's land market. Li (1998) and Zhu (1999b, 2002) argue that the dual land market does not guide efficient utilization of land resources, and has contributed to the oversupply of commodity buildings in many cities in the early 1990s. Therefore, the dual land market is threatening to corrupt the nascent land market. This dual-track system, however, greatly facilitated the early reform in the land market and helped maintain social stability. As Stiglitz (1994) argues, the gradual reform in China provides some people with strong incentives, and mitigates some resistance from other people. A gradual transition may facilitate this learning process of both the individual and organizations, through avoiding the problem of 'information overload'.

Therefore, the dual-track system seems a part of reform strategy to achieve the objective of clearly defined property rights in land, but should be only tentative and transitional. To complete its transition to a market economy, China needs further intuitional reforms. Due to historical reasons, the *danwei* still hold much land and are seeking opportunities to capitalize their land assets through cooperation with developers. Moreover, the reform of collective land seems a more challenging task, suitable for the long-term agenda of the government. Unfortunately, current economic theories have little knowledge about the transitional economy, and even less about the timing and process of transitional institutions (Cheung, 1982; Stiglitz, 1994; Qian, 1999). In this respect, a deep investigation of China's dual-track reform approach may add some knowledge to economic theories.

Table 8.4   Growth of private sectors in China

Year	1993	2010	Average annual growth speed (%)
Number of private enterprises	156800	8455200	26.44
Registered assets (billion yuan)	681	19210	21.71
Number of employees (million)	3.72	94.18	20.94

Source: China Statistics Yearbook (1994–2012).

8.4.3   The Increasing Role of the Non-State Sector[8] in Real Estate Development

China presents an interesting case study in promoting new private enterprises. It did not focus its attention on privatizing existing state enterprises, and the existing state enterprises have declined in importance as a result of the growth of new enterprises (Stiglitz, 1994). During the pre-reform era there were no private enterprises in China. Since the 1978 economic reform, along with the rise of its political position, the non-state sector has played an increasingly important role and contributed to employment and tax revenue, with private business becoming an important impetus to economic development (Table 8.4). According to Kanamori and Zhao (2004), taking into account holding companies, foreign-funded companies, township-owned business and private business in rural areas, private business accounted for 60 per cent of the country's gross domestic product (GDP) in 2004.

The development of the non-state sector has experienced several stages since 1978. From 1978 to 1982, although a series of policy measures were launched, and a private sector was developed, there were no explicit economic and political guarantees. In 1982 the Constitutional Amendment Act stated, 'The private economy is a supplement to the socialist state-owned economy'. Realizing the importance of private sectors in economic development, the Communist Party Congress promoted the role of private enterprises from 'supplement' to 'important component' in 1998. Since then the Chinese government has adopted some concrete measures to boost private business in terms of legislation, administration, foreign trade and financing services. In November 2002, the Sixteenth Congress of the Communist Party of China explicitly proposed to 'improve the legal system to protect private property rights'.

Under the favourable macro-environment, the non-state sector in the real estate industry has been growing very rapidly. In Guangzhou, the

Table 8.5   The ownership structure of top 30 real estate enterprises in Guangzhou

Year	SOEs		Non-state enterprises (including overseas real estate enterprises)	
	Number	Share (%)	Number	Share (%)
1995–1996	19	63.3	11	36.7
1998–1999	8	26.7	22	73.3
1999–2000	6	20.0	24	80.0
2000–2001	4	13.3	26	86.7
2002–2003	2	6.7	28	93.3

Sources: Guangzhou Statistics Bureau, Guangdong Real Estate Association (2002).

investment of the non-state real estate sector amounted to 58.62 per cent in total real estate investment in 1995; two years later, its share increased to 65.1 per cent, and continued growing to 87 per cent and 95.2 per cent in 2000 and 2003, respectively (Guangdong Real Estate Association, 2002). Meanwhile, the investment of SOEs in real estate development has substantially decreased, and their dominant role in the real estate market of the early 1990s has been greatly weakened. Since the mid-1990s the Guangzhou Statistical Bureau and the Guangzhou Construction Committee have jointly ranked real estate enterprises based on several indices such as annual sales area, real estate investment and credibility. Table 8.5 shows this ranking result since 1995. In 1995, only 11 developers of the 30 top real estate developers were in the non-state sector, but in 2003, 28 were in the non-state sector. In general, SOEs' roles in urban physical development have been diminishing. Non-state-owned entities and private firms are replacing SOEs as main actors in the new economy. The *danwei* are fading out and SOEs are gradually discarding their *danwei* responsibilities and becoming independent enterprises (Zhu, 2005).

The participation of non-state sectors in the real estate industry has dramatically contributed to local economic growth. According to the Guangzhou Statistics Yearbook, the tax from the non-state real estate sector amounted to 86.48 per cent, 90.61 per cent and 92.35 per cent of taxes from all real estate development companies in 2001, 2002 and 2003, respectively. Besides these direct contributions, the growth of the non-state sector has helped to boost the marketization process. While the SOEs dominated the real estate market in the early 1990s, LURs were mainly acquired through negotiation, and planning parameters were subject to frequent changes due to connections of SOEs with government departments. It was difficult for non-state sector developers to acquire LURs, particularly in good city locations. Since the late 1990s, auction and tender have become the main ways of achieving LURs, and created more equitable opportunities for the private sector to enter the real estate market. Furthermore, the active participation of the non-state sector is beneficial to the further clarification of property rights in land. Non-state sectors are more conscious of their *ex ante* property rights than SOEs, which have more *ex post* bargaining power. In order to compete with the stronger private market, SOEs have to introduce market-oriented management practices, and thus have been undergoing dramatic reforms.

SUMMARY

Empirical analysis, investigating the evolution of property rights in land from the perspective of institutional changes, suggests that as the economy develops and commercialization progresses, property rights become more precisely defined compared with those in the early reform period. The increasingly professional land management scheme, such as land supply and planning control, and the gradual formalization of informal property rights, such as the LURs of *danwei* and the collective land in the city area, together with the growing role of the non-state sector in the real estate sector, have reflected a gradual learning curve of the government in responding to the market.

The institutional evolution of China has been a very interesting phenomenon. With a gradual reform approach, China avoided the fate of East European reform prior to 1990. Through analysing the evolution of property rights in land, this research reveals that the incentive of local government generated by decentralization, the double-track system in the land market, the increasing role of the non-state sector and the bailing out of SOEs in real estate development form the major institutional changes in the land market, and can help explain the achievements and problems in the land market as well.

In an imperfect world, the transaction cost of setting up well-defined property rights is very high, and the establishment has to depend on social, cultural and political factors. Constrained by these factors, the Chinese government has adopted a realistic gradual approach. As a consequence, the economic growth has been breathtaking, but is often at the expense of equity, fairness and long-term urban development. Certain parties have to bear the cost of government activities without sufficient compensation, thus leading to unfairness and the potential risk of political chaos. Although transitional institutions facilitate economic activities during the dynamic transformation, the informality of the institutional environment creates uncertainty. Uncertainty could cause the newly established market many risks (Schotter, 1981). In this respect the government should take a more direct and active role in the clarification of property rights in land, so that a balance between social and economic interests can be struck.

NOTES

1. After 2004 the calculation of the city built-up area includes two new districts, the Panyu district and Huadu district, that used to be county-level cities. Therefore, the data of the built-up area after 2004 is not included here.
2. According to Provisions for Basic Agricultural Land (1998), basic agricultural land is land with good quality and output, and it is designated in the Overall Land Use Plan to guarantee basic demands of food products in certain areas.
3. When the UPB is providing planning parameters, it usually refers to the approved site development control plan, but does not have to adhere to this plan. In other words, it has discretion to make decisions according to the individual application.
4. For instance, the average new commodity housing price was 4618 yuan/m² in Guangzhou in 2004, and the penalty, 35.42 yuan/m², only amounted to 0.77 per cent.
5. Source: interviews with the employees of the GZUPB in December 2011.
6. Source: Guangzhou Economic Planning Commission (1997).
7. After 1997, the LURs of industrial land have to be acquired through tender or auction.
8. The definition of 'private sector' is unclear in China due to the mixed ownership in joint ventures. The official statistics only regard domestic Chinese enterprises as 'private enterprises'. This underestimates the real development of the private sector. Considering that some de facto private enterprises have been registered as collective enterprises to receive preferential tax treatment, this author uses the term 'non-state sector' to include the collective enterprises, private enterprises, foreign-funded enterprises and shareholding enterprises listed in the official statistics.

9. Conclusion

In the preceding chapters, betterment and compensation schemes under China's land use rights (LURs) system have been examined from the perspectives of institutional arrangements and property rights evolution. This chapter summarizes the findings of this book and a set of conclusions is drawn from them. Finally it recommends some future research topics.

9.1 SUMMARY

This book has three main elements, as follows. The framework of the New Institutional Economics was adopted to analyse the property rights in land under the LURs system. In particular, the role of the state in the land market was examined to explore the impacts of government intervention on land markets. This book reveals that the state has taken advantage of the ambiguous property rights in land, somewhat ignoring issues of betterment and worsenment, to achieve wide discretion in development control in pursuit of the objective of rapid urban growth. Moreover, constrained by the high cost of measures such as establishing an integrated GIS system, and improving valuation and management skills, issues of capturing betterment and compensating worsenment have not been high on the agenda of the government.

The analysis of property rights evolution indicates that an imprecise property rights system might be a second-best institution under the transitional period in China when the cost of well-defined property rights is too high to afford. Moreover, it provides some evidence that property rights in land have been moving towards more precise definition, consistent with the economic theories that consider clearly defined property rights to be essential for economic growth. In order to establish a fairer and more efficient land market, however, further institutional changes and clarification of property rights in land are inevitable.

Through empirical analysis and case studies, the research in this volume develops approaches that are specifically designed to assess the extent of betterment and worsenment engendered by government activities at both macro and micro levels, which fills the knowledge gap of the lack of betterment and worsenment research under the LURs system. These evaluation approaches can have wider application in other countries and cities.

Originating from the observation of widening inequity and increasing uncertainty associated with the failure of the government to adequately address betterment and compensation issues, this book has attempted to assess betterment and compensation schemes and explore their implications under China's LURs system. The theoretical framework of the New Institutional Economics was adopted to analyse institutional arrangements for addressing betterment and compensation at three levels in China: national, municipal and project levels.

At the national level, various betterment and compensation schemes were examined, and their merits and shortcomings discussed. Then the role of the state in the land market was described, and obstacles to addressing betterment and compensation, such as non-disclosure of information and ambiguities of property rights in land, were presented to explain the government's failure to adequately deal with these issues. At the municipal level, Guangzhou was selected as a case study. Some indicators, such as the contribution of land revenue to local revenue and the percentage of land revenue in funding urban infrastructure facilities, were adopted to assess to what extent the government has captured surplus land value. This book finds that the assessment of compensation at the municipal level is a very difficult, if not impossible, task. Therefore, it has mainly analysed the compensation policies from a descriptive perspective and introduced several cases to assess worsenment and compensation. At the project level, repeat-sales and hedonic regression models were applied to assess the impacts of the Metro Line 2 (ML2) and Inner Ring Road (IRR) on property values. The results of the repeat-sales analysis reveal that since its completion up until 2004, the ML2 has contributed to a positive value growth of the commodity dwelling units within walking distance of its metro stations, and the IRR has led to a negative property value decrease of the commodity dwelling units which directly face the elevated road. The Hedonic regression analysis of the ML2 provides strong evidence that the construction of the ML2 has had positive impacts on values of residential properties within walking distance of metro stations. This finding is consistent with the observation that in a dense city where public transport has been dominant, the construction of a metro line can have substantial influences on the property market.

Taking the Guangzhou land market as a case study, this book has explored the evolution of property rights in land from different perspectives, including land administration, formal rules, informal property rights, and increasing participation of the private sector in the real estate industry. The property rights framework of land in Guangzhou has reflected the characteristics of path-dependence, which North (1981, 1990)

defines as the dependence of economic outcomes on the path of previous outcomes, rather than simply on current conditions. In other words,
history matters. The abolition of negotiation in land supply of the primary
market involving the state and developer, the gradual release of planning
information, and the phasing-out of the state-owned enterprises (SOEs)
in the real estate industry have contributed to reducing the uncertainty
in the land market and protecting property rights in land. Nevertheless,
although gradually adapted to the land market mechanism, the property
rights framework in land features problems of uncertainties caused by the
wide discretion of local authorities. Further institutional changes, such as
the disclosure of more information and the restriction of the discretion
of local government, are envisaged to help move to more open market
dealings in the near future.

This book not only describes the results of extensive empirical analysis
but also establishes the linkage between theoretical and empirical analyses.
While empirical findings are inevitably context-dependent, the analytical
framework of property rights and the state, and a policy-oriented comparison of international experiences developed in this book, are widely
applicable to the cities and countries where a public land leasehold system,
or equivalent, has been adopted.

Finally, limitations of this research have to be addressed. The most
conspicuous factor weakening the robustness of this thesis is the data
problem. Constrained by the unavailability and non-disclosure of data,
the quantity and quality of data used in this research are far from satisfactory. Betterment and compensation issues depend highly on local context:
political, economic and social environments. The neglect of the Chinese
government in addressing these issues provides little empirical evidence to
assess relevant policies, which makes the research on them very complex
and difficult. In terms of either breadth or depth, this research is still not
sufficient, but it represents an initial attempt to explore these complex
issues. The author sincerely hopes that with more available data and the
increased attention of the Chinese government in addressing betterment
and compensation, scholars, including the author herself, can carry on this
meaningful research with more insight and evidence.

9.2   POLICY IMPLICATIONS

9.2.1   The Role of the State

One considerable concern of the role of the state in the economy is fear
that local authorities may become too greedy and exert undue leverage on

developers in the hope of gain. Under the growth-led approach, Chinese governments are more concerned about economic growth than equity and fairness, leading to the neglect of betterment and worsenment issues. Nevertheless, pushed by the increasing growth of the non-state sector, and motivated by the long-term goal of sustainable economic development, the state must strike a balance between growth and equity, discretion and market certainty.

The theme of discretion and certainty

Ham and Hill (1985) define 'discretion' thus: 'A public officer has discretion whenever the effective limits of his power make him free to make a choice among the public courses of action or inaction.' Discretion is necessary to free decision-makers from the inflexibility of rules, but the rules have to ensure that discretion is not merely a matter of personal whim that results in injustice and reduces the possibility of redressment (Booth, 1996).

The Chinese government has enjoyed wide discretion, which is understandable in the present era of rapid change when inflexible rules often seem too rigid. The lack of transparency and supervision of decision-making in land management, however, provides a protective umbrella for the abuse of power in the land market for organizational or personal financial interests. Therefore, on the one hand, discretion facilitates flexible city growth; on the other hand, it leads to much uncertainty in the market. Uncertainty results in the absence of a predictable and transparent environment that is essential for effective market activities.

In the UK, where a discretionary planning system is also adopted, the agency discretion offered by British legislation is set within narrow limits set out, for example, by the central government in Circulars and Policy Guidance Notes, opinions of the electorate, and case law that has defined parameters of discretion. In China, however, there are many fewer restrictions on the government's discretionary power. The absence of certainty is just as much a problem for public decision-makers as for private developers. Both developers and government need certainty if the industry is to function effectively. Developers need to know what they can do with the rights they purchase from the government, and the government needs to know what it can charge them. Therefore, both flexibility and certainty are needed for land market development in the long run.

The theme of accountability

Whenever there is discretion to act, the question of how decision-makers can be held to account remains crucial. Under the British discretionary planning system, there are three tools available to account for local discretionary power: politically, at local elections; policy, laid down both locally and nationally through the appeals system; and judicially, when decisions are challenged on the grounds of their legality rather than in relation to policy. In particular, a local public inquiry is an important means for exploring the policy grounds of a decision. This has shown considerable resilience and has been widely accepted as a fair and open means of reaching a decision (Booth, 1996).

Qian (1999) argues that the biggest challenge for China to complete its market transition is the establishment of the rule of law. The law should be applied to the government, which provides a foundation for secure private property rights against government intrusion. In China, the absence of public participation in land and planning management and an independent judicial system has been blamed for the failure of the government to account for its vast discretionary power. Under the current one-party political system and institutional arrangements, the judiciary is still manipulated by local government. As a corollary, the punishment for improper decisions by local authority (officials) is surprisingly slight, which indirectly aggravates violation of rules and weak law enforcement. Moreover, non-disclosure of information makes it easier for policy-makers to shed their accountability. Transparency in the procedures, therefore, can greatly contribute to accountability, which will be discussed below.

Reduction of corruption

Corruption is a noteworthy problem in government, affecting fair play in the real estate market. Corrupt behaviour not only causes unfair competition but also affects the development of a healthy property market. Besides, there is a loss to the government of both revenue and people's confidence (Chan, 1999). One way of reducing corruption may be by reducing the level of government economic activity. Since 1998, the Chinese State Council has required all government departments and army forces to disengage their affiliated economic enterprises. In 1999, 19 458 military-affiliated enterprises were withdrawn, and 12 109 enterprises were required to break off their relations with the army. Central government department-affiliated enterprises with 2.85 million employees, whose assets totalled 707.4 billion yuan, were required to disconnect from government departments (http://news.xinhuanet.com/newscenter/2004-09/20/content_1998524.htm, accessed 11/10/2005). Local authorities were also required to no longer be involved in economic activities and to withdraw from government-affiliated enterprises. The military, police and judicial branches of the government now solely rely on tax revenues to maintain their operations, rather than on business incomes (Qian, 2000).

Another way to reduce corruption is to narrow the scope of government authority in regulating the market sector, such as the granting of licences and permits to operate private businesses which provide bureaucrats with opportunities for corruption (Chow, 2004). For instance, requiring auction and tender, instead of negotiation, is one measure towards achieving this. Nonetheless, in order to forestall serious corruption, these measures alone are not sufficient and further institutional changes are necessary.

9.2.2 The Information Infrastructure

There are two major aspects to be addressed in terms of information infrastructure under the LURs system of China. One is the establishment of an integrated geographic information system (GIS) system; the other is information transparency.

As mentioned in Chapter 6, land cadastre and management information is scattered through different government departments and not shared. This situation has impinged on the land management system and is adverse for both commercial and academic purposes. The integration of all land information in a GIS system should be on the early agenda of the government. The municipal government can be the agency for organizing a common GIS system which can incorporate many subsystems, such as land title registration, topography, planning control parameters and population, on the basis of a common platform. Such a unified system can provide a coordinated database and help the government identify the critical limiting factors for land markets as well as the maximum potential for land use. The establishment of this unified GIS system, however, would be a very difficult task, given the diversity of organizational interests in China. The second-best, and perhaps more realistic, strategy is that data structure, classification and coding of different departments should be standardized to facilitate exchanges among them (World Bank, 1993).

A basic market rule, which is crucial for protection of property rights, is that information should be transparent and open. The lack of publicity has allowed many avoidable contradictions and problems to recur (Li, 1998). The oversupply of land and the high property vacancy rate in Guangzhou in the early 1990s can be partly attributed to the lack of information transparency.

Driven by the incentive to pursue high profits, real estate developers very often take advantage of loopholes of information opaqueness and release false information to cheat housing purchasers. There have been many reported frauds in real estate transactions owing to the lack of accessibility to sufficient information. By forcing the disclosure of the property registration system to the public, the law would provide better protection for both investors and consumers. Since the middle of 2004, the Ministry of Land Resources has required all land management departments at the provincial and local levels to publish 24 different types of information on the Internet, including relevant laws and regulations, land use plans, land supply information, LURs granted, the approval of land for development, and benchmark prices of land. Although thus far the information system has not been satisfactory, some progress has been made and more than half of provinces and cities have published the required data on the Internet. It is anticipated that more information will be published in the future, so that market openness can be improved.

In some East Asia countries and cities, such as Singapore and Hong Kong, government intervention has historically been strong in the land market. According to Western standards, they cannot be considered as democratic societies (Castells et al., 1990), and public participation in the land market is much less in Singapore and Hong Kong than in the USA and the UK. Nevertheless, due to highly transparent information, the Singapore and Hong Kong governments have been very efficient and clean (Lang, 2006). A well-informed market makes for a more stable market, which in the long run will produce more land revenue for local governments (Li, 1998). Compared with other institutional changes in property rights in land, such as *danwei* and collective land reform, the establishment of information systems might encounter less resistance from land users in China. In this regard, local governments should take an active and pragmatic role to boost the information transparency in the land market.

9.2.3   Further Clarification of Property Rights in Land

Although its real estate market has achieved rapid growth, the Chinese government has not fully recognized the importance of protecting property rights. In order to promote the sustainable development of land markets, further reform measures to clarify the property rights in land should be considered, as follows.

Firstly, a scheme that can internalize externalities should be gradually introduced to the Chinese land market. New measures such as a property tax or betterment levy can be introduced to capture surplus land value. Meanwhile, the taxation system requires fundamental changes. Miscellaneous fees and taxes that are unrelated to the market value of property and are levied solely to generate local revenue should be gradually abolished to simplify and enhance the credibility of the taxation structure. Land development rights should be protected, and local authorities should be required to compensate the worsenment generated by their activities. This compensation may slow city growth, but it also puts some restrictions on the discretionary power of the government, and thus pushes the government to make more reasonable decisions.

Secondly, with the establishment of a land market structure, informal property rights in land, such as *danwei* land and the collective land in *chengzhongcun*, should be gradually clarified and formalized. The phasing-out of SOEs and increasing difficulties for *danwei* to acquire free land can further the marketization process in the real estate market. Meanwhile, the Measures for the Transfer of the Collective Developable Land Use Rights in Guangdong Province, issued by the Guangdong provincial government, are encouraging attempts to clarify property rights in collective land. The extension of collective land reform to the nation can be envisaged in the future.

Thirdly, laws and regulations should be written with more clarity and consistency. While some ambiguities of Chinese laws or regulations originate from unpredictability in a period of rapid change, others are simply due to a lack of understanding of market rules by decision-makers; for example, information rules slowing the release of information, and the lack of financial considerations in planning control. Moreover, the institutional capacity to enforce rules should be enhanced. The introduction of public participation in land management can enhance the institutional capacity, support the rule of law and associated needs for transparency and accountability, and then create law enforcement capacity independent of government. Public participation, however, is deemed to be a gradual and long-term process in the current political framework of China, which is beyond the scope of this volume.

Institutional changes are necessary for successful economic reform, but in order to strike a balance between incentives to spur growth and imperatives of social equity, further institutional changes and more formalized property rights are essential to ensure that growth continues down the right path (Oi, 1996). Although Chinese are proud of their past achievements, comparing those of other post-command economies, local authorities have to watch out for the real competitors. In order to create an internationally competitive real estate economy, China has a long way to go to establish a regulated market economy and greater clarity in property rights in land.

9.3   FUTURE RESEARCH TOPICS

9.3.1   Institutional Arrangements in the Transitional Economy

In the transition from the command economy to the market economy, China has no peers. In general, Chinese economic reform is characterized by gradualism and a problem-solving approach, and the evolution of China's property rights is characterized by the spontaneous emergence of various forms of formal and informal property rights, which have been very contentious. Some scholars argue that the gradual approach and informal property rights have proved to be an effective way to avoid disorder and maintain social and political stability during the transitional period (Liew, 1995; Li, 1996; Qian, 1999; Kanamori and Zhao, 2004). Some insist that only well-defined, enforced and transferable property rights would maximize social welfare, thus achieving the goals of social and economic development (Putterman, 1996; Zhu, 2004a; Wang et al., 2004).

The experience of Chinese economic reform, particularly the coexistence of China's miraculous economic growth and ambiguous property rights, appear to deviate from the mainstream economic theories that regard well-defined property rights as a precondition of economic growth. Qian (1999) claims that China's reform experience has not been properly accounted for by the mainstream economics and that mainstream economists tend to underestimate the significance of China's economic reform. Chow (2004) notes that although there are problems and obstacles due to inertia, political and economic vested interests, such problems associated with many aspects of China's reform process have not prevented China's economic and political system from improving steadily. According to Seabrooke and How (2004), traditional microeconomic analysis focuses on transactions rather than transaction process. The author argues that the reason why the existing theories cannot explain the experience of China is that no theory focuses on the process or particular context of institutional change. Most theories identify the appropriate/inappropriate institutional arrangements to minimize transaction costs based on specific assumptions (Hong, 1995), but cannot illustrate what steps can be adopted to achieve the goal of well-defined property rights. In other words, economic theories portray an end-of-state picture of institutions, but cannot provide a step-by-step action plan to achieve it. As Cheung (1982) points out, economic theory is unable to specify the timing of change. The designing of institutions largely depends on an understanding of institutional change processes by decision-makers after considering their own specific political, economic, social and cultural contexts. In China, the costs of institutional changes, such as the cost of obtaining correct information and the cost of persuading or forcing the privileged group to acquiesce, are declining, yet nobody knows precisely to what extent these costs have been reduced, and when and how they can be reduced to the same level as those in the USA and some European countries. This is largely due to the intricate interweaving between Chinese politics and the economy.

In dealing with the uncertainty of policy implementation, the Chinese government usually adopts an experimental approach to test what the results might be and what kind of resistance might be encountered in relatively small areas, after which, nationwide reform can be considered and implemented, which has proved to be quite effective in institutional reform. Qian (1999) argues that experiments are second-best arrangements but are very effective in providing incentives, and thus lead to the emergence of a variety of transitional institutions, many of them taking unconventional forms. The special economic zones, the land leasing experiment in Shenzhen, and the trial of auction and tender in developed cities, are strong examples. The collective land reform in Guangdong province and the introduction of property tax in some cities will be future examples.

The relationship between property rights and economic growth in the transitional economy is a complex subject, and has important implications for other countries that have been or will be launching institutional reforms. The experiences and lessons of property rights evolution in China will certainly assist policy-makers elsewhere in launching institutional reforms. How the framework can be designed to instruct the process of institutional change to achieve the objective of clear property rights has been a fascinating and challenging task, and this book represents only an initial step towards a large topic, which can be a fruitful opportunity for future studies.

9.3.2 Extension of Betterment and Compensation Study to Other Countries and Cities

A second topic is to investigate whether the analytical framework in this book can be extended to other countries and cities where a public land leasehold system, or equivalent, has been adopted. The experiences and lessons of assessing and addressing betterment and compensation developed under the LURs system can add some valuable knowledge to international land markets. A critical issue in addressing betterment and compensation is whether the costs of enforcement and possible impacts on real estate markets go beyond the benefits. The theoretically rational policies may encounter great difficulties in reality, and engender unexpected problems, such as reducing incentives to invest in real estate markets and entailing public resistance. Therefore, the application of policies to address betterment and compensation must consider different local contexts.

The major differences between China and other countries and cities with public land leasehold systems are the degree of government intervention in the land market and the strength of property rights in land. These differences may make it difficult to compare various approaches adopted in these countries, yet the evaluation and institutional analytical frameworks developed in this book may have wider application in other contexts. Close scrutiny of these betterment and compensation approaches and their impacts would add to our knowledge of how to maximize the benefits of a public leasehold system.

Finally, looking back with pride and scrutiny, China's land market has made great progress in the past two decades, yet the issues of betterment and compensation have not attracted sufficient attention. Historical evidence reveals that land value appreciation is usually faster than GDP growth in developing countries, particularly in the fast-growing cities (Zhu, 1999b: 152). As the landowner and the investor in infrastructure facilities, government should be capable of capturing surplus land value and compensating worsenment due to its own activities. The introduction of measures of internalizing these externalities can contribute to the certainty of land markets and clarity in property rights in land, which are obviously critical for the long-term land market development and the general economy as well.

References

Adams, J.S., J.L. Cidell, L.J. Hansen, H.J. Jung, Y.T. Ryu and B.A. Van Drasek (1999) 'Development impact fees for Minnesota? A review of principles and national practices', TRG Report No. 3, http://www.cts.umn.edu/trg/research/reports/TRG_03.html, accessed 8/7/2004.

Alchian, A.A. (1977) *Economic Forces at Work*, Liberty Press.

Alexander, G.S. (2006) *The Global Debate over Constitutional Property: Lessons for American Takings Jurisprudence*, University of Chicago Press.

Alterman, R. (2011a) *Takings International: A Comparative Perspective on Land Use Regulations and Compensation Rights*, American Bar Association Press.

Alterman, R. (2011b) 'Land use regulations and property rights: the "windfalls capture" idea revisited', in N. Brooks, K. Donaghy and G.J. Knaap (eds), *The Oxford Handbook of Urban Economics and Planning*, Oxford University Press, pp. 755–786.

Archer, R.W. (1974) 'The leasehold system of urban development: land tenure, decision-making and the land market in urban development and land use', *Regional Studies*, 8, 24–59.

Atmer, T. (1987) 'Land banking in Stockholm', *Habitat International*, 11(1), 47–55.

Bailey, M.J., R.F. Muth and H.O. Nourse (1963) 'A regression method for real estate price index construction', *Journal of the American Statistical Association*, 58, 933–942.

Banister, D. and J. Berechman (2000) *Transport Investment and Economic Development*, UCL Press.

Banister, D. and N. Lichfield (1995) 'The key issues in transport and urban development', in D. Banister (ed.), *Transport and Urban Development*, E & FN Spon, pp. 1–16.

Bao, H.J. and X.D. Hu (2003) 'Establishment of a social security system for farmers whose land is acquired', *China Real Estate Research (Zhongguo Fangdichan Yanjiu)*, 2003(4), 1–27 (in Chinese).

Barber, G.R. (2005) 'Bundle of rights approach to value', http://www.privatelandownernetwork.org/plnlo/bundleofrights.asp, accessed 15/7/2005.

Barzel, Y. ([1989] 1997) *Economic Analysis of Property Rights*, 2nd edn, Cambridge University Press.

Bertaud, A. and B. Renaud (1992) 'Cities without land markets', World Bank Discussion Paper No. 227.

Bertaud, A. and B. Renaud (1997) 'Socialist cities without land markets', *Journal of Urban Economics*, 41, 137–151.

Bird, R.M. (2004) 'Getting it right: financing urban development in China', Working Paper 04-35, Andrew Young School of Policy Studies, December.

Blanchard, O. and S. Fischer (1993) *NBER Macroeconomics Annual 1993*, National Bureau for Economic Research.

Booth, P. (1996) *Controlling Development: Certainty and Discretion in Europe, the USA and Hong Kong*, UCL Press.

Boutin, K. (1999) 'The real impact of impact fees', http://www.ncrealtors. org/searchpubs/THR/2002/thr-0302/impact.htm, accessed 12/10/2004.

Bover, O. and P. Velilla (2002) 'Hedonic house prices without characteristics: the case of new multiunit housing', Working Paper No.117, European Central Bank, January.

Bromley, D.W. (1991) *Environment and Economy: Property Rights and Public Policy*, Basil Blackwell.

Bryant, R.W.G. (1972) *Land: Private Property Public Control,* Harvest House, Montreal.

Buchanan, J.M. (1975) *The Limits of Liberty: Between Anarchy and Leviathan*, University of Chicago Press.

Burton, J. (1978) 'Epilogue: externalities, property rights, and public policy: property rights of the spoliation of nature', in Steven N.S. Cheung (ed.), *The Myth of Social Cost: A Critique of Welfare Economics and the Implications for Public Policy*, Hobart Paper 82, the Institute of Economic Affairs, London, pp. 69–82.

Cai, M. (2011) 'Local determinants of economic structure: evidence from land quota allocation in China', http://extranet.isnie.org/uploads/ isnie2012/cai.pdf, accessed 15/7/2013.

Callies, D.L. and M. Grant (1995) 'Paying for growth and planning gain: an Anglo-American comparison of development conditions, impact fees, and development agreements', in R.H. Freilich and D.W. Bushek (eds), *Exactions, Impact Fees and Dedications: Shaping Land-use Development and Funding Infrastructure in the Dolan Area*, State and Local Government Section/American Bar Association, pp. 357–383.

Cao, G., C. Feng and R. Tao (2008) 'Local "land finance" in China's urban expansion: challenges and solutions', *China and World Economy*, 16(2), 19–30.

Cao, J. (2003) 'An investigation of property market institutions in China', PhD thesis, University of Portsmouth.

Castells, M., L. Goh and R.Y.-W. Kwok (1990) *The Shek Kip Mei Syndrome: Economic Development and Public Housing in Hong Kong and Singapore*, Pion.

Cervero, R. and M. Duncan (2001) 'Transit's value-added: effects of light and commuter rail services on commercial land values', http://www.apta.com/research/info/briefings/documents/cervero_duncan.pdf, accessed 14/11/2005.

Chan, N. (1999) 'Land-use rights in Mainland China: problems and recommendations for improvement', *Journal of Real Estate Literature*, 7(1), 53–63.

Chen, A. (1998) 'China's urban housing market development: problem and prospects', *Journal of Contemporary China*, 7(17), 43–60.

Chen, G. (1993) 'An analysis on China's real estate market price bubbles and its remedy', *SZ-HK Property Valuation and Market Review*, 3(2), 13–16

Chen, L. and M. Berrell (2004) 'China's expanding real estate market: are the current growth rates healthy?', 16th Annual Conference of the Association for Chinese Economics Studies, Australia.

Cheung, S.N.S. (1970) 'The structure of a contract and the theory of a non-exclusive resource', *Journal of Law and Economics*, 13, 49–70.

Cheung, S.N.S. (1978) 'The myth of social cost: a critique of welfare economics and the implications for public policy', Hobart Paper 82, Institute of Economic Affairs, London.

Cheung, S.N.S. (1982) 'Will China go "capitalist"? An economic analysis of property rights and institutional change', Institute of Economic Affairs, London.

China Atlas (2002) Chinese Map Press.

China Land and Mine Resources Law Center (2007) 'The evolution of land policy's involvement in macro-control policies of China', *China Land*, 6, 53–56 (in Chinese).

Chow, G.C. (2004) 'The role of planning in China's market economy', International Conference on China's Planning System Reform, 24–25 March, Beijing.

Cmnd. 5124 (1972) *Development and Compensation – Putting People First*, HMSO.

Coase, R.H. ([1937] 1973) 'The nature of the firm', in *The Firm, the Market, and the Law* (1973), University of Chicago Press, pp. 33–56.

Coase, R.H. ([1960] 1973) 'The problem of social cost', in *The Firm, the Market, and the Law* (1973), University of Chicago Press, pp. 95–156.

Corkindale, J. (2004) 'The land use planning system: evaluating proposals for reform', produced for the lunch seminar of the Department of Land Economy, University of Cambridge, 21 April.

Cullingworth, B. and V. Nadin (2006) *Town and Country Planning in the UK*, 14th edn, Routledge.

Dai, Y. (1999) 'Land leasing and existing Chinese annual rent system', *China Land Science (Zhongguo Tudi Kexue)*, 13(5), 27–33 (in Chinese).

Deák, C. (1985) 'Rent theory and the price of urban land: spatial organization in a capitalist economy', Dphil dissertation, King's College University of Cambridge, http://www.usp.br/fau/docentes/depprojeto/c_deak/CD/3publ/85r-thry/index.html, accessed 12/8/2014.

Delafons, J. (1969) *Land-use Controls in the United States*, 2nd edn, MIT Press.

Demsetz, H. (1967) 'Toward a theory of property rights', *American Economic Review*, 57(2), 347–359.

Demsetz, H. (1990) *Ownership, Control, and the Firm: The Organization of Economic Activity Volume 1*, Basil Blackwell.

Deng, X., J. Huang, S. Rozelle and E. Uchida (2010) 'Economic growth and the expansion of urban land in China', *Urban Studies*, 47, 813–843.

Denzin, N.K. (1970) *The Research Act in Sociology*, Aldine.

Ding, C. (2003) 'Land policy reform in China: assessment and prospects', *Land Use Policy*, 20, 109–120.

Doebele, W.A. (1982) *Land Readjustment: A Different Approach to Financing Urbanization*, Lexington Books.

Doebele, W.A. (1987) 'The evolution of concepts of urban land tenure in developing countries', *Habitat International*, 11(1), 7–22.

Donahue, C. (1980) 'The future of the concept of property predicted from its past', in J.W. Penncock and J. Chapman (eds), *Property*, New York University Press, pp. 28–68.

Dowall, D.E. (1993) 'Establishing urban land markets in the People's Republic of China', *APA, Journal of the American Planning Association*, 59(2), 182–192.

Duncan, S. (1988) 'Land policy in Sweden: separating ownership from development', in S. Barrett and P. Healey (eds), *Land Policy: Problems and Alternatives*, Avebury, Gower Publishing Company, pp. 308–344.

Dunkerley, Harold B. (1983) *Urban Land Policy: Issues and Opportunities*, Oxford University Press.

Economakis, G.E. (2003) 'On absolute rent: theoretical remarks on Marx's analysis', *Science and Society*, 67(3), 339–348.

Eggertsson, T. (1990) *Economic Behavior and Institutions*, Cambridge University Press.

Eggertsson, T. (1993) 'Mental models and social values: North's institutions and credible commitment', *Journal of Institutional and Theoretical Economics*, 149(1), 24–28.

Eggertsson, T. (1996) 'A note on the economics of institutions', in Lee J. Alston, Thráinn Eggertsson and Douglass C. North (eds), *Empirical Studies on Institutional Change*, Cambridge University Press, pp. 6–24.

Emsley, S. (1998) 'Renewing the case for Marx's concept of absolute rent: towards an historical interpretation', paper presented at the Conference of the International Working Group on Value Theory / Eastern Economic Association.

Engels, F. ([1884] 2010) *The Origin of the Family, Private Property and the State*, reissue edition, Penguin Classics.

Epstein, R.A. (1985) *Takings: Private Property and the Power of Eminent Domain*, Harvard University Press.

Evans, A.W. (1983) 'The determination of the price of land', *Urban Studies*, 20, 119–129.

Evans, A.W. (1999) 'On minimum rents: part 1, Marx and absolute rent', *Urban Studies*, 36(12), 2111–2120.

Farrier, D. and P. McAuslan (1975) 'Compensation, participation and the compulsory acquisition of "homes"', in J.F. Garner (ed.), *Compensation for Compulsory Purchase: A Comparative Study*, United Kingdom National Committee of Comparative Law, pp. 43–72.

Farvacque, C. and P. McAuslan (1992) 'Reforming urban land policies and institutions in developing countries', Urban Management Program Paper 5, World Bank.

Feder, G. and D. Feeny (1991) 'Land tenure and property rights: theory and implications for development policy', *World Bank Economic Review*, 5(1), 135–153.

Fischel, W. (1995) *Regulatory Takings: Law, Economics, and Politics*, Harvard University Press.

Flechner, H.L. (1974) *Land Banking in the Control of Urban Development*, Praeger Publishers.

Foldvary, F.E. (2005) 'Geo-rent: a plea to public economists', *Econ Journal Watch*, http://econjwatch.org/articles/geo-rent-a-plea-to-public-economists, accessed 12/10/2012.

Foster, S.R. (2011) 'The social function of property: a comparative law perspective', http://ssrn.com/abstract=1960022, accessed 12/1/2013.

Furubotn, E.G. and S. Pejovich (1972) 'Property rights and economic theory: a survey of recent literature', *Journal of Economic Literature*, 10(4), 1137–1162.

Furubotn, E.G. and S. Pejovich (1974) (ed.) *The Economics of Property Rights*, Ballinger Publishing Company.

Gaffney, M. (1987) 'Alfred Russel Wallace's campaign to nationalize land', paper presented at the annual meeting of AAAS, Pacific Division, San Diego, CA, 17 June.

Gao, S.L. (2003) 'An exploration of improving Chinese land taxation system', *China Real Estate* (*Zhongguo Fangdichan*), 2003(1), 28–30 (in Chinese).

Garner, J.F. (1975) 'Compensation for compulsory purchase: a comparative study', United Kingdom National Committee of Comparative Law.

Gatzlaff, D.H. and M.T. Smith (1993) 'The impact of the Miami metrorail on the value of residences near station locations', *Land Economics*, 69(1), 54–69.

George, H. ([1879] 1886) *Progress and Poverty*, reprint, Kegan Paul, Tench & Co.

Glaeser, E.L. (2007) 'Restricting residential construction', in Gregory K. Ingram and Yu-hong Hong (eds), *Land Policies and Their Outcomes*, Lincoln Institute of Land Policy, pp. 21–45.

Gomez-Ibanez, J.A. (1996) 'The debate over impact fees', Illinois Real Estate Letter, University of Illinois at Urbana-Champaign.

Green, B.D. (1986) *Land Compensation: A Study of Compensation Determination*, Granta Editions.

Guangdong Land Society (1996) *Study and Exploration of Land Management*, Guangdong Map Press (in Chinese).

Guangdong Real Estate Association (2002) 'The development and reform of real estate enterprises in Guangzhou' (in Chinese).

Guangzhou Real Estate Association (1997) 'Investigation on real estate fee charging in Guangzhou', unpublished report.

Guangzhou and Shenzhen Local Tax Bureaus (2005) http://www.gzds.gov. cn/bsfw/12366zx/12366zxzx/12366_sszc/201407/t20140725_1282840. htm, accessed 8/13/2014.

Guangzhou Economic Planning Commission (1997) *Guangzhou Land Use Planning Atlas*, unpublished.

Guangzhou Public Security Bureau (2004) http://news.ifeng.com/society/ 5/200909/0915_2579_1349326_11.shtml, accessed 15/9/2010.

Guangzhou Urban Planning and Survey Institute (2003) 'Report on urban villages in Guangzhou', unpublished report.

Guangzhou Urban Planning Bureau (GZUPB) (2000) 'Research on land supply of Guangzhou', unpublished report.

Guiliano, G. (1995) 'Land use impacts of transportation investments: highway and transit', in S. Hanson (ed.), *The Geography of Urban Transportation*, Guilford Press, pp. 305–341.

Hagman, D.G. and D.J. Misczynski (1978) *Windfalls for Wipeouts: Land Value Capture and Compensation*, Chicago, IL: American Society of Planning Officials.

Haila, A. (1988) 'Land as a financial asset: the theory of urban rent as a mirror of economic transformation', *Antipode*, 20, 79–102.

Haila, A. (2007) 'The market as the new emperor', *International Journal of Urban and Regional Research*, 31(1), 3–20.

Hallett, G. (1985) *Land and Housing Policies in Europe and the USA: A Comparative Analysis*, Routledge.

Ham, C. and M. Hill (1985) *The Policy Process in the Modern Capitalist State*, Wheatsheaf.

Han, S. (2000) 'Shanghai between state and market in urban transformation', *Urban Studies*, 37(11), 2091–2112.

Han, S. and Y. Wang (2003) 'The institutional structure of a property market in inland China: Chongqing', *Urban Studies*, 40(1), 91–112.

Harvey, R.O. and W.A.V. Clark (1972) 'Controlling urban growth: the New Zealand and Australian experiment', in Richard B. Andrews (ed.) *Urban Land Use Policy: The Central City*, Free Press, pp. 242–247.

Heikkila, E.J. (2007) 'Three questions regarding urbanization in China', *Journal of Planning Education and Research*, 27(1), 65–81.

Hill, R.C., J.R. Knight and C.F. Sirmans (1997) 'Estimating capital asset price indexes', *Review of Economics and Statistics*, 79(2), 226–233.

Ho, S.P.S. and G.C.S. Lin (2003) 'Emerging land markets in rural and urban China: policies and practices', *China Quarterly*, 175, 681–707.

Hobbes, T. ([1651] 2012) *Leviathan*, Oxford University Press.

Hong, Y. (1995) 'Public land leasing in Hong Kong: flexibility and rigidity in allocating the surplus land value', unpublished MIT PhD dissertation.

Hong, Y. (1998) 'Transaction costs of allocating increased land value under public leasehold systems: Hong Kong', *Urban Studies*, 35(9), 1577–1595.

Hu, Angang (2002) 'Public exposure of economic losses resulting from corruption in the late 1990s', *Jiangsu Social Science*, 3, 51–53.

Hua, S. (2013) *Transition of Urbanization and Land Trap* (*Chengshihua Zhuanxing yu Tudi Xianjing*), Oriental Press (in Chinese).

Jacobsen, F. and C. McHenry (1978) 'Exactions on development permission', in Donald G. Hagman and Dean J. Misczynski (eds), *Windfalls for Wipeouts: Land Value Capture and Compensation*, American Society of Planning Officials, pp. 342–366.

Jaèger, J. (2003) 'Urban land rent theory: a regulationist perspective', *International Journal of Urban and Regional Research*, 27(2), 233–249.

Jaffe, A.J. and D.J.R. Louziotis (1996) 'Property rights and economic efficiency: a survey of institutional factors', *Journal of Real Estate Literature*, 4, 137–159.

Kanamori, T. and Z. Zhao (2004) 'Private sector development in the People's Republic of China', Asian Development Bank Institute.

Kent, P. (2004) 'An institutional analysis of the subject matter of real estate transactions', in W. Seabrooke, P. Kent and H.H.H. How (eds), *International Real Estate: An Institutional Approach*, Blackwell Publishing, pp. 73–92.

Kiser, L.L. and E. Ostrom (1982) 'The three worlds of action: a metatheoretical synthesis of institutional approaches', in E. Ostrom (ed.), *Strategies of Political Inquiry*, Sage Focus Editions, pp. 179–222.

Koslowski, R. (1992) 'Market institutions, East European reform, and economic theory', *Journal of Economic Issues*, 26(3), 673–705.

KraÈtke, S. (1992) 'Urban land rent and real estate markets in the process of social restructuring: the case of Germany', *Environment and Planning D: Society and Space*, 10, 245–264.

Kwan, C. (2003) 'Building an all-round well-off society – the shift from efficiency to equity', http://www.rieti.go.jp/en/china/03042401.html, accessed 14/2/2006.

Lang, X. (2006) 'Capitalism in China, socialism in the USA', address given at Tsinghua University, 10 February.

Latham, K., S. Thompson and J. Klein (eds) (2006) *Consuming China: Approaches to Cultural Change in Contemporary China*, Routledge.

Leaf, M. (1998) 'Urban planning and urban reality under Chinese economic reforms', *Journal of Planning Education and Research*, 18, 145–153.

Leitner, M.L. (1995) 'The "gameboard" and the rules of the game', in R.H. Freilich and D.W. Bushek (eds), *Exactions, Impact Fees and Dedications: Shaping Land-use Development and Funding Infrastructure in the Dolan Area*, State and Local Government Section/American Bar Association, pp. 51–59.

Li, D.D. (1996) 'A theory of ambiguous property rights in transition economies: the case of the Chinese non-state sector', William Davidson Institute Working Papers Series 8, William Davidson Institute at the University of Michigan Stephen M. Ross Business School.

Li, J. (2004) *Renovation of Chengzhongcun*, Science Press (in Chinese).

Li, L. (1995) 'The official land value appraisal system under the land-use rights reform in China', *Appraisal Journal*, January, 102–110.

Li, L. (1998) *Urban Land Reform in China*, St Martin's Press.

Li, S. (2000) 'The housing market and tenure decisions in Chinese cities: a mulitivariate analysis of the case of Guangzhou', *Housing Studies*, 15(2), 213–236.

Liew, L.H. (1995) 'Gradualism in China's economic reform', *Journal of Economic Issues*, 29(3), 883–895.

Lin, G.C.S. (2007) 'Reproducing spaces of Chinese urbanisation: new city-based and land-centred urban transformation', *Urban Studies*, 44, 1827–1855.

Lin, J.Y. (2006) 'China's macroeconomic conditions in the first half of 2006: policy options and reflection on macroeconomic theories', http://www.cenet.org.cn/article.asp?articleid=25136, accessed 15/2/2008.

Ling, L. and D. Isaac (1994) 'The development of urban land policy in China', *Property Management*, 12(4), 12–17.

Liu, L. (2010) 'Real estate industry as a pillar industry of China' (*Fangdichanye yijing chengwei woguo zhongyao de zhizhu chanye*) *China Investment* (*Zhongguo Touzi*), 1, 102–105 (in Chinese).

Liu, S., X. Li and M. Zhang (2003) 'Scenario analysis on urbanization and rural–urban migration in China', Chinese Academy of Science, August, http://www.iiasa.ac.at/Publications/Documents/IR-03-036.pdf, accessed 12/8/2004.

Liu, W. (2003) 'The changes of land banking', *China Real Estate Finance*, 3, 18–21 (in Chinese).

Llewelyn, D., D. Banister and P. Hall (2004) 'Transport and city competitiveness – literature review', http://www.ucl.ac.uk/~ucft696/Competitiveness.pdf, accessed 15/10/2004.

Locke, J. (1690) *Two Treatises of Government*, http://oregonstate.edu/instruct/phl302/texts/locke/locke2/locke2nd-a.html, accessed 12/5/2013.

Lomasky, L.E. (1990) *Persons, Rights, and the Moral Community*, Oxford University Press.

Loughlin, M. (1988) 'Apportioning the infrastructure costs of urban land development', in Susan Barrett and Patsy Healey (eds), *Land Policy: Problems and Alternatives*, Avebury, Gower Publishing Company, pp. 229–248.

Lv, X. and E.J. Perry (eds) (1997) *Danwei: The Changing Chinese Workplace in Historical and Comparative Perspective*, M.E. Sharpe.

Malthus, T. (1798) *An Essay on Principle of Population*, Oxford World's Classics reprint, http://www.esp.org/books/malthus/population/malthus.pdf, accessed 12/12/2013.

Marshall, A. ([1890] 1997) *Principles of Economics*, rev. edn, Prometheus Books.

Marx, K. (1844) *Economic and Philosophic Manuscripts of 1844*, http://www.marxists.org/archive/marx/works/download/pdf/Economic-Philosophic-Manuscripts-1844.pdf, accessed 20/11/2013.

Marx, K. ([1863] 1988) 'Theories of surplus value', *Collected Works of Marx and Engels*, Vols 30, 31 and 32, International Publishers.

Marx, K. (1894) *Capitalism*, Vol. III.

Marx, K. and F. Engels (1961) *Writings on the US Civil War*, http://www.marxists.org/archive/marx/works/1861/us-civil-war/index.htm, accessed 14/2/2004.

McKean, R. (1972) 'Property rights within government, and devices to increase government efficiency', *Southern Economic Journal*, 39, 177–186.

Melnick, M.N. (1995) 'New avenues for special assessment financing', in R.H. Freilich and D.W. Bushek (eds), *Exactions, Impact Fees and Dedications: Shaping Land-use Development and Funding Infrastructure in the Dolan Area*, State and Local Government Section/American Bar Association, pp. 167–191.

MLR (2005) http://news.xinhuanet.com/fortune/2004-07/26/content_16 52373.htm, accessed 8/13/2014.

Montgomery, J.R. (1987) 'The significance of public landownership: local authority land trading in Oxford and Sheffield', *Land Use Policy*, January, 42–50.

Morgan, P. and S. Nott (1995) *Development Control: Law, Policy and Practice* 2nd edn, Butterworth.

Motha, P. (1981) *Singapore Property Market in the 80's*, Select Books.

Niskanen, W.A. (1973) *Bureaucracy – Servant or Master?* Hobart Paperback 5, IEA.

North, D. (1981) *Structure and Change in Economic History*, Norton.

North, D. (1990a) 'A transaction cost theory of politics', *Journal of Theoretical Politics* 2(4), 355–367.

North, D. (1990b) *Institutions, Institutional Change and Economic Performance*, Cambridge University Press.

North, D. (1993a) 'Epilogue: economic performance through time', in Lee J. Alston, Thráinn Eggertsson and Douglass C. North (eds), *Empirical Studies on Institutional Change*, Cambridge University Press, pp. 342–355.

North, D. (1993b) 'Institutions and credible commitment', *Journal of Institutional and Theoretical Economics*, 149(1), 11–23.

North, D. (1994) 'Economic performance through time', *American Economic Review*, 84, 356–368.

Oi, J.C. (1992) 'Fiscal reform and the economic foundations of local state corporatism in China', *World Politics*, 45(1), 99–126.

Oi, J.C. (1996) 'The role of the local state in China's transitional economy', in A.G. Walder (ed.), *China's Transitional Economy*, Oxford University Press, pp. 170–187.

Omura, M. (2004) 'Property rights and natural resource management: a theoretical and empirical investigation into their linkages and evolution', PhD thesis, Department of Land Economy, University of Cambridge.

Parker, H.R. (1965) 'The history of compensation and betterment since 1900', in P. Hall (ed.), *Land Values: The Report of the Proceedings of a Colloquium Held in London in March 1965*, Sweet & Maxwell, pp. 53–70.

Payne, G. (1997) *Urban Land Tenure and Property Rights in Developing Countries: A Review*, Intermediate Technology Publications.

Payne, G. (2001) 'Urban land tenure policy options: titles or rights? *Habitat International*, 25, 415–429.

Petty, W. (1662) *A Treatise of Taxes and Contributions*, EEBO Editions, ProQuest.

Pigou, A.C. ([1920] 1929) *The Economics of Welfare*, 3rd edn, Macmillan.

Plunkett, T.J. (1972) 'Tax and development', in Richard B. Andrews (ed.), *Urban Land Use Policy: The Central City*, Free Press, pp. 248–252.

Prokhorov, A. (1969) *The Great Soviet Encyclopedia*, 3rd edn, Macmillan Publishers.

Pugh, C. (1995) 'Housing policies and the role of the world bank', *Habitat International*, 15(1ER), 275INK.

Putterman, L. (1996) 'The role of ownership and property rights in China's economic transition', in A.G. Waldern (ed.), *China's Transitional Economy*, Oxford University Press, pp. 85–102.

Qian, Y. (1999) 'The institutional foundations of China's market transition', Working Papers 99011, Stanford University.

Qian, Y. (2000) 'The process of China's market transition (1978–98): the evolutionary, historical, and comparative perspectives', *Journal of Institutional and Theoretical Economics*, 156(1), 151–171.

Qian, Y. and B.R. Weingast (1997) 'Federalism as a commitment to preserving market incentives', *Journal of Economic Perspectives*, 11(4), 83–92.

Quigley, J.M. (2007) 'Regulation and property values in the United States: the high cost of monopoly', in Gregory K. Ingram and Yu-hung Hong (eds), *Land Policies and Their Outcomes*, Lincoln Institute of Land Policy, pp. 46–65.

Ricardo, D. ([1817] 1821) *On the Principles of Political Economy and Taxation*, 3rd edn, Batoche Books.

RICS Policy Unit (2002) 'Land value and public transport – Stage One report', http://www.ucl.ac.uk/~ucft696/land_value.pdf, accessed 12/11/2005.

Riker, W.H. and I. Sened (1996) 'A political theory of the origin of property rights: airport slots', in Lee J. Alston, Thráinn Eggertsson and Douglass C. North (eds), *Empirical Studies on Institutional Change*, Cambridge University Press, pp. 283–303.

Royal Town Planning Institute (RTPI) (2000) 'Planning gains and obligations: a policy paper', http://www.rtpi.org.uk/resources/policy-statements/2000/dec/pol20001202.pdf, accessed 15/4/2005.

Ryan, A. (1987) 'Property', in J. Eatwell, M. Milgate and P. Newman (eds), *The New Palgrave: A New Dictionary of Economics*, Vol. 13, Macmillan Press, p. 1029.

Shepsle, K.A. (1992) 'Discretion, institutions and the problem of government commitment', in P. Boudrieu and J.S. Coleman (eds), *Social Theory for a Changing Society*, Westview Press, pp. 245–263.

Schotter, A. (1981) *The Economic Theory of Social Institutions*, Cambridge University Press.

Scully, G.W. (1988) 'The institutional framework and economic development', *Journal of Political Economy*, 96(3), 652–662.

Seabrooke, W. and H.H.H. How (2004) 'Real estate transactions: an institutional perspective', in W. Seabrooke, P. Kent and H.H.H. How (eds), *International Real Estate: An Institutional Approach*, Blackwell Publishing, pp. 3–34.

Sened, I. (1997) *The Political Institution of Private Property: Theories of Institutional Design*, Cambridge University Press.

Shoup, D.C. (1983) 'Intervention through property taxation and public ownership', in Harold B. Dunkerley and Christine M.E. Whitehead (eds), *Urban Land Policy: Issues and Opportunities*, Oxford University Press, pp. 132–152.

Song, S.F., G.S. Chu and R.Q. Cao (1999) 'Real estate tax in urban China', *Contemporary Economic Policy*, 17(4), 540–551.

Startup, T. and A. Rossiter (eds) (2003) 'The role of property in financing infrastructure', paper for seminar at the Social Market Foundation, 29 July.

Stiglitz, J. (1977) 'The theory of local public goods', in M.S. Feldstein and R.P. Inman (eds), *The Economics of Public Services*, Macmillan, pp. 274–333.

Stiglitz, J. (1994) *Withering Socialism*, MIT Press.

Strong, A.L. (1979) *Land Banking: European Reality, American Prospect*, Johns Hopkins University Press.

Strong, A.L. (1987) 'The Pinelands – America's largest "transfer of development rights" programme?' *Habitat International*, 11(1), 63–71.

Tan, S. (1999) 'Suggestions on Chinese land taxation system reform', *China Land Science*, 13(6), 16–20 (in Chinese).

Tang, B., H.T. Choy and J.K.F. Wat (2000) 'Certainty and discretion in planning control: a case study of office development in Hong Kong', *Urban Studies*, 37(13), 2465–2483.

Tang, W. (2000) 'Chinese urban planning at fifty: an assessment of the planning theory literature', *Journal of Planning Literature*, 14(3), 347–366.

Tang, Y. (1989) 'Urban land use in China', *Land Use Policy*, 6(1), 53–63.

Thünen, J.H.V. (1826) *The Isolated State*, http://global.britannica.com/EBchecked/topic/675933/The-Isolated-State.

Tian, L. (1998) 'Villages in metropolises: on the contradictory and harmonious development in the period of countryside–city transformation', *Urban Planning Forum* (*Chengshi Guihua Huikang*), 115(3), 54–56 (in Chinese).

Tian, L. (2007) 'Impacts of public transit on residential property values in the land market of China: evidence from two transport projects in Guangzhou', *Journal of Property Research*, 23(4), 347–366.

Tian, L. (2008) 'Chengzhongcun land market in China: boon or bane? A perspective of property rights', *International Journal of Urban and Regional Research*, 32(2), 282–304.

Tian, L. and W. Ma (2009) 'Government intervention in city development of China: a tool of land supply', *Land Use Policy*, 26, 599–609.

Tiebout, C. (1956) 'The pure theory of local expenditures', *Journal of Political Economy*, October, 416–424.

Tong, J. and F. Qu (2003) 'Research on Chinese land fee: a case of Jiangsu Province', *China Real Estate*, 2, 22–26 (in Chinese).

Tongji University (2003) 'Research report on the reform of planning obligations in residential area in Guangzhou' (in Chinese).

Tse, R.Y.C. (1998) 'Housing prices, land supply and revenue from land sales', *Urban Studies*, 35(8), 1377–1392.

Turgot, A.R.J. ([1766] 2012) *Reflections on the Formation and Distribution of Wealth*, reprint, Foreign Language Teaching and Research Press.

Uthwatt et al. (1942) 'Final report of the Expert Committee on Compensation and Betterment', Cmd. 6386, Reports from commissioners, inspectors and others.

Vandergeest, P. (1997) 'Rethinking of property', *Common Property Resource Digest*, April, No. 41, 4–7.

Vogel, E.F. (1989) *One Step Ahead in China: Guangdong under Reform*, Harvard University Press.

Wakeford, R. (1990) *American Development Control: Parallels and Paradoxes from an English Perspective*, HMSO.

Walker, A. and L. Li (1994) 'Land use rights reform and the real estate market in China', *Journal of Real Estate Literature*, 2(2), 199–211.

Wallace, A.W. (1883) 'Land nationalization', *Pall Mall Gazette*, 5594, 2a–b.

Wallace, A.W. (1883) 'The "why" and the "how" of land nationalisation', Part I, *Macmillan's Magazine*, 48(287), 357–368; Part II, *Macmillan's Magazine*, 48(288), 485–493.

Wang, C. (2001) 'An introduction of annual rent into LURs system', *China Real Estate*, 245(15), 32–36 (in Chinese).

Wang, C. (2003) 'Economic growth under decentralization: old wine in new bottles? Another look at fiscal incentives in China', paper at workshop on National Market Integration, Beijing, September.

Wang, H. (2001) *Weak State, Strong Networks: The Institutional Dynamics of Foreign Direct Investment in China*, Oxford University Press.

Wang, X., H. Han and J. Bennett (2004) 'China's land use management', Australian Centre for International Agricultural Research (ACIAR) Project, ADP/2002/021.

Wang, Y. (1999) *There's no Free Lunch: China's Reform Cost and International Comparison*, China Finance Press (in Chinese).

Webb, E.J., D.T. Campbell, R.D. Schwartz, and L.Sechrest (1966) *Unobtrusive Measures: Non-reactive Research in the Social Sciences*, Rand McNally.

Wegnener, M. (1995) 'Accessibility and development impacts', in David Banister (ed.), *Transport and Urban Development*, E&FN Spon, pp. 157–162.

Weimer, D.L. (ed.) (1997) *The Political Economy of Property Rights: Institutional Change and Credibility in the Reform of Centrally Planned Economies*, Cambridge University Press.

Weingast, B.R. (1993) 'Constitutions as governance structures: the political foundations of secure markets', *Journal of Institutional and Theoretical Economics*, 149(1), 286–311.

World Bank (1993) 'China: urban land management in an emerging market economy', World Bank.

World Bank (2002) *Building Institutions for Markets: World Development Report 2002*, Oxford University Press.

World Bank (2007) *World Development Report 2006 on Equity and Development*, http://siteresources.worldbank.org/INTWDR2006/Resources/WDR_on_Equity_FinalOutline_July_public.pdf, accessed 8/13/2014.

Wu, F. (1998) 'Polycentric urban development and land use change in a transitional economy: the case of Guangzhou, PRC', *Environment and Planning*, 30, 1077–1100.

Wu, F. (2002) 'China's changing urban governance in the transition towards a more market-oriented economy', *Urban Studies*, 39(7), 1071–1093.

Wu, F. and A.G.O. Yeh (1999) 'Urban spatial structure in a transitional economy: the case of Guangzhou, China', *APA Journal*, 65(4), 377–394.

Wu, W. (1999) 'Reforming China's institutional environment for urban infrastructure provision', *Urban Studies*, 36(13), 2263–2282.

Xie, Q., A.R. Chanbari and B. Redding (2002) 'The emergence of the urban land market in China: evolution, structure, constraints and perspectives', *Urban Studies*, 39(8), 1375–1398.

Xinhua (2005) 'Investment growth to slow down', http://english1.mofcom. gov.cn/aarticle/counselorsreport/westernasiaandafricareport/200503/20 050300022606.html, accessed 15/2/2008.

Xinhua (2006) 'Land supply tightened to curb economic overheating', 5 September, http://english.gov.cn/2006-09/05/content_378180.htm, accessed 15/2/2008.

Xu, J. and M. Ng (1998) 'Socialist urban planning in transition: the case of Guangzhou, China', *Third World Planning Review*, 20(1), 35–51.

Yandle, B. (ed.) (1995) *Land and Rights: the 1990s Property Rights Rebellion*, Rowman & Littlefield.

Yang, R. and Q. Yang (2000) 'Gradual reform model: the role of local government in institutional change of China', *Economic Research Journal* (*Jingji Yanjiu*), 3, 1–9 (in Chinese).

Ye, L. and A. Wu (2014) 'Urbanization, land development and land financing: evidence from Chinese cities', *Journal of Urban Affairs*, Special Issue, 36(s1), 354–368.

Yeh, A.G.O. (1994) 'Land leasing and urban planning: lessons from Hong Kong', *Regional Development Dialogue*, 15(2), 3–21.

Yeh, A.G.O. and F. Wu (1996) 'The new land development process and urban development in Chinese cities', *International Journal of Urban and Regional Research*, 20, 330–353.

Yin, R. (1994) *Case Study Research: Design and Methods*, Sage.

Zhang, L., S. Zhao and J. Tian (2003) 'Self-help in housing and *Chengzhongcun* in China's urbanization', *International Journal of Urban and Regional Research*, 27(4), 712–737.

Zhang, T. (2000) 'Land market forces and government's role in sprawl', *Cities*, 17(2), 123–135.

Zhang, Z. (2003) 'Several issues of Chinese real estate taxes and fees', *China Real Estate Research*, 3, 140–170 (in Chinese).

Zhao, S. (2007) 'Impacts of benchmark price of industrial land' (*Gongye dijia xinzheng de duochong yingxiang*), *China Land (Zhongguo Tudi)*, 2, 33–35 (in Chinese).

Zheng, J. (2001) 'Research on the land relocation for urban factories: a case study of Guangzhou', PhD dissertation, Zhongshan University, China (in Chinese).

Zhou, X. (2004) 'Urban land management: from a perspective of taxation system reform', speech by the Director of China's People Bank, 6 December (in Chinese).

Zhu, J. (1994) 'Changing land policy and its impact on local growth: the experience of the Shenzhen Special Economic Zone, China in the 1980s', *Urban Studies*, 31, 1611–1623.

Zhu, J. (1997) 'The effectiveness of public intervention in the property market', *Urban Studies*, 3(4), 627–646.

Zhu, J. (1999a) 'Local growth coalition: the context and implications of China's gradualist urban land reforms', *International Journal of Urban and Regional Study*, 23(3), 534–548.

Zhu, J. (1999b) 'The transition of China's urban development: from plan-controlled to market-led', Praeger.

Zhu, J. (2002) 'Urban development under ambiguous property rights: a case of China's transition economy', *International Journal of Urban and Regional Research*, 26(1), 58–79.

Zhu, J. (2004a) 'From land use right to land development right: institutional change in China's urban development', *Urban Studies*, 41(7), 1249–1267.

Zhu, J. (2004b) 'Local developmental state and order in China's urban development during transition', *International Journal of Urban and Regional Research*, 28(2), 424–447.

Zhu, J. (2005) 'A transitional institution for the emerging land market in urban China', *Urban Studies*, 42(8), 1369–1390.

Zhu, K. and P. Roy (2007) 'Securing land rights for Chinese farmers: a leap forward for stability and growth', Cato Development Policy Analysis Series, No. 3, 15 October, Social Science Research Network, available from: http://ssrn.com/.

Zou, B. and H. Chen (2003) 'Dilemma and future of Shenzhen statutory land use plan', http://www.upr.cn/html/thinking/baijia/3.htm, accessed 30/7/2004 (in Chinese).

Index